PENGUIN BOOKS

SEXUAL IDENTITY CONFLICT IN CHILDREN AND ADULTS

A graduate of Syracuse University and of the Johns Hopkins University School of Medicine, Richard Green was formerly Associate Professor of Psychiatry in Residence and Director of the Gender Identity Research Treatment Program at U.C.L.A. He is currently a Professor in the Department of Psychiatry and Behavioral Science at the State University of New York, at Stony Brook. Dr. Green also serves as Editor-in-Chief of *Archives of Sexual Behavior*. He has written more than fifty papers and articles and is coeditor, with John Money, of *Transsexualism and Sex Reassignment* (1969).

RICHARD GREEN, M.D.

SEXUAL IDENTITY CONFLICT IN CHILDREN AND ADULTS

Penguin Books Inc
Baltimore • Maryland

Penguin Books Inc
7110 Ambassador Road
Baltimore, Maryland 21207, U.S.A.
Penguin Books Canada Limited
41 Steelcase Road West
Markham, Ontario, Canada L3R 1B4

First published by Basic Books, Inc., New York, 1974
Published by Penguin Books Inc, 1975

To my mother and father
who first taught me
the meanings of sexual identity

CONTENTS

FOREWORD

Robert J. Stoller, M.D.

Three parts of the process of discovery in the study of human behavior are important for us here. The first is naturalistic: one observes something. Second is abstraction: using previous experience, he concludes he has found something new. The third confirms the finding: others now can repeat the observation. The process works effectively for discoveries in the visible world, as when a new land or species is found. It is probably next best for working out natural laws, like those inherent in the acceleration of falling bodies, in entropy, or in evolution, and weakest with teleology—motivated behavior, whether of energy, matter, or man.

These obvious thoughts may help us orient Dr. Green's study. It reports how he goes about building reliable techniques for confirmation (or, equally, disconfirmation) and what he has found so far. Above all, he wants to satisfy the recurrent demand, unfilled by the single case, for significance in statistics, logic, and sensibleness. For this task he must learn how to ask his questions so that the answers do not serve mainly to disguise the subjects' emotions, thoughts, fantasies, opinions, and history. Then he must mobilize enough cases to convince the justly skeptical.

The urge to do this, as you will see, comes from Green's familiarity with an abundance of unconfirmed theories on the development of deviations of masculinity and femininity. The theories some of us have produced are quite good, even if they contradict each other, but it is clear that this activity should be leavened with reliable data.

The workers tested in this book are mainly the learning theorists, of whom Freud is by far the most profound. It is to him that we are indebted for one of the greatest discoveries in the history of psychology —that the experiences of infancy and childhood help lay down the

Robert J. Stoller is Professor, Department of Psychiatry, School of Medicine, University of California. Los Angeles.

foundations of personality. Not that others had not noticed this, more or less; but none systematized and deromanticized what had been at best only casual or poetic observations. Freud told us, in a manner that prevents us from escaping the insight, what are these earliest events and what is their significance to the child and his family. Then he created a brilliant, encompassing theoretical structure to make sense of these data. As a result, no one in his right mind—including those who are angered by or ignore Freud and psychoanalysis—denies that the external events of the first years of life as they impinge upon the child contribute to the creation of personality. By now, interest in infancy and childhood as crucial determinants of identity is acceptable. But, as always when great scientific discoveries consolidate, an industry is established that provides occupation for large numbers of drones, softly chewing their way into the academic woodwork.

For me, biased by being a psychoanalyst and thus a clinician, it seems that most of the best work in child development—the great observations and the great explanations—has been done by analysts. This is not to say that the observations need be accepted as the truth or that the explanations are complete and correct; we shall need studies like Green's to establish such ratings. The marvelous contribution made by Freud and his creative followers was the provocativeness of their ideas, the scope of their explanations, the stimulus—goading—they gave others, the opening of new perspectives, the demand for new concepts, the challenge to think and argue, the offering of enriching possibilities for the researcher and clinician, the theoretician and naturalist.

But to the analytic concepts must then be added another body of crucial work: the experiments and hypotheses of the more traditional learning theorists—the behaviorists, ethologists, and many others. Their great argument with analysis has been on the subject of intrapsychic conflict as the cause of personality development, normal or abnormal. Most learning theorists say that behavior is modified by nonpsychodynamic processes; that is, simple or complicated stimuli impinging on any organism—including man—cause change in behavior regardless of what the organism thinks it thinks about it. For the analyst, however, humans fantasy, anticipate, and remember by means of symbols, and processes such as these add up to something new in the evolutionary scale: complex mental life. In turn, this mode of behavior (of thinking) has led to another new quality: psychic conflict.

Perhaps, then, the disagreement between the dynamic psychologies like analysis and the purer learning theories—those most amenable to a

scientific methodology—is on the old philosophic question of the nature
of humanness, and especially of choice. Each camp, in creating its
grand scheme, has tended to leave out the other's findings. Green's
review of their work regarding gender identity puts the two under one
cover, a step, I hope, toward the day when they become—together—a
new psychology. We may find then that large parts of gender identity,
probably those earliest to appear, are created by imprinting, conditioning, and other nonpsychodynamic learning processes. Then we shall
link these with other parts, motivated by awareness, conscious and
unconscious, of our past, by our attempts to reconstruct that past into
a new intrapsychic organization, and by our judging the world through
that private, idiosyncratic, rich perspective.

In the meanwhile how to take all this systematically into account is
the task with which Green is concerned. Original, provocative ideas
have been found in the past in the exciting but scientifically treacherous
laboratory of psychoanalytic practice and more recently, more safely, in
the direct observation of infants and children with their families and
peers. But without some way to protect ourselves against our corruptible
benefactor, the human imagination, all is private fantasy. So to keep us
honest, we need the second methodology: confirmation. It is constructed to help us find whether a discovery is real. Can someone else
see it and see it pretty much as did the discoverer; can we find laws
governing the observations and make reliable predictions from them;
can we reproduce the circumstances of the discovery? Psychoanalysis
has created no such methodology for itself, and psychoanalysts in general take no joy in such labor. And since both discovery and confirmation are necessary for our task of understanding the development of
personality and since there are few geniuses so constructed that they
can combine the attributes of the explorer *and* the scientist, the two
tasks are parceled out.

The confirmatory work dynamic psychiatry requires of the scientific
method has only come decades after the free-swinging, exhilarating
activities of the discoverers. In that part of his research that is unique—
the techniques he has devised and the data derived from the interviews
with the children, with the consorts of adult patients, from the group
treatment of children and of mothers and fathers, and from the psychological tests—Green not only exemplifies and honors the hard labors
that have been lying in wait for us but marks the beginning, I hope, of
a new and difficult phase in the study of gender identity development:
He is taking declarations and changing them to the questions they

really always were. But more; it would be a shame, since it is done before one's eyes rather than described, for the reader to miss Green's message that the whole area of personality development needs such research. This book implies the lack, demonstrates a better way, and even gives us information. It is thus a landmark.

Green has reported his findings in a clear, simple, quiet manner. He is also sensible enough continually to mark the paths still to be traveled, the questions unanswered, the techniques requiring refinement, the cautions to be built into the research and to be used in evaluating the findings. He helps teach us how to judge what he has done and yet foregoes the pleasure of propagandizing his audience; in this regard, after he has said what he wishes, he leaves us alone with our thoughts.

You should recognize that this foreword loses objectivity because my hypotheses about etiology, diagnosis, and treatment are among those Green is testing. Still it is perhaps not improper when I note that beyond his working with techniques I admire and at times have also used, he has had the fortitude to create original and unique tests. As different from some of us, he not only advocates certain moral positions (like being scientific) but also acts on his principles. He does what must be done to the preliminary findings and ideas of those of us offering theories about family influences as sources of masculinity and femininity: he invents ways to check statements that are of only modest value when left unchecked.

For instance, I find his distinctive data, those which examine the feminine boys with psychological tests and by controlled questionnaire study of the families, most valuable for me. I developed a hypothesis about causes of marked femininity in males based on histories given by a mother in analysis and by families seen in extended evaluation or psychotherapy. It derives from history and observations changed by being run through a psychoanalyst's mind. It is a helpful thesis. But since others have also expounded good explanations, only reliable data will help us select the most likely, in time clearing the way for a new wave of more informed data. It is here that Green enters; he is developing a method to test such possibilities (and while we are friends, he is not the sort to bend his findings to make me happy). His methodology has broad application; it can question theorists—from behaviorists to psychoanalysts, anyone who asks a question that can be converted into a testable hypothesis—and it can look for data in an *organized* way.

You may believe—I do—that transcripts do not fully reveal what people communicate to each other (and anyway are boring to read at length), that interviews with people one does not know well fail to uncover important factors, that psychological tests are stilted, that only a trusting relationship favors the emergence of a person's true experiences, and that these restrained investigations cannot make conscious unconscious processes as can analysis. Yet by using all these techniques, by fortifying them with extensive interviews and psychotherapy, by specifically avoiding using only the same techniques another researcher has employed to develop his theory, and especially by a natural inclination for experimentation and controls, Green puts into his research an objectivity that is just what is needed. (And he also gets us closer to his raw data, for instance in using extended quotations, than researchers of psychology usually do. That is more important than the dangers of tiring a reader.) You will see, as you read, that he is constantly inventing and modifying his techniques, for he too is aware of these restricting factors just listed.

Stressing the scientific function—theory testing—reported in this book emphasizes what interests me most in it. That, however, takes up only a part of Green's effort. He has a larger purpose, to review for a more general audience the work done in recent years on sex and gender. And so we have here a beautiful and full exposition of the theories, research strategies, and findings now at work in the study of the development of gender identity. Nowhere else will one find the subject described and clarified so fully and intelligently—and then extended with significant new findings. And this is a time for new findings in the study of sexual behavior. The dominating position taken by psychoanalysts has given way, and our changing society has heaved up researchers and propagandists who mark, as much as move, the new permissive era in sexual behavior. With so many people looking, it must happen that new things are found, some of which are unsettling. That is the case with the information this book takes up: that marked disturbances of masculinity and femininity exist in children and are not "just a phase" or the later confabulation of an adult to justify his persisting in cross-gender behavior; that these conditions are manifest as soon as anything appears that can be labeled gender behavior, sometimes as early as a year or so of age; that the earlier the onset, the more irreversible, so that no psychiatric treatment later in life will encourage sex-appropriate behavior to form; that some of these conditions are not the same as the perversions of erotic desire with which we are familiar but are, from the start, ways of life, identities.

And, finally, it presents the more hopeful ideas that the study of these people can help unravel the development of gender identity congruous with one's sex, that is, normal development.

Green pieces all this together in the best way, by letting us share what was actually said, not putting us at the mercy of an impressionistic summary. As a result, you will be well informed when you have finished reading. He is on to something new and valuable. The study of the development of masculinity and femininity has more solid foundations now than ever before.

PREFACE

The purpose of this book is to give a comprehensive description of what is comparatively rare behavior. It describes children and adults who clearly prefer living the sex role opposite to that expected by nature of their anatomy. How this preference comes about is a mystery.

Sexual identity—also termed gender identity—is a fundamental personality feature. It may be considered as encompassing three components: (1) an individual's basic conviction of being male or female; (2) an individual's behavior which is culturally associated with males or females (masculinity and femininity); and (3) an individual's preference for male or female sexual partners.

The forces that operate to shape sexual identity are my principal research interest. In this pursuit, I have employed two strategies: (1) studying persons whose development is atypical, and (2) initiating study early in life, as the atypicality appears. A virtue of strategy 1 is that by setting up for comparative analysis the most disparate groups possible, prospects for discerning the origins of those differences should be maximized. A virtue of strategy 2 is that by directly observing the emergence of an atypical identity, more direct examination of causative factors becomes possible.

This project began with a study of adults who requested sex-change operations. Data were collected on their recalled childhood behavior and early family experiences. From this, a composite picture was drawn of children at "high risk" for later atypical sex-role development. Over the next five years, a sample of such children was gathered. Psychological testing procedures were devised for assessing the children's behavior, interviewing and testing formats were constructed for understanding their parents, and methods were developed for observing families in both home and laboratory settings.

The research project is an ongoing one. New families as well as new procedures continue to be added and follow-up evaluations are made to assess those children previously seen.

A major focus of this book is the atypical child. Adults with similar preferences are described chiefly with two purposes in mind: (1) to illustrate how deeply pervasive such cross-sexed identity can be—as seen by the adults themselves and also through the eyes of their most intimate companions, and (2) to illustrate the early age of onset of this atypical identity.

In documenting these phenomena I have selected a style of data presentation that may please some and annoy others. It seems to me that a historic failing in reporting psychiatric research has been that the great bulk of clinical data has been advanced in the "take my word for it" approach. Summary clinical descriptions of patients are given as seen, recalled, and ultimately reported by the writer. Behavior is interpreted with glibness—"the ensuing hours confirmed the impression that . . ." or "provided additional support for the thesis that. . . ."*

Each scientist has his own tools and techniques for recording data. The chemist has his spectrometer, the psychologist his written test response, the ethologist his camera, and the interviewer his record of the spoken word. It is the latter which I have liberally used here. In this book, I want to portray a number of male and female adults and children who are discontented with the gender role expected of them. I want to demonstrate how early in life this discontentment begins. And I have let the people themselves describe it. Beyond these descriptions, I have also presented a strategy for gathering clues that point to how and why this atypical development evolves.

RICHARD GREEN, M.D.

---

* Notable exceptions include Laing and Esterson's *Sanity and Madness in the Family*, Ackerman's *Treating the Troubled Family*, Stoller's *Sex and Gender*, and Hatterer's *Changing Homosexuality in the Male*.

ACKNOWLEDGMENTS

During my more naive days, I used to wonder why authors of scholarly works were always confessing their indebtedness to those whose inspiration and guidance paved the way. It was always reminiscent of the manner in which Academy Award winners parade a list of names "who made this great moment possible." I no longer wonder why.

As a fledgling medical student at Johns Hopkins, in 1958, I was taken under the wing of a pioneering researcher into the vagaries of psychosexual development. I had just completed an anatomy paper on hermaphrodism. I was interested in psychiatry. I was assigned an advisor who had just published important works on sexual identity in hermaphroditic children. Serendipitously, in the course of that study, a boy had been referred as a suspected anatomic hermaphrodite because of his feminine behavior. However, he was found to be anatomically normal, and, if hermaphroditic, was more properly what has been called a "psychic hermaphrodite." At John Money's suggestion, we studied this boy and his parents. Thus began my focus on the development of masculinity and femininity.

The years as a medical student at Johns Hopkins were crucial. John Money provided the encouragement to learn and reward for effort sufficient to motivate a commitment to psychologic research at a time when a myriad of career opportunities were being presented. He taught me the care of the researcher, the importance of recording data systematically, organizing it, and remaining objective in its assessment. And, he has been a friend.

Though psychiatric specialty training at the University of California, Los Angeles, was selected primarily for geographic reasons, chance had it that there resided the one psychiatric researcher committed to the study of the development of masculinity and femininity.

The years at UCLA have been crucial. Robert Stoller has provided the support, guidance, and unfailing confidence in me that permanently set the course of my career. He has taught me the importance of studying people in depth, the value of the recorded transcript as data, and has provided me with numerous ideas to explore. Countless discussions over the years have so blurred the boundaries of the origins of many of my thoughts that many of his have been unconsciously expropriated as my own. And, he too has been a friend.

I must also acknowledge Harry Benjamin. Vibrant still in his tenth decade, "the Father of Transsexualism" catalyzed within me a unique empathy for the adult driven to changing sex. Much of the historical and cross-cultural material in Chapter 1 was originally collated for his *Transsexual Phenomenon*, and while extensively revised here, remaining sections reappear with his permission.

My salary was paid from 1969 to 1973 by the National Institute of Mental Health under the terms of a Research Scientist Development Award. The award number was MH 31-739. I am very grateful for this support, facilitated by Drs. Bert Boothe and Mary Haworth, because it permitted a full-time commitment to the research described in this book. This pioneering Development Award Program, shared by a relatively small number of psychiatric researchers, produced significant contributions in many areas of behavioral science. Regrettably, the program was eliminated from the federal budget in 1973. My research expenses have been paid by the Foundations' Fund for Research in Psychiatry. The grant number was G69-471. I am also very grateful for this support, facilitated by Dr. Clark Bailey. I appreciate the confidence shown me by the NIMH and FFRP and hope they both got their money's worth.

Several persons who have helped in various phases of preparation of this work have made an otherwise impossible task merely improbable.

General. Thelma Guffan, my secretary, handles, on a daily basis, the infinitely numerous and bothersome details that would have by now consumed me and this work. Katharine Smith, companion during the years this material was collected, took a raincheck on needs that could have only been met by the attention required to generate these pages. So did her daughters, Lisa, Arlette, and Marina.

Specifics. Transcribers of taped interviews to the typewritten page: JoAnn Goldberg, Eileen Kelley. Retyping abridged transcripts: Thelma Guffan, Eileen Kelley, Katharine Smith. Drawing psychological picture tests and graphs: Libby Hayes. Collection of psychologic test data: Marielle Fuller, Jared Hendler, Brian Rutley, Katharine Smith. Particular thanks to Marielle for committing an extraordinary amount of time to the otherwise thankless task of collecting data.

Earlier manuscript versions were read by Martin Hoffman, Robert J. Stoller, and Richard Whalen. Their suggestions rescued me from even more perilous pedantic pitfalls. Diane Settlage's skill in the use of the English language reduced some chapters from twenty-one pages to eighteen pages without in any way reducing their content.

Lastly, I am grateful to my publishers, initially Arthur Rosenthal, and more recently Erwin Glikes, in New York, their copyeditor Claude Conyers, and Colin Haycraft in London and his editor, Isaac Marks. Arthur and Isaac in particular conceived the idea for this book, suffered through a prolonged period of gestation, survived a harrowing stretch of labor, and finally were in attendance at the time of birth.

PROLOGUE

A MOTHER OF AN ELEVEN-YEAR-OLD BOY

Mother: My boy is showing feminine tendencies and has ever since he was *two* years old. It started out real *cute*. His sister had dress-up clothes at her grandparents, and when he got to be about two years old, he'd dress up in these clothes and hats and high heels, and he was just real cute. We thought it was something he'd *pass*. Now he will be *eleven* years old this month, and he does this in secret. I just felt like *now* was the time to investigate it.

A FATHER OF A SEVENTEEN-YEAR-OLD BOY

Doctor: Perhaps you could fill me in a bit on why your son was seen here ten years ago?
Father: He had a lot of these feminine traits. Which at that time, at that age didn't bother me overly because *all* boys go through periods of acting like girls.
Dr.: What sort of feminine traits did he have?
Father: He just acted like a girl.
Dr.: Beginning at what age?
Father: I'd guess maybe five, six, seven years old.

THE SON

Son: Since I was about eight, you know, I thought, "Well, it would be better if I did have the operation done."
Dr.: What if someone were to say to you now, at seventeen, "OK, you could have a sex-change operation"?
Son: I would take it.
Dr.: Why?
Son: Because I think I'd be more happier that way.

AN ADULT FEMALE

Female: I remember that I never played with dolls. And I know when my parents got my brother his set of Western guns, well, I got one too. Everything my brother got, I got. It had to be boy things.

Dr.: Do you remember anything about the kind of clothing you were wearing?

Female: Every time anyone came over to see me I was always in cut-off jeans or in jeans or shorts and never in feminine clothes, so they would always talk, "Look at tomboy." I just took it from there. Then I started liking the girl next door, and at that time I just couldn't figure out why. I thought that it was just a feeling that I would get over, but I didn't.

This person is now a husband and adoptive father. . . .

SEXUAL IDENTITY CONFLICT IN CHILDREN AND ADULTS

1

HISTORICAL AND CROSS-CULTURAL SURVEY

The following chapters describe children and adults who are discontented with their expected sex roles in today's society. Is this a contemporary phenomenon ushered in by current societal forces? Hardly. Males and females discontented with the sex roles expected of them because of their anatomy are unique neither to our culture nor our time. Evidence from classical mythology, ancient, Renaissance, and more recent history, as well as cultural anthropology points to its longstanding and widespread occurrence.

WESTERN CULTURE

Mythology and Ancient History

·In classical mythology the transsexual influence, the wish to be of the other sex, is personified by Venus Castina, the goddess who responded with sympathy and understanding to the yearnings of feminine souls locked in male bodies (Bulliet, 1928). Specific myths involving sex change, not only as a result of desire but also as punishment, are numerous. Among the best known is the story of Tiresias, a Theban soothsayer. One version tells that he was walking on Mt. Cyllene when he came upon two snakes coupling; he killed the female, and for this act the gods punished him by changing him into a woman. Later, having come to look favorably on his new form, he testified that woman's pleasure during intercourse was ten times that of man, thus angering the gods, who promptly punished him again—by changing him back into a man (Leach, 1949).

Another mythical account concerns the Scythians, whose rear guard pillaged the temple of Aphrodite at Ascelon. The goddess is alleged to have been so enraged that she made women of the plunderers, and, as reported by Herodotus in the fifth century B.C., decreed that their posterity should be similarly affected. Hippocrates, more than a century later, was intrigued to find among the Scythians "No-men" who resembled eunuchs. "They not only follow women's occupations but show feminine inclinations and behave as women. The natives ascribe the cause to a deity . . ." (Hammond, 1887). Basically agreeing, he theorized an etiology:

We believe that this illness like any other comes from the Gods. . . . Here is, I believe, how this impotence happens: It is the result of the perpetual horseback riding of the Scythians. When they go to a woman and cannot perform they do not worry at first and simply rest, but if two or three or even more attempts do not succeed, they feel they have committed some offense against God to whom they attribute their affliction, so they don women's clothing, admit their impotence, and from then on live as women, doing their kind of work. This illness among the Scythians afflicts not the poor but the nobles and the powerful and the rich, horsemanship being the cause, and if the poor are less subject to it it is because they do not ride.

Thus Hippocrates suggested that testicular trauma, followed by episodes of impotence, would be so psychically traumatic as to discourage all masculine behavior.

Among the Scythians Hippocrates further described women who "ride, are adept at archery and throw the javelin. They participate in wars so long as they are virgins and do not marry until they have killed three enemies." Also reputed to have lived in Scythia, near the Black Sea, was the race of warrior women known as the Amazons. Perhaps the best-known example of women in men's roles, these females excluded men from their society, reproducing by temporary unions with members of neighboring tribes. Boys born of these unions were either killed or sent to their fathers' tribes. Girls were trained in exercises of war and hunting, and so that they might better draw the bow, their right breasts were burned off when they were eight years old. From this practice comes their name, derived from the Greek (*a*, without; *mazos*, breast).

Such accounts as these, ranging from the purely mythological to the semi-historical, illustrate the antiquity of the transsexual theme in man's fantasy. Less fanciful and better documented accounts exist in other writings from the legacy of ancient Greece and Rome.

Philo, the Jewish philosopher of Alexandria, who lived about a thousand years ago, commented thus upon some males of his Hellenistic society who were discontented with the male role: "Expending every possible care on their outward adornment, they are not ashamed even to employ every device to change artificially their nature as men into women—some of them craving a complete transformation into women, they have amputated their generative members" (cited by Masters, unpublished).

The Roman poet Manilius described similar young men in first-century Rome: "These [persons] will ever be giving thought to their bedizenment and becoming appearance; to curl the hair and lay it in waving ripples—to polish the shaggy limbs—Yea! and to hate the very sight of [themselves as] a man, and long for arms without growth of hair. Woman's robes they wear . . . [their] steps broken to an effeminate gait . . ." (cited by Masters, unpublished). And Juvenal, in "Against Hypocritical Queens", concludes a lengthy diatribe on some effeminate young patricians of Rome with these peevish questions:

> *But why*
> *Are they waiting? Isn't it now high*
> *time for them to try*
> *The Phrygian fashion to make*
> *the job complete . . .*
> *Take a knife and lop off that*
> *superfluous piece of meat?* *

Besides such literary descriptions as these, one finds even among the histories of Roman emperors stories of changes of sex. One of the

---

* From *The Satires of Juvenal* (translated by Hubert Creekmore), pp. 40-41. Copyright © 1963 by Hubert Creekmore. Reprinted by arrangement with New American Library, 1301 Avenue of the Americas, N.Y., N.Y.

earliest sex-conversion operations may have been performed at the behest of one of the Caesars, the infamous emperor Nero. During a fit of rage, Nero is said to have kicked his pregnant wife in the abdomen, killing her. Filled with remorse, he attempted to find someone whose face resembled that of his slain wife. No such woman was discovered, but a young male ex-slave was found who bore the dead wife a strong resemblance, and so Nero ordered his surgeons to transform the man into a woman. Following the "conversion" Nero and the new "woman" were married. A later emperor, Heliogabalus, had aspirations to change his own sex. He is reported to have been officially married to a powerful slave and then to have taken up the tasks of a wife. He is described as having been "delighted to be called the mistress, the wife, the Queen of Hierocles" (Bulliet, 1928), and is said to have offered half the Roman empire to the physician who could equip him with female genitalia (Benjamin and Masters, 1964).

Medieval History

From the Middle Ages in Europe one account stands out; it is perhaps apocryphal but nonetheless remarkable. Centering on the ninth-century figure known as Pope John VIII, the story goes that this person, nominated as successor to Pope Leo IV in 855, was, in fact, a woman. In a report published with the approval of Pope Julius III, it was stated that "she gave birth to a baby and died, together with her offspring, in the presence of a large number of spectators" (De Savitsch, 1958; Durrell, 1962).

Throughout medieval Europe the belief was widespread that sex changes could be performed on both human and beast by witchcraft and the intervention of demons. Witches were claimed to be the possessors of drugs that had the capacity to reverse the sex of the recipient. Some said that males could be transformed into females and females into males, but others argued that the change worked in only one direction. They declared that the devil could make males of females but could not transform men into women, because it is nature's way to add on rather than to take away. The *Malleus Maleficarum* (The Witches Hammer, 1489), the book that served as the source of "treatment" of the insane for nearly three hundred years, contains an eyewitness account of a girl changed into a boy, by the devil, in Rome (Masters, 1962).

Modern History

A number of public transsexual figures were known—some famous—in France from the sixteenth through the eighteenth centuries. Among the notable Frenchmen of the seventeenth century, the Abbé de Choisy, also known as François Timoleon, has left for posterity a vivid, firsthand account of a strong cross-gender wish. During his infancy and early boyhood, his mother had dressed him completely in girls' clothing. As a youth, he continued the practice, and at eighteen his waist was "encircled with tight-fitting corsets which made his loins, hips, and bust more prominent." As an adult, he played comedy as a girl and reported: "Everybody was deceived; I had lovers to whom I granted small favors." At thirty-two he became the ambassador of Louis XIV to Siam. Regarding his sexual identity, he wrote (Bulliet, 1928):

I thought myself really and truly a woman. I have tried to find out how such a strange pleasure came to me, and I take it to be in this way. It is an attribute of God to be loved and adored, and man—so far as his weak nature will permit—has the same ambition, and it is beauty which creates love, and beauty is generally woman's portion—I have heard someone near me whisper "There is a pretty woman." I have felt a pleasure so great that it is beyond all comparison. Ambition, riches, even love cannot equal it.

Another abbé, the Abbé d'Entragues, attempted to simulate feminine facial beauty, to make himself "pale and interesting," by undergoing frequent bleedings (De Savitsch, 1958), and yet another, Becarelli, a false messiah, boasted of possessing a drug that could "change sex." Although sexual anatomy was not changed, men who took the drug temporarily believed themselves transformed into women and women thought themselves transformed into men (Masters, 1962).

One of the most famous examples of cross-gender behavior in history is the Chevalier d'Eon, whose surname provided the eponym *eonism* (transvestism). He is reported to have made his debut into history in woman's garb as the rival of Madame de Pompadour as a pretty new mistress for Louis XV. When his secret was made known, the king capitalized on his initial mistake by turning the chevalier into a trusted diplomat. On one occasion, in 1755, he went to Russia on a secret mission disguised as the niece of the king's accredited agent, and the following year he returned to Russia attired as a man to complete the mission. Following the death of Louis XV he lived permanently as a woman. There was great uncertainty in England, where he spent his final years, as to whether his true anatomic sex was male or whether the periods when he dressed in male attire were, in fact, the periods of impersonation. At his death, the Chevalier d'Eon had lived forty-nine years as a man and thirty-four years as a woman (Bulliet, 1928; De Savitsch, 1958; Gilbert, 1926).

A person whose whole adult life was lived as Mlle. Jenny Savalette de Lange died at Versailles in 1858 and was discovered to be a man. During his lifetime he had managed to get a substitute birth certificate designating himself female, was engaged to men six times, and was given a pension of a thousand francs a year by the king of France with a free apartment in the château of Versailles (De Savitsch, 1958).

America, too, has had its examples of prominent persons with cross-gender identities. The first colonial governor of New York, Lord Cornbury, arrived in the New World from England in full woman's dress and so appeared during his time in office. And, a century later, during the Civil War, Mary Walker became the first American woman to be commissioned an Army surgeon and the only woman expressly granted congressional permission to wear men's clothing (Brown, 1961). Dr. Walker, once referred to by humorist Bill Nye as a "self-made man," dressed in men's clothes for fifty years and claimed to have twice been proposed marriage by Chester Arthur, President of the United States (Yawger, 1940).

TRIBAL CULTURES

The universality among primitive peoples of the transsexual theme has come to light as anthropologists have studied isolated and widely separated cultures. The prevalence of metamorphoses of males into females in tribal cultures has been succinctly explained by Frazer (1955):

There is a custom widely spread among savages in accordance with which some men dress as women and act as women throughout their life. . . . These unsexed creatures often, perhaps generally, profess the arts of sorcery and healing; they communicate with spirits, and are regarded sometimes with awe and sometimes with contempt, as beings of a higher or lower order than common folk. Often they are dedicated and trained to their vocation from childhood.

The emphasis here is on male-to-female transsexuality, specifically as an attribute of the shaman, a priest-doctor with magical powers. Evidence has also been found, however, of female-to-male cross-gender identity, albeit not so frequently.

North American Indians

The original settlers of the North American continent have long been the subjects of cultural anthropologists. During the early decades of this century, particularly, extensive information on their traditions and practices was gathered. Even then, extensive cross-gender behavior was evident. "In nearly every part of the continent there seem to have been, since ancient times, men dressing themselves in the clothes and performing the functions of women . . ." (Westermarck, 1917).

Among the Yuma Indians there existed a group of males called the *elxa*, who were considered to have suffered a "change of spirit" as a result of dreams occurring at the time of puberty. A boy or girl who dreamed too much "would suffer a change of sex." Such dreams frequently included the receiving of messages from plants, particularly the arrowseed, which is believed to be liable to change sex itself. One boy's "dream of a journey" implied his future occupation with women's work. "When he came out of the dream he put his hand to his mouth and laughed . . . with a woman's voice and his mind was changed from male into female. Other young people noticed this and began to feel towards him as a woman" (Ford, 1931). The female counterparts of such boys were reported to be girls who as small children had played only with boys' toys. It was alleged (Ford, 1931) that such women never menstruated and that their secondary sexual characteristics were underdeveloped or, in some instances, male (perhaps some form of hermaphroditism or virilism).

In the Yuma culture it was believed, further, that the Sierra Estrella, a mountain, had a transvestite living inside who had the power to "sexually transform men." Signs of such transformation were said to come "early in childhood"; older people allegedly knowing by a boy's actions that he would "change sex." *Berdache* was the term for those males who behaved like women (Bulliet, 1928). The tribe also included women who passed for men, dressed like men, and married women (Spier, 1933).

Among the Cocopa Indians, there were males (*elha*) reported to have shown a feminine character "from babyhood." As children they were described as talking like girls, seeking the company of girls, and doing things in women's style. Females known as *war'hemeh* had male playmates, made bows and arrows, had their noses pierced, and fought in battles. "Young men might love such a girl, but she cared nothing for him, wished only to become [a] man" (Gifford, 1933).

Mohave Indian boys who were destined to become shamans would "pull back their penis between their legs and then display themselves to women saying, 'I too am a woman, I am just like you are.' " These boys refused to play with boys' toys, would not wear pants, and insisted on skirts. Similarly, there were girls who rejected dolls, refused skirts, copied boys' behavior, and refused to work with bark or do other feminine chores (Devereux, 1937).

For those Mohave boys who were to live as women, there was an initiation rite during the tenth or eleventh year of life: "Two women lift the youth and take him outdoors. . . . One puts on a skirt and dances, the youth follows and imitates. . . . The two women give the youth the front and back pieces of his new dress and paint his face. . . ." Such persons spoke, laughed, sat and acted like women, and assumed a name befitting a person of the opposite sex. They insisted that their genitals be referred to by female terminology. After finding a husband, they would simulate menstruation by scratching between their legs with a stick until blood was drawn. When they were "pregnant," "menstruations" would cease. Before "delivery" a bean preparation would be ingested that would induce violent stomach pains dubbed "labor pains." Following this would be a defecation, designated a "stillbirth," which was later ceremoniously buried. There would then ensue a period of mourning by both husband and "wife" (Devereux, 1937).

Brief mention has been made of similar practices in other tribes. The "men-women" of the Yukis and other California Indians formed a regular social grade. Dressed as women, they performed women's tasks. Two reasons were given for the origin of this class of men: masturbation and a wish to escape the responsibilities of manhood. When such an Indian would show a desire to shirk his manly duties, he would be made to take his position in a circle of fire, and a bow and a "woman-stick" would be offered to him. He would have to make a choice between these sexual symbols and forever after abide by that choice (Powers, cited by Crawley, 1927). Among the Crow, "men-women" were in charge of cutting the sacred tree used in the sundance; in the Yuki tribe they taught the young and preserved and transmitted the history of memorable tribal events; and among the Yakuts they tended to the dead and led the singing during burial ceremonies (Dubois, 1969).

The Pueblo culture, too, allegedly embraced the concept of "man-woman," but the decision on such a mixed identity was made by the tribe, not the individual. A very powerful man, "one of the most virile," was chosen. He was masturbated many times a day and made to ride horseback almost continuously. The effects of this procedure have been described (Hammond, 1887):

Gradually such irritable weakness of the genital organs is engendered that, in riding, great loss of semen is induced. . . . Then atrophy of the testicles and penis sets in, the hair of the beard falls out, the voice loses its depth and compass. . . . Inclinations and disposition become feminine. [He] loses his position in society as a man   his endeavor seems to be to assimilate himself as much as possible to the female sex, and to rid as far as may be all the attributes, mental and physical, of manhood.

Among the Chukchees living near the Arctic Coast, men and women shamans were alleged to undergo a partial, or even complete, change of sex. Transformation by various degrees would take place by tribal command made during early youth. In the first stage, a boy would impersonate a woman only in the manner of braiding and arranging his hair. In the second, he adopted female dress, and in the third the young man left off all pursuits and manners of his sex and took up those of a woman. "At the same time his body alters, if not in its outward appearance, at least in its faculties and forces. The transformed person . . . becomes . . . fond of . . . nursing small children. Generally speaking, he becomes a woman with the appearance of a man." The "soft-man" after a time would take a husband and, as a "wife," would tend house, performing all domestic pursuits and work. Legend had it that some would even acquire the organs of a woman (Bogoras, 1907).

Handsome boys being brought up entirely in the manner of girls were called *shupans* by the Aleuts. These boys' beards would be carefully plucked out, and their hair cut in the manner of women (Langsdorf, cited by Crawley, 1927). Between age ten and fifteen, they were married to some wealthy man (Westermarck, 1917). It was further reported that sometimes if parents had wished for a daughter, and were disappointed by having a son, they would make the newborn into a *shupan* (Bloch, 1933).

The attitudes of the early European explorers of North America were considerably less tolerant than those of the various tribes of natives. When the Spaniards invaded the Antilles and Louisiana they found men dressed as women who were respected by their societies. Thinking they were hermaphrodites, or homosexuals, they slew them (Dubois, 1969).

South American Indians

Practices and traditions similar to those of the tribes of North America have been found among the Indians of South America, although they have been less extensively studied. Believing in sorcery, the Patagonian Indians, for example, chose candidates for their shamans from among children who had had St. Vitus' dance (A. Bastian, cited in Crawley, 1927).

In some South American tribes, females, too, have adopted a cross-gender identity. In Brazil, women were observed who abstained from every womanly occupation and imitated men in all roles. They wore their hair in masculine fashion and "would rather allow themselves to be killed than have sexual intercourse with a man. Each of these women had a woman who served her and with whom she was married . . ." (De Magalhaens, cited by Crawley, 1927; Westermarck, 1917). Also in Brazil may have existed historical counterparts to the legendary Amazons of Greece. The great river rising in the Peruvian Andes and flowing across the continent to the sea was given its name by early Spanish explorers, who claimed to have seen female warriors along its banks.

EASTERN CULTURES

In the Orient, themes of transsexual behavior thread the literatures of both the Far and the Near East. The erotic and amorous literatures of ancient China and Persia, particularly, abound with references to eunuchs and transvestites. Nowhere in the East, perhaps, is cross-gender behavior more remarkable than in the customs and beliefs of the multitude of village cultures on the subcontinent of India.

One folk tale of East Indian lore is a striking parallel to the Tiresias myth of ancient Greece. According to legend, a king was transformed into a woman by bathing in a magic river. As a woman he bore a hundred sons whom he sent to share his kingdom with the hundred sons he had sired as a man. Later, the former king refused to be changed back into a man because "a woman takes more pleasure in the act of love than does a man." Unlike Tiresias, the transformed king was allowed to remain female (Leach, 1949).

A curious footnote to the Tiresias myth is a superstition still current in South India, where many believe that it is unlucky to see snakes coupling. Tiresias is said to have been transformed into a woman as punishment for killing a female snake in the act of coupling; in contemporary India some say that the witness of such an act will be punished with homosexuality (Graves, 1955).

About a hundred years ago in South India, an observer reported performances by male singers and dancers in female dress, who were described variously as either "natural eunuchs" or males castrated during boyhood. These males were apparently similar to the *hinjras*, "Indian male homosexual transvestites," who appear at private and public celebrations in erotic parodies of women's songs and dances. Every group of villages is reputed to have one or two males who live this societal role (Shortt, 1873, cited in Crawley, 1927).

More recently, in mid-twentieth-century North India, the city of Lucknow witnessed a great many eunuchs appearing at the polls in the lines of female voters. The eunuchs, who were dressed in women's garments, were reported to have been "amazed" at finding themselves listed as male voters. "Only after the insistence of the police officers . . . did they bow to the law. . . . These eunuchs, though they resist further surgery to make them more female, have their male genitalia amputated, and the pubic area reshaped to give it the look of the female vagina." The event is celebrated by a grand feast restricted to eunuchs (Siddigui and Rehman, 1963).

Thus, many people have lived out their lives in an opposite-sexed role in many places and in many times. With rare exceptions, persons behaving as members of the other sex have been integrated into the larger society, which has created a specialized role for their atypical behavior. By contrast, contemporary Western society has been less tolerant of atypical sex-role adoption, as shown by clinical material in the following chapters.

Regrettably missing from these historical and cross-cultural accounts are data on the origins of such behavior. How did it come about? What early experiences were associated with the desire to adopt the opposite sex role? This process is not clear. What is clear, however, are two points: (1) the early age of onset of cross-gender behavior and (2) its apparent lifelong endurance. Contemporary material in the following chapters confirms these historical and cross-cultural records on both counts.

2

PSYCHOLOGIC
THEORIES

Explorers searching for the experiential roots of masculinity and femininity have employed a variety of strategies. Some have focused on behavior of the newborn and the different styles with which parents interact with male and female babies. Others have reconstructed, from the memories and current feelings of adults, early life determinants of gender-role development. Others have designed experiments, based on theories of learning, to test ways in which children learn to behave as boys or girls. Still others have made observations in widely divergent cultures and challenge the universality of the findings of almost everyone else.

NEONATAL AND INFANT STUDIES

Not only do differences exist from birth *between* sexes and *within* sexes, but parents respond differently to infant boys compared to infant girls. Here may be the beginnings of gender identity.

To what extent are babies of the *same sex* different at birth, and how durable are these differences? Human newborns show consistent individual differences during the first days of life. Babies tend to respond in characteristic ways: most babies can be characterized as either slightly, moderately, or intensely responsive to *any* stimulus, regardless of the stimulus (Bridges and Birns, 1963). These differences present at birth probably reflect individual differences in temperament. It seems likely therefore that similar environmental changes will have d:fferent effects on different babies. This last inference must be kept in mind when one attempts to relate specific early experiences to subsequent behavior.

That differences exist between infants as a *function of their sex*, may be apparent within the first days of life. Girls have been found to have lower thresholds to touch and pain, and are thus more irritable when handled (Bell and Costello, 1964). They also sleep longer (Moss, 1967). Boys appear to have greater muscular development in that they are more able to raise their head when placed on their stomach (Bell and Darling, 1965). Taste preferences also differ. Newborn females are more responsive to sweet; they (and not boys) increase their intake of a formula when a sweetener is added (Nisbett and Gurwitz, 1970). This preference by females for sweet is not limited to the newborn period but persists well into adulthood (Panborn, 1959).

Studies have also found differences in the behavior of mothers to their firstborn infant depending on whether it is male or female (Moss, 1967). At three weeks, boys' limbs are exercised and stretched more than those of girls. At three months, girls are more often vocally imitated than boys, that is, a mother is more likely to repeat a female infant's sounds, thus increasing the baby's babbling (Todd and Palmer, 1968). These early differences in mother-infant behavior as a function of the baby's sex may be an early contribution to boys' greater use of large muscle groups and girls' greater verbal capacity on I.Q. tests (Garai and Scheinfeld, 1968). However, that these differences in maternal actions may depend on whether the infant is the firstborn child was shown in a later study. Here the difference in mothers' talking to their male and female infants disappeared when the child was the secondborn (Thoman, Leiderman, and Olson, 1972). To make the situation even more complex, fathers were found to talk more to their infant sons. However, since their degree of talking to children of either sex is so low, their input into the child's being trained to verbalize is rather negligible (Rebelsky and Hanks, 1971).

Another sex difference appears to exist at three months: the degree to which boys and girls respond to different types of reward. Male and female infants were rewarded by a visual or auditory cue for looking at an object. The visual reward consisted of a change of a white circle into a colored face; the auditory reward was a soft tone. Girls learned to look at the object only when rewarded with the tone, whereas boys learned only when rewarded with the circle that changed into a face (Watson, 1966).

Boys and girls also appear to have different "musical preferences" at quite an early age. Heartbeat deceleration is believed to be a measure of increased attention in infants. At six months, girls were shown to exhibit greater cardiac deceleration while listening to modern jazz, but boys "attended" more to some interrupted tone (Kagan and Lewis, 1964).

Even though the specific meanings of these findings may seem obscure, the general finding that sex differences may exist at birth bears an important implication. Sex-linked temperamental differences may contribute to differing ways males and females respond to similar environmental input. They may influence interactional styles with parents that constitute early learning experiences. And, if early, presumably innate, behavioral variables clearly discriminate males from females, atypical neonates could be studied from infancy on. Would a male who falls within the female range for these variables later be a feminine boy? Further, if mothers interact differently with newborn males and females, will a mother who treats a young son in the way mothers typically treat a daughter impart a feminizing influence?

Sex differences in children's styles of play and interaction with their mothers have been observed somewhat later than neonatally, but still earlier than commonly assumed: at *thirteen months*. Mothers and children were observed in a playroom with a set of blocks, a pail, a lawnmower, a stuffed dog, a pegboard, and a wooden bug pull-toy. In this setting each mother was instructed to take her child from her lap, place it on the floor, and watch it play. Upon being removed from their mothers' laps, girls were more reluctant to move away. Once they did, they made more visual and physical returns. Girls also touched their mothers more during the test period and spent more time (when not touching) closer to them in the room. After fifteen minutes a barrier was set up separating children and toys. Girls cried and motioned for help; boys moved to the ends of the barrier (perhaps trying to get around it). Play styles also differed: girls tending to sit passively and play with the toys; boys tending to be more active, swinging and banging them about.

These same children had also been observed with their mothers at six months of age. At that time, mothers of daughters touched and talked to their children more than did mothers of sons. Thus, the girls' greater propensity for staying near their mothers at thirteen months may be related to the mothers' earlier greater physical closeness (Goldberg and Lewis, 1969). The finding of differential physical contact between mothers and infant males and females has a parallel with nonhuman primates. Infant male monkeys also spend less time in physical proximity to their mothers (Jensen et al., 1968; Mitchell, 1968). In the squirrel monkey, at least, it is the infant male, not the mother, who appears to initiate this earlier physical separation (Rosenblum, forthcoming, 1974). Should such differences exist across species, this is additional evidence for noncultural or primarily biological contributions to early sex differences.

That mothers and infants mutually influence each other's behavior is shown by a study of foster mothers and their infants. Foster mothers with two infants of the same sex were observed. Some foster mothers showed a high degree of consistency in feelings, attitudes, stimulation, and infant-care practices from child to child, but others showed strikingly different patterns of behavior to each child. Differing responses from two foster mothers toward the *same* infant were also noted. The authors of this study emphasized that neither infant nor mother appeared to be the sole determinant of the relationship; rather it resulted from a subtle interaction of both mother and infant characteristics (Yarrow and Goodwin, 1956). This interrelation must be kept in mind when reading descriptions of mother-infant and mother-child interaction.

PSYCHOANALYTIC THEORIES

Psychoanalytic theories of gender-identity development derive from the writings of Sigmund Freud. Freud's training in biology and his knowledge that before birth all mammals have primordial male *and* female anatomic structures led him to postulate a similar psychic bisexuality. Whether the male or female psychologic components would assume ascendancy resulted from the child's drives and ensuing experiences with parents. The critical period for this psychosexual differentiation was believed to take place during the first five to six years.

Freud observed that, for both male and female infants, the first other person to be "identified" with and "loved" is the mother. Male and female children were seen as developing similarly for the first three years, through postulated oral and then anal stages of development and up to the onset of the phallic stage. (The names for these stages correspond to the body zone to which the child was primarily directing attention.) By the end of the third year significant differences in male-female development were considered to be unfolding. Crucial to this phase was the child's awareness of anatomic genital differences between males and females. For the male child, awareness of the existence of persons without a penis evoked "castration fear," fear that something destructive could happen to a part of his body from which he was deriving considerable pleasure. For the female, awareness that males have something where she apparently has nothing aroused "penis envy."

Children of both sexes were believed to enter into a love and jealousy relationship with their parents. For the boy, love for his mother is accompanied by the wish to replace his father. Fear that his father, who is also admired, would retaliate against this wish was seen as arousing anxiety that the punishment would be loss of the boy's penis. During this phase, which lasts from about three and a half to six years, the boy ultimately reaches a compromise. He will behave as a male (like father) and will later seek out another female (perhaps like mother). On the other hand, the girl, blaming her mother for her lack of a penis, turns to her father as an object for love. Realizing the impossibility of her aspiration to replace her mother, she then identifies with her and will later seek out another more suitable male. These were believed to be the normal phases of psychosexual development. Freud (1935) wrote:

> The erotogenic zones are not all equally capable of yielding enjoyment; it is therefore an important experience when . . . the infant in feeling about on its own body discovers the particularly excitable region of its genitals. . . .
> If then a boy discovers the vagina in a little sister or playmate he at once tries to deny the evidence of his senses; for he cannot conceive of a human being like himself without his most important attribute. Later, he is horrified at the possibilities it reveals to him . . . he comes under the dominion of the castration complex. . . .
> Of little girls we know that they feel themselves heavily handicapped by the absence of a large visible penis and envy the boy's possession of it; from this source primarily springs the wish to be a man. . . .
> We call the mother the first love-object . . . with this choice of the mother as love-object is connected . . . "the Oedipus complex" . . . [the meaning of which] the name tells you: you all know the Greek myth of King Oedipus, whose destiny it was to slay his father and to wed his mother. . . .

Freud's stress on penis envy as pivotal in the female's development has been criticized by other psychoanalysts, especially women. Karen Horney objected:

Although the concept of penis-envy is related to anatomical differences, it is nevertheless contradictory to biological thinking. It would require tremendous evidence to make it plausible that women physically built for specifically female functions, should be psychically determined by a wish for attributes of the other sex. . . . There is no reason to think that this wish is any more significant than the equally frequent wish (by males) to have a breast. . . .

Additionally, she challenged Freud's notion that little girls pass through a masculine phase prior to the emergence of their femininity: "Among the views in question I include Freud's statement that 'it is well known that a clearly defined differentiation between the male and the female character is first established after puberty.' On the contrary I have always been struck by the marked way in which little girls between their second and fifth years exhibit specifically feminine traits" (Horney, 1933).

Clara Thompson stressed the cultural meaning of "penis envy." "One can say the term 'penis-envy' is a symbolic representation of the attitude of women in this culture, a picturesque way of referring to the type of warfare which so often goes on between men and women. . . . The attitude called 'penis-envy' is similar to the attitudes of any under-privileged group toward those in power" (Thompson, 1942).

Some contemporary analysts depart from Freud's theory with particular reference to the age of onset of gender identity development and differences between boys and girls. Stoller (1968) writes:

Freud may have distorted his whole description of the development of "sexuality" in both boys and girls by his insistence on beginning the story in certain regards only after the child was two or three years old.

One gets the impression from observing little girls . . . that they show definitive signs of femininity long before the phallic and Oedipal phases and that one can trace these early traits of femininity from at least the first year or so of life. . . . If the observation is correct, then this fundamental building block in Freud's theory of the development of femininity—penis-envy and castration complex—becomes only *one aspect* of this development rather than the *origin* of it. . . .

It would seem that for Freud there is no such thing as a woman with aspects of femininity that are primary and not just the result of . . . disappointment. . . . Such an approach fails to take into account the long period of time when the infant girl would have no more reason to complain about her femaleness than she would about any part of her body.

Stoller has focused his studies on the etiology of a feminine identity in males, and puts particular emphasis on early parent (especially mother)-son interaction:

The essential psychodynamic process seems to be excessive identification with their mothers, caused by the inability of these mothers to permit their sons to separate from their mother's bodies. Although the normal infant's increasing capacity to move into and deal with reality is matched by his mother's ability to let him farther out on his tether before she has to rescue him, these mothers cannot permit such freedom, they treat the infant as if he were part of their own body. . . .
The most fundamental way in which these mothers produce this blurring of ego boundaries between themselves and their infant son is by literally keeping the child up against their bodies for far more hours of the day and night than occur in normal mother-infant relationships. . . .

Regarding the father's involvement in such a family, he notes: "They are . . . if not *physically* absent from family interaction, at least *dynamically* absent."

Another contemporary psychoanalyst, Kleeman, studying the origin of gender identity in normal girls, also departs from traditional psychoanalytic theorizing. He observes that "by one year the flirting, coyness, contact with glances, seeking-kisses behavior [by the girl] with her father and not with mother may be striking so that the girlishness can be very clear-cut . . ." (Kleeman, 1971a).

Prior to a stage where castration anxiety may be manifest, the girl shows "unmistakable pride and pleasure in her own body and specifically her exterior genital area." An interesting developmental milestone for the theory of castration anxiety occurs when "at about seventeen months maturational capacities include being able to point out missing parts, such as a piece gone from a teddy bear's nose. . . . This mental ability opens the way for *possible* [italics added] castration anxiety later . . ." (Kleeman, 1971a).

Departing from Freud, Kleeman writes, "The *beginnings* of the Oedipus complex evident in the third year . . . appear at a time when the foundations of core gender identity are already well laid. . . . My thesis is that castration anxiety and envy of the male can be observed at an early age but are not necessary conditions to the emergence of [a female] core gender identity." He reports observations on a normal girl who was without opportunity to see a nude male until twenty-two months of age, but who had already begun showing clear-cut evidence of behaving as a female (Kleeman, 1971b).

THEORIES OF DEVELOPMENTAL PSYCHOLOGISTS

Many psychologists conceptualize gender identity development in terms of learning theory. They propose that the child learns to be a boy or a girl by the manner in which it is treated by its parents. While analytic theory does not deny the importance of the parent-child relationship, or the relevance of parental expectations, it gives more emphasis to posited early instinctual drives.

The social-learning view of sex differences can be simply stated. When a boy behaves like a "little man," say, by not crying when hurt, this "brave" behavior is reinforced. If, on the other hand, he does not behave in a masculine-stereotyped fashion, perhaps crying when hurt, this behavior may be negatively reinforced, that is, by his being called a "sissy." The development of the appropriate sex-role identification for the girl is, in many ways, the converse of that for the boy. However, the girl does not receive comparable reinforcement for adopting the feminine role, or comparable punishment for adopting the masculine one, since our culture is masculine-centered and masculine-oriented (Lynn, 1959).

The social-learning view thus rests its case on the thesis that (1) children want approval, (2) parents give them approval if they adopt socially appropriate gender-typic behavior, (3) therefore, males learn to be boys and females learn to be girls.

Identification with the appropriate sex-role model is seen as critical in these theories. Those factors believed to be essential for identification are (1) the model must be perceived as nurturant to the child, (2) the model must be in command of goals desired by the child, especially power, love, and competence in areas the child regards as important, and (3) the child must perceive some objective bases of similarity between himself and the model (Kagan, 1958).

A somewhat different view of the sex-typing process based on the child's mental capacity has also been put forth. Here the phase of sex-role development a child is in at a particular time is not merely based on availability of models with various attributes for social learning but is also related to the child's developmental stage intellectually. Thus there is predicted an interaction between mental age and various aspects of sex-role behavior (Kohlberg and Zigler, 1967).

Not all writers stress the importance of *both* parents, or the availability of a male model for masculine gender identity development. Colley (1959) proposes a "parthenogenic" theory of sex-role emergence:

> Our theoretical plan allows for the total absence, physical or psychological, of one parent without disturbing the child's [sexual identity], provided there is one appropriately identified parent with whom the child experiences close interaction. One parent may supply sufficient differential response to the child . . . even in a father's absence . . . mother will respond to a boy "as if" he were a male and will expect him to treat her as a male would treat a female.

Several experiments have been conducted to assess gender identity in children as a function of their parents' roles and attitudes In one, father-present and father-absent boys aged nine to twelve were compared. Father-absence was associated with less participation in contact sports, more time in nonphysical, noncompetitive activities, and more feminine scores on the It-Scale (a psychologic test that shows significant differences between boys and girls). This was especially true for boys without father substitutes, who were separated from their fathers before four years of age. Children's masculinity and femininity ratings were also assessed as a function of the *dominant parent* within the home. Parents were rated by their friends on a list of attributes, and their children were rated on the same attributes by their teachers. Boys who came from homes considered to be mother-dominated were rated as less masculine on the It-Scale and those from father-dominated homes more like father than mother. Boys from father-dominated homes identified equally with both parents, while girls in mother-dominated homes identified more with mother (Hetherington, 1966, 1965).

Even younger (age five) father-absent and father-present boys have been compared, along with the role played by the mothers of the father-absent boys in promoting masculinity. Kindergarten boys whose fathers were absent for at least one year were found to be more feminine on the It-Scale and also on their game preferences than father-present boys. Boys whose fathers were absent two or more years were even more feminine than those whose fathers were absent from one to two years. The mothers' attitudes toward certain behaviors such as their sons wrestling, climbing, picking up heavy objects and pushing back other boys were also assessed. For father-absent boys, mothers who were more encouraging of assertive behavior had boys whose game preferences were more masculine and who were rated as more masculine by their teachers. However, for those boys with fathers living in the home, their mothers' encouragement of assertive behavior was not correlated with the boys' rating of masculinity (Biller, 1969). Thus in the absence of a father, the mother's influence on male-type behavior is considerably augmented.

The attitude of *both* parents in relation to a young child's masculinity and femininity has also been studied. Nursery school children were observed in a variety of play and test situations and their parents interviewed. Various hypotheses relating parental attitudes and the child's gender-role behavior were tested. One hypothesis was that if parents expected strong behavioral differences in young boys compared to young girls, the more distinctive would be their children's behavior. For girls, there was some "slight support of the hypothesis"; however, for boys, there was no significant correlation. A second hypothesis was that if parents have highly stereotyped ideas of their *own* gender role, this would be transmitted to their children and the children would develop more strongly stereotypic gender roles. There was "no support whatsoever for this hypothesis."

An hypothesis that did find support was the following: since males are believed to be more sexually aggressive, parental encouragement or inhibition of sexual behavior should be positively correlated with masculinity or femininity, respectively. Interviews assessed maternal and paternal attitudes toward the child's household nudity, masturbation, and social sex play. The gender-role measures for the children included their behavior during nursery play sessions, toy preferences, and future occupational choices. "There was clear evidence that parental sex anxiety induces femininity in *both* boys and girls. The influence of the father was substantially greater than that of the mother for both sexes." Thus a father with considerable sex anxiety tended to have more feminine sons (and daughters). Similarly, mother's insistence on good table manners, severity in toilet training, and punishment of aggression toward parents was associated with femininity in *both* boys and girls (Sears, Rau, and Alpert, 1965).

ANATOMICALLY INTERSEXED CHILDREN

Anatomically intersexed infants provide the opportunity to study the relative influences of several determinants of sex. In such an "experiment," a child's assigned sex at birth may contradict at least one anatomic variable for sex determination. Seven variables that contribute to the "sex" of a person have been enumerated: chromosomal configuration (XX or XY), gonads (ovaries or testes), internal reproductive structures (uterus or prostate, etc.), external genitalia (penis and scrotum, or clitoris and labia), hormonal secretion (predominantly androgens [male hormones] or estrogens [female hormones]), sex assigned at birth, and psychologic sex or gender identity (Money, Hampson, and Hampson, 1955). Since intersexed newborns may be raised as boys or girls while contradicting at least one variable of sex determination, it is possible to study the relative influence of anatomic variables compared to the psychologic variable—how the child is reared.

Several combinations have been studied. There were forty-four cases of chromosomal and gonadal females born with excessive male hormone production (the adrenogenital syndrome) and ambiguous external genitalia. Thirty-nine were assigned as female at birth. Thirty-seven developed a female identity. By contrast, all five assigned and reared as males developed a male gender identity. In an additional twenty-five cases the external genital appearance did not agree with the sex of rearing, e.g., a child with a greatly enlarged clitoris raised as a girl or a boy with a very small phallus raised as a boy. Twenty-three developed a gender identity consistent with the sex of rearing. Another group of twenty-one males were born with undescended testes and either a penis with the urethral opening along the underside (hypospadias) or else with a very small phallus (a predominantly female appearance). Fifteen were assigned and reared as females. Twelve developed a female identity. All six reared as males developed a male identity. Thus it was possible, in the intersexed human, for consistent environmental input, pointing in the direction of being a boy or a girl, to overrule the biological contributions to sexual identity.

In summary, the following statement on the establishment of gender identity was put forth (Money, Hampson, and Hampson, 1967):

Our findings indicate that neither a purely hereditary nor a purely environmental doctrine of the origins of gender role and orientation is adequate. Gender role and orientation is not determined in some automatic, innate, or instinctive fashion by chromosomes, gonadal structures, or hormones. However, sex of assignment and rearing does not automatically and mechanically determine gender role as there is a small group of patients whose sexual outlook diverged somewhat from that of the sex to which they had been assigned. It appears that a person's gender role and orientation becomes established as that person becomes acquainted with and deciphers a continuous multiplicity of signs that point in the direction of his being boy or girl. These signs range all the way from nouns and pronouns differentiating gender to modes of dress, haircut, and modes of behavior. The most emphatic sign is the appearance of the genital organs.

Should these signs be ambiguous (if the parents receive a mixed message from the physician as to the child's sex, or if they doubt the physician's judgment as to the correct sex) then a mixed (or hermaphroditic) sex identity is transmitted and subsequently incorporated by the child (Stoller, 1968).

OBSERVATIONS OF ANTHROPOLOGISTS

Cross-cultural studies permit observation of gender identity development under circumstances in which variables, standard in traditional Western culture, are altered.

The cues used in different societies in the assignment of gender role vary widely. Where bravery is the determining point, as among Plains Indians, a timid male child might be assigned a "transvestite" or cross-dressing role, to which he would adjust by identifying with other transvestites, rather than with either warriors or women (Mead, 1961).

Where men and women are differentiated in areas involving softness and harshness in clothing, "tactile sensitivity in a male child may be the first cue . . . assigning him to a feminine role." In those societies in which religious functions are marked by ecstatic trance behavior and cross-dressing for both sexes, "early occurrence of states of catalepsy, dissociation, or hallucinatory experiences may trigger that sex-role assignment" (Mead, 1961).

Pubertal initiation rites in some cultures are seen as ensuring identification of the young male with the adult males of that society. Varieties of initiation practices, some of which are very harsh, have been correlated with varying patterns of early mother-son and mother-father relationships.

In some societies during the first postpartum years the mother and baby son share the same bed to the exclusion of the father. Concurrently, there is a taboo restricting the mother's sexual behavior. For example, Whiting, Kluckhohn and Anthony (1958) report:

[In New Guinea] the Kwoma infant sleeps cuddled in his mother's arms until he is old enough to be weaned, which is generally when he is two or three years old. The father, in the meantime, sleeps apart on his own bark slab bed. Furthermore, during this period, the Kwoma mother abstains from sexual intercourse with her husband. The Kwoma mother not only sleeps with her infant all night but holds it in her lap all day without apparent frustration.

The hypothesis was advanced that such an early life pattern for the male would make it necessary for him, when he reached adolescence, to have a harsh initiation rite. This ritual was seen as putting a final stop to his wish to return to his mother's arms and lap, preventing an open revolt against his father who had displaced him from his mother's bed, and ensuring identification with the adult males of the society.

Support for this hypothesis has been found. Of twenty societies studied where mother and baby shared the same bed for a year to the exclusion of the father, *and* where mother's sexuality was restricted, fourteen were found to have harsh initiation ceremonies. In societies in which there was only one of these early life experiences—that is, either a postpartum sex taboo or an exclusive mother-son sleeping arrangement—the initiation rites, though held, were attenuated. Where there was neither earlier life experience, only two of twenty-five societies had such initiation ceremonies (Whiting, Kluckhohn and Anthony, 1958).

It would be helpful to know more about the gender identity of young males in those societies in which mothers and sons share the same bed to the exclusion of the father, particularly in view of Stoller's findings of extensive mother-son contact summarized earlier. Are such young males feminized? If they are masculine, this would not necessarily constitute a refutation of Stoller's thesis, however. Comparability is lacking in assessing the psychologic effects of an exclusive mother-son relationship in a society in which such behavior is *routine* and in one in which it is *exceptional* and derives from an idiosyncratic need of the mother or characteristic of the son.

Selected clinical material in this text may be marshaled by those who stress one or another theory of sex-role development. Some children are described as having been so temperamentally different from birth that their parents responded to their uniqueness. Others are not. Some males are reported as being treated by their mothers during their first two years in ways that could be seen as inhibiting psychological separation. Others are not. Some children appear to have received positive reinforcement toward cross-sexed behavior during their first five to six years. Others do not. Some have fathers who appear to have been unavailable for role modeling or identification. Others do not.

All the above theories, arising from various starting points, need not be construed as mutually incompatible. Sex differences in the newborn may exist that begin to set a train of events in motion. Parents may not respond to male and female babies in the same way. In turn, differential responses of children will influence parents. These findings are integral to the theories of psychoanalysts, learning theorists, and others.

While psychoanalysis pays considerable attention to postulated unconscious instinctual drives, it hardly ignores early life experiences by which a child learns crucial things about itself and others. And while learning theorists stress models of interaction for the acquisition of behavior, they are not blind to symbolic or less readily apparent meanings of events that help determine *what* people learn, what they *fail* to learn, or what they *remember*.

Finally, anthropologists help keep everyone intellectually "honest" by guarding against the inclination to generalize observations beyond the culture under study.

3

BIOLOGIC STUDIES

Biologically oriented researchers continue their quest for a physiological, anatomical, or hormonal basis of unusual sexual behavior. History's pendulum continues its swing. At the close of the nineteenth century, biologists reigned and Krafft-Ebing's view that male and female sex centers in the brain controlled behavior was typical of its time. Even Freud postulated a biological foundation for the direction of human sexuality. Thus, sensory overendowment in the region of the anus was thought to predispose males to homosexuality. Over the decades, disappointments in not finding biological differences between homosexuals and heterosexuals, coupled with the advent of psychoanalytic and learning theory formulations, resulted in a full swing. Postnatal experiences were the sole determinants of sexual orientation.

A rapprochement may be upon us. Animal research of the 1960s and hormonal assays of the 1970s have ushered in a gradual return to the middle. Animals have been bred that behave contrary to what might be expected by nature of their anatomy, because of changing sex hormone levels before birth. A behaviorally masculine female rhesus monkey results if she is exposed to high levels of male hormone as a fetus. And, a behaviorally feminine male rat or dog results when deprived of male hormone during a comparable period.

In humans, circulating levels of sex hormones have become amenable to ultrasensitive assay. While previous methods involved breakdown products extracted from whole-day urine samples, newer techniques permit exquisite determinations from small samples of blood. Suddenly, differences in clinical subgroups have been reported, and the study of human sexual behavior has entered a new phase of speculation and research.

During these latter years, isolated patient examples and small patient series have occasionally been published correlating a neuroanatomic abnormality or an unusual hormonal status with atypical sexuality. While many of the case reports are more intellectually titillating than scientifically conclusive, they cannot go unnoticed. They demand attention in any integrated attempt to fathom the determinants of masculinity and femininity.

NEUROANATOMIC ABNORMALITIES
AND ATYPICAL SEXUAL BEHAVIOR

The presence within the same person of both a physically demonstrable brain abnormality and unusual sexual behavior tempts one to draw a causal relation between the two. Unquestionably, space-occupying tumors can cause personality change, as can patterns of abnormal electrical discharge. Furthermore, from animal experimentation it is clear that there are discrete areas within the brain responsible for some aspects of sexual behavior. Thus it is possible that in humans a lesion could, if properly located, have an effect on sexual behavior.

Unfortunately, detailed clinical histories of patients with atypical sexual behavior and brain pathology are usually missing from case reports. Typically it is reported: "The patient showed no evidence of cross-dressing prior to the onset of his cerebral pathology at age thirty-five." Researchers would be on more solid ground if details were known of cross-dressing activities in childhood and the extent of any undue interest in cross-dressing in subsequent years, even if not practiced. Implications differ considerably whether transvestism with concurrent brain pathology occurs in a person with no previously latent impulses to cross-dress, or in someone with a longstanding preoccupation suddenly rendered less capable of suppression. Furthermore, it is also known that adults with no previous history of atypical sexuality may begin showing such behavior relatively late in life without evidence of anatomic brain pathology.

The Temporal Lobe

With increased sophistication in electroencephalographic techniques for measuring brain waves, interest has focused on abnormal rhythms in association with atypical sexuality Dysrhythmias are of considerable interest because they may represent subtle evidence of brain pathology, possibly present in populations of seemingly healthy persons. Furthermore, the abnormal locus is accessible to experimental manipulation by the use of drugs that may modify electrical discharge and by restricted surgical removal of abnormal cells.

An oft-quoted case report is that of a man sexually aroused by safety pins who also had temporal lobe epilepsy. A "perverse form of erotic gratification, the contemplation of a safety pin, [had] become attached to the onset of the epileptic seizure. . . ." Surgical removal of the left anterior temporal lobe relieved both the epilepsy and the unusual pattern of sexual arousal (Mitchell et al., 1954).

The case report of a thirty-eight-year-old woman with "sexual seizures" in association with destruction of one temporal lobe is of interest both for the vivid detail of the "automatic" sexual behavior and the subsequent amnesia, characteristic of temporal lobe epilepsy. The patient had primary syphilis at sixteen. At thirty-six she complained of a four-year history of a feeling of itching in the pubic area, accompanied by a feeling that a red hot poker was being inserted into her vagina. The patient would then spread her legs apart, beat both hands on her chest, and "verbalize her sexual needs (often in vulgar terms)." She would have no memory for these episodes. Neurological tests revealed bilaterally dilated brain ventricles and changes consistent with tissue loss in the right temporal lobe. This was thought to be due to syphilis. An anticonvulsant drug brought the seizures under some degree of control (Freeman and Nevis, 1969).

Removal of specific brain areas resulting in changes in sexual behavior is a longstanding observation. Over thirty years ago, Kluver and Bucy (1939) described, in the male monkey, a behavior pattern produced by bilateral removal of the temporal lobe areas. Three to six weeks later these monkeys displayed considerable masturbation and mounting of both males and females. In the human, a case has been reported of a nineteen-year-old male who had a similar operative procedure and who two weeks later showed atypical sexual behavior. He reported his attention was attracted by the sexual organs of an anatomic diagram hanging on the wall and displayed to his doctor that he had spontaneous erections, followed by masturbation and orgasm. He also showed, after surgery, heterosexual indifference, in contrast to his previous behavior, and made homosexual invitations (Terzian and Dalle Ore, 1955).

The role of the temporal lobe in persons requesting sex-change surgery has been studied. One report described nearly half of twenty-six subjects who cross-dressed and wanted sex change as having abnormal electrical patterns (Walinder, 1965). However, no matched controls were included in that series, and the criteria of abnormality are not known. Furthermore, another study failed to find the same incidence of abnormality (only two of fifteen transsexuals) (Blumer, 1969).

A larger survey looked at the medical records of eighty-six men in an anti-epileptic clinic in Czechoslovakia. A history indicating brain damage (usually from infection or trauma) was found more often among epileptics who manifested a deviation in sexual behavior than among epileptics with nondeviant sexuality. When comparing sexually typical and atypical men with temporal lobe epilepsy, those with atypical sexuality had developed epilepsy earlier in life (Kolarsky et al., 1967). However, before implicating abnormal brain foci in producing both epilepsy and unusual sexuality, it should be noted that only 10 percent of the epileptic men showed such behavior, an incidence which may be no higher than the nonepileptic population.

Sexual arousal to hair in association with a left temporal lobe tumor has also been described. The patient from age four experienced an intense preoccupation with women's long hair. By ten he had intermittently dressed in women's clothes and, in his twenties, would pay prostitutes to allow him to stroke their hair while being masturbated. Psychologic treatment for the hair fetish resulted in loss of symptoms for eighteen months. Subsequently, major seizures ensued during sleep, and the hair fetish returned. Though his electroencephalogram showed a normal electrical pattern, he was found three months later to have a brain tumor. Both the seizures and the hair fetish came under some degree of control with medical treatment (Ball, 1968).

Focal Brain Destruction As Treatment

Neuroanatomical knowledge gained from animal research has been recently applied to treatment of atypical human sexuality. In the rat, and other species, the ventromedial nucleus of the hypothalamic portion of the brain plays a role in regulating sex hormone secretion. Extending the implications of this finding to the human, a team of surgeons treated a forty-year-old male attracted to young boys by destroying the nucleus in one side of his brain. A seven-year postoperative follow-up report indicated a reduction in sexual drive and capacity for erection and an absence of previous sexual orientation. Urinary hormone levels and seminal fluid were described as normal.

A second patient treated more recently by the same team had a sexual attraction to early adolescent males coupled with an aversion to females. He regarded his behavior as an organic disease and "at once agreed to a stereotaxic procedure to remove the 'sex-behavior center.'" At short-term follow-up (six months) he reported no homosexual fantasies and no further revulsion to women. A third patient was an elderly male also sexually attracted to young boys who subsequently reported a sex drive diminished in intensity, but not direction (Roeder and Muller, 1969).

The extent to which the results of this procedure are due to interference with the central regulation of male hormone secretion (with its resultant loss of sex drive) or to a direct destructive influence of a hormone sensitive brain area, or to the high motivation for change and expectation of help by patients who agree to such a procedure is difficult to assess. Also, the fact that one-sided brain lesions in animals do not appear to affect sexual behavior makes interpretation of this report difficult.

NEUROENDOCRINE ABNORMALITIES
AND ATYPICAL SEXUAL BEHAVIOR

Recent studies have focused on the interaction between sex hormones and the developing brain in determining later sexuality. Sex hormones may differentiate the central nervous system in a manner analogous to that in the peripheral reproductive system (Grady, Phoenix, and Young, 1965). Thus, while it was previously known that male hormone was required for the genitalia to proceed along male lines, recent findings suggest that male hormone may also be required for the brain to differentiate in a male-type direction.

Of considerable significance for understanding sexual development is that the basic biologic disposition of mammalian embryos is female. No gonads and no sex hormones are required for a fetus to develop in a female direction. For maleness to emerge, androgenic or male hormones must act at critical developmental periods. This was demonstrated initially in the rabbit when a male fetus castrated *in utero* subsequently developed along female lines (Jost, 1947). In the human, the syndromes of Turner (gonadal dysgenesis) and testicular feminization (androgen insensitivity) strikingly illustrate the analogous phenomenon. Children with Turner's syndrome generally have but one sex chromosome (X), develop neither functional ovaries nor testes (and thus do not secrete gonadal hormones), and appear to be female at birth (Money, 1968). Children with testicular feminization are chromosomally male (XY), have testes that secrete normal amounts of testosterone, but their body cells are unable to utilize it (Simmer, Pion, and Dignam, 1965; Rivarola et al., 1967). At birth they appear to be normal females (Money, 1968).

Excessive Male Hormone in the Female

Early evidence that prenatal levels of androgenic hormone may influence postnatal sex-related *behavior* was first demonstrated in the guinea pig and then the nonhuman primate. In the primate, a "tomboy" female rhesus monkey results if the fetus is exposed to large amounts of male hormone from injections given her mother. Normal preadolescent male and female rhesus monkeys behave quite differently, much in the same way as do boys and girls. The male monkey more often participates in rough-and-tumble play, chasing activity, and threatening behavior. Females who have received male hormone *before* birth, however, in addition to being genitally virilized, are considerably more "masculine" in their behavior. Comparable amounts of male hormone given *after* birth, on the other hand, do not appear to have the same masculinizing effect (Young et al., 1964).

These nonhuman primate studies provide speculative appeal for a related phenomenon operating in man. Although it is not possible to conduct parallel experiments with humans, there are some circumstances in which human females have been exposed to unusually high levels of male hormone before birth.

In the adrenogenital syndrome a defect in the production of some adrenal hormones results in excessive production of others that are genitally masculinizing. This overproduction begins before birth and continues postnatally, unless treated. Fifteen preadolescent girls exposed to excessive androgen before birth, but not after, have been studied. The diagnosis of adrenogenital syndrome had been made in infancy so that androgen excess was medically terminated. This natural experiment is somewhat analogous to the monkey procedure mentioned earlier. There girls were compared with fifteen girls in whom there was no evidence of male hormonal excess before birth. These androgen-exposed girls showed much less interest in doll play, more interest in boys' toys, less satisfaction in being girls, and were more likely to be considered tomboys (Ehrhardt, Epstein, and Money, 1968). However, the investigators point out that seven of the fifteen androgenized girls had been thought to be boys at birth but were reassigned as girls before seven months. Since the parents knew of the genital masculinization at birth, "this knowledge may have insidiously influenced their expectancies and reactions regarding the child's behavioral development."

Also studied were a group of twenty-three adult females who were exposed to excessive androgen levels not only prenatally but, because they were not treated during childhood, for at least eight years *after* birth as well. Sexual preferences as adults were assessed. Of the twenty-three, only two had had frequent homosexual contacts, and neither was exclusively homosexual. None were transsexual and desirous of sex-change surgery (Ehrhardt, Evers, and Money, 1968). Thus high androgen exposure before and after birth does not appear to result in homosexuality or transsexualism in the female.

Finally, a group of ten girls, aged three to fourteen was studied which had been exposed to progestins before birth—administered to prevent abortion in the mother. Progestins, although "female" hormones in that they are similar to progesterone, have a masculinizing effect. Nine of the girls showed a strong interest in boys' toys; six an interest in organized team sports, and nine liked to compete with boys in sports. Only two liked frilly dresses and nine were called "tomboy" by their parents and/or themselves. However, in one family a sister who had *not* received progestin was at least as tomboyish as her hormone-exposed sister (Ehrhardt and Money, 1967). Thus, this latter study, as well as that of the girls with the adrenogenital syndrome, is suggestive of a masculinizing effect on behavior as a result of high prenatal doses of androgen.

Deficient Male Hormone in the Male

TESTICULAR FEMINIZATION

The testicular feminizing syndrome (androgen insensitivity) is a human parallel to animal laboratory studies in which male fetuses are deprived of male hormone. These persons, unable to utilize androgen, have undescended testes and the male chromosome pattern XY. At birth, they appear to be normal infant females, are designated female, raised as girls, and later show appropriately feminine behavior. At puberty they develop feminine breasts presumably via the chemical breakdown of testosterone (secreted by the testes) to female hormones. The absence of menstruation (there is no uterus), or removal of an inguinal mass found to be a testis, frequently leads to the diagnosis. Such persons are very feminine, are not aware they are chromosomal and gonadal males, and live their lives as sterile women. It is possible that the absence of male-hormonal influence on the fetal nervous system enhances their capacity to adjust so readily to the female role (Money, Ehrhardt, and Masica, 1968).

TRANSSEXUALISM

A neuroendocrine basis for transsexualism, where the preferred sex role is opposite to anatomic determinants, is a provocative concept. From animal work it is evident that at least in some species there exists a period of behavioral sexual differentiation in response to male hormone exposure, as well as a period of genital differentiation, and that these two critical time periods may be separate (Whalen, Peck, and LoPiccolo, 1966). Thus it is possible to approach in the laboratory a model of transsexualism in which a "female mind exists in a male body" and vice versa. This could result from a male hormone deficiency at a critical developmental period, resulting in an anatomically normal-appearing male with an unmasculinized or undifferentiated nervous system. However, it is not necessary to postulate a global neural organization in a male or female direction as the effect of an excess or deficiency of androgen. The effect could be on nonspecific variables such as aggressivity and activity. These factors might subtly influence early mother-child and peer-child relations. For example, a passive boy might be treated more delicately by his parents and might find the games and companionship of girls more agreeable than the rough-and-tumble of more aggressive boyhood. Evidence presented in this text demonstrates the importance of such early experiences in shaping gender identity and gender role activities.

In the great majority of cases of transsexualism there is presently no evidence that such a hormonal imbalance may have existed. However, there are a few patients in whom there is some basis to make this speculation. Recently there has been reported a series of three males desirous of living as women in whom a testicular defect was discovered (Baker and Stoller, 1968).

Case One appeared to be a normal male at birth and was so raised. However, he developed a feminine social orientation, and behaved as a girl from age four. At twenty-eight, after he had requested surgical sex reassignment to live as a female, microscopic examination of the testes revealed an abnormality with a relative excess of "Sertoli" cells. There is uncertainty as to whether such testes produce abnormal amounts of female hormone; however, it is of interest that Sertoli-Cell tumors in dogs *are* feminizing.

Case Two also appeared to be a normal male at birth but insisted during childhood on behaving as a girl. During adolescence his body became feminized with small but feminine breasts with well developed nipples. Facial hair did not appear until his twenties. At thirty, he requested sex reassignment to live as a female. Testicular examination and chromosomal study revealed an intersexed state, XXY, and small, underfunctioning testes.

Case Three, similarly feminine during childhood, was subsequently diagnosed as having a pituitary gland deficiency, one consequence of which was lowered testicular androgens. As an adult he reported feeling like a woman unless his usual low levels of androgen were supplemented by injections. (It was not possible to rule out the effects of suggestion here on enhanced feelings of masculinity.)

These cases of a female identity in a male, all with evidence of deficiently functioning testes, may represent the clinical result of male hormone deficiency at a critical period in central nervous system development. Or, they may represent the combined effect of specific experiential childhood factors superimposed on a receptive brain substrate with the latter influenced by fetal male hormone deficiency. *Or*, they may represent the coincidental existence of two independent phenomena, feminine identification and hypogonadism.

Most recently, another sample of males desirous of sex change has been studied using sophisticated biochemical measures. Both the pattern of sex hormone secretion and the responsivity of certain tissues to male hormone have been measured. Earlier studies of rodents indicated that a male, deprived of androgen at a critical developmental period, released gonad-stimulating substances in a cyclic pattern similar to the normal female, rather than in the steady male pattern (e.g., Harris, 1964). In rats the pattern is determined by androgen action on the hypothalamus. An indirect way of assessing whether there may have been a deficiency of hypothalamic exposure to androgen during the early development of male transsexuals thus presented itself: determining the release pattern of these substances. The hypothesis was not confirmed. The pattern was revealed to be tonic, i.e., normal male.

In a second strategy, scrotal skin of transsexuals and nontranssexuals was exposed to radioactively labeled androgen, and the quantity later present in the tissues was assessed. Here, again, no differences between the two groups were found (Gillespie, 1971). However, since the peripheral reproductive organs of male-to-female transsexuals are typically normal, there is little reason to suspect a deficiency in androgen utilization at such sites. These studies complement the earlier finding that the concentration of male hormones in plasma and female hormones in urine was the same for male transsexuals and nontranssexuals (Migeon et al., 1969). When coupled with the finding noted earlier that females with the andrenogenital syndrome (and thus exposed to high levels of male hormone) do not become female-to-male transsexuals, and yet another finding that female-to-male transsexuals had normal plasma male hormone levels (Jones, 1971), these are important negative reports. They must be considered by those who would ascribe transsexualism to a purely endocrine etiology.

HOMOSEXUALITY

A revival of interest in a hormonal basis of homosexuality has been spurred by the development of ultrasensitive measures of gonadal hormones. Several provocative studies have been reported. In one, twenty-four-hour urine samples from forty males were analyzed for levels of two breakdown products of the principal male hormone, testosterone. The ratio of urinary etiocholanalone versus androsterone differed for the homosexuals and heterosexuals. Caution must be exercised, however, before concluding that the different ratio is directly related to sexual preferences. Three *hetero*sexuals reported in the same study, who were severely depressed, also had urinary levels like the homosexuals, as did one heterosexual diabetic (Margolese, 1970). Additionally, a more recent study has been unable to confirm this finding (Tourney and Hatfield, 1972). However, a third study (Evans, 1972) did replicate the Margolese finding, thus leaving the issue unsettled.

Loraine and co-workers (1970) compared a small number of hetero- and homosexual females and males. Levels of male hormone were higher and female hormone lower in four homosexual females, while male hormone was lower than normal in two homosexual males.

A most provocative study has compared thirty young adult male homosexuals with fifty male heterosexuals for plasma testosterone levels and additionally has examined the semen of the homosexuals. Those males who were exclusively or almost exclusively homosexual had testosterone levels approximately one half that of the heterosexuals. Additionally, there was a correlation between sperm count and degree of homosexuality, with fewer sperm being associated with a greater degree of homosexual orientation (Kolodny et al., 1971). Again, caution must be exercised pending confirmation on other subjects with rigorous attention paid to possibly confounding variables, such as stress. It could be, for example, that greater stress experienced by homosexuals, because of societal prohibitions, influences the findings. Evidence exists from other studies that stress lowers the secretion rate of testosterone. In the male rodent, for example, exposure to a variety of stressors not only lowers plasma testosterone but also decreases testicular size (Christian, 1955; Bardin and Peterson, 1967). Additionally, in the human male, exposure to military training and actual combat has been shown to significantly lower both urinary excretion rates and plasma levels of testosterone (Rose et al., 1969; Kreuz et al., 1972). More recently, another team of investigators (Tourney and Hatfield, 1972) has been unable to confirm the Kolodny finding.

ESTROGEN-PROGESTERONE TREATMENT OF DIABETIC WOMEN

During the past two decades pregnant diabetics at the Joslin Clinic in Boston have been given high doses of estrogen along with smaller amounts of progesterone. Hormones were administered during pregnancy in an effort to reduce the high fetal mortality rate associated with diabetes. Forty males born of these pregnancies (twenty aged sixteen; twenty aged six) have been compared with same-aged boys of untreated mothers. Both age groups of hormone-treated boys were found to be less aggressive and less athletic (Yalom, Green, and Fisk,

1973). However, the degree to which chronic illness (diabetes) of the hormone-treated mothers (rather than hormones) affected their sons' behavior is uncertain.

OVERVIEW

The additional hormonal dimension required to differentiate male characteristics may help explain why, at the clinical level, psychosexual anomalies are commoner in males (e.g., homosexuality, fetishism, transsexualism, pedophilia, sadism, voyeurism, etc.). In a dual system in which one path automatically evolves and the alternate requires specific influences at specific intervals, more errors are probable along the latter path. An additional nonhormonal hurdle for the male infant may be the necessity of psychologically differentiating himself from the first person with whom he is intimate—a female (Greenson, 1967).

While the measurement of gonadal hormones has been greatly simplified by new techniques, understanding their role has been rendered even more complex. Specific hormonal forms appear to act at specific sites and to affect specific functions. One androgen may be critical for masculine differentiation of the genital system and another for defeminizing specific areas of the brain (Goldfoot, Feder, and Goy, 1969; Luttge and Whalen, 1970, 1971). Thus any hormonal differences shown in human subgroups must take into account laboratory findings on the possible sites and modes of action of the compounds under study.

SEX CHROMOSOMES AND SEX BEHAVIOR

It is a comparatively recent development that chromosomes have become individually visible. Only within the last few years have the consequences of omissions and excesses of chromosomal elements become known. As the incidence of sex chromosome anomalies in the male is about one in five hundred consecutive births, the number of persons so affected is considerable. Controversy exists over the possible interrelation of these chromosomal abnormalities and cross-gender behavior. Several male patients have been described with an extra X chromosome (presumably a step toward genetic femaleness) who are also transvestites or transsexuals (Money and Pollit, 1964; Baker and Stoller, 1968). However, it is difficult to rule out sampling bias as the numbers are small, and such patients are more likely to find their way into the literature. It is also difficult to control for the influence of the somatic manifestations of having an extra X chromosome (a degree of female-type breast development, small genitalia) on a male's self-concept. The issue may be settled by prospective studies in which males identified at birth as having an extra X chromosome undergo longitudinal psychologic study.*

The importance of direct chromosomal observation notwithstanding, that ability may historically come to be but a small beginning. The person with testicular feminization has a normal male chromosomal pattern $(44 + XY)$. Yet, hidden within a normal-appearing chromosome is an invisible genetic defect that renders that male incapable of realizing its masculine potential.

The manner in which gonadal hormones, brain anatomy, and sexual behavior are interrelated defies precise description. If man were solely dependent on relatively simple chemical-cellular interactions, responding as lower animals in a relatively more programmed manner, delineating key mechanisms would be difficult enough. In the human, overlaid with the profound influences of a lifetime of interpersonal experiences and mediated by a more sophisticated central nervous system network, the task of orderly arrangement of all the operant influences approaches the insurmountable. For the present we must content ourselves with descriptions of case reports that alert us to the finding that striking relationships among gonadal hormones, anatomical structures, and sexual behavior may exist. Each new finding merely enlarges the complexity with which the relationship can be viewed. It would be equally hazardous to accept a purely neuroanatomic or neuroendocrine basis of human sexual behavior as it would be to discard all the above findings as irrelevant and inconsequential to man when viewed against psychoanalytic or learning theory formulations.

---

* S. Walzer, personal communication, 1972.

4

MEN WHO WANT
TO BECOME
WOMEN

The adult male who feels himself to be more a woman than a man, so much a woman that he cannot bear to live as a man, presents an extraordinary dilemma for medicine and society. Striving for full acceptance by society as a woman, he seeks medical help. Typically he requests female hormones to bring his body contours closer to female proportions, pleads for genital surgery to remove all male anatomic insignia, and seeks a birth certificate designating female status.

The purpose of this chapter is not to debate the ethical issues enveloping such a person but rather to indicate, through excerpts from six case histories, the pervasiveness of cross-sexed identity in adult males, men who suffered sexual identity conflict as children and who never "outgrew it." Five of the six state that they have felt feminine as far back as they can remember. As children they were considered to be "sissies." They preferred the activities, dress, and companionship of girls; in short, they wanted to *be* girls. Their childhood memories are strikingly similar to the stories and parental descriptions of feminine boys in Chapters

10–16. Excerpts from their case histories are therefore given here at some length as Examples 4-1–4-6 to set the stage for subsequent data.

Tempting as it may be to relate theories of psychosexual development to what one learns from these patients, this is fraught with hazards. These are people who came to be interviewed because they wanted something—sex-change procedures—and they told their stories within that context. Even if they made no conscious distortions, the mere passage of time undoubtedly obscured their memories to some degree. Thus, considerable barriers intercede in the researcher's attempts to obtain valid descriptions of childhood experiences and parental behavior. However, what one does obtain from the stories of these adult males is a first approximation of what to look for in boys on their way toward very extensive adult femininity. In that way we may learn more about the process of atypical sex-role development.

Example 4-1

The subject of the following interview is a male-to-female transsexual whose childhood memories are fairly typical. Among them are praying to become a girl, an intimate relationship with a little girl— disguised in boyfriend-girlfriend terms—and being cross-dressed by a sister.

Male-to-Female Transsexual: Well, my problem to begin with is of very long standing. In fact, all my conscious life, I have been aware that I was of the wrong sex, and I can remember quite clearly back as far as my third birthday. I have scattered little memories of this and that, beginning with my parents. They were sort of expecting a girl when I arrived.

Interviews with parents of feminine boys, presented in Chapters 11, 14, and 15, reveal that parents who have wished for a girl may, in fact, convey this message to their young son.

Doctor: How do you know this?
M-F TS: They had the name picked out. I was to be named Mary Joan after my two grandmothers, but it was never a big issue. Nobody ever set me down and said, "You should have been a girl." The only time I can ever recall as a child having been involuntarily dressed as a girl was a very, very dim little memory when I was either three or four, and my sister just played one afternoon, and she put one of her dresses on me and started playing around, saying, "This is my little sister." I believed her. It was just right for me, because it happened to be a dress that I had seen her wear and I had wished I could have one like it, so without my even asking her she

put it on me and played with me like a doll. Then she said, "OK," and took it off me. I was frankly a little *disappointed*.

A few of the boys described in Chapters 11 and 15 were also cross-dressed by a sister.

Dr.: What else do you remember?
M-F TS: I remember being on our front porch. We had a high front porch, and we were skipping along there, and she was holding my hand; she was telling the other kids—she was four years my senior—she was having fun introducing me as her new little sister. . . . Then I started grabbing garments surreptitiously from my sister and my mother and trying them on, usually in the bathroom.
Dr.: At what age?
M-F TS: Five, and from then on. Nobody knew. They never caught me. Nobody said anything or inferred that there was anything wrong. My mother taught me sewing. I was quite a good seamstress, and—
Dr.: Did she teach your older brother sewing also?
M-F TS: No.
Dr.: Why didn't she teach him?
M-F TS: Possibly because I was interested. They [subject's brother and sister] were both in school while I was still at home.

A preschool child with school-aged siblings and none younger has more opportunity for the undivided attention of his mother.

M-F TS: I suppose I ran my first seam on a sewing machine before I was in kindergarten. I loved to sew and always have. Even at five I made little things.
Dr.: When you were a kid, what type of friends did you have?
M-F TS: When I was in kindergarten, I would have crushes on the girls, and I would look at them, and I would imitate them. I developed in kindergarten a speech impediment from imitating a little black, curly-headed girl. I would imitate the way she kind of had a slight *lisp*, and I don't think I've ever gotten over it. And it was because I wanted to be like her. Yet I called her my girlfriend. I would talk about the only thing that made sense to me —boy/girl—and that was to go out and get married. That's all I could see going on around me. And if I wanted her around me that was the way to perpetuate it, and the way I could get the closest to her. But I really *imitated* her.

The origin of the lisp (sibilant "s") in the effeminate male is obscure, as women *per se* do not speak in this manner. A young boy with such a lisp is described in Chapter 16, which focuses on group therapy with feminine boys.

Dr.: What other early memories do you have?

M-F TS: There was a place way up in the branches of a tree where I grew up that branched out close enough I could lie in it like a hammock. I would lie there and look up through the leaves to the sky and pray. I would promise, and I would offer anything if God would do a miracle for me and make me a girl some day. Any day.

Dr.: Why?

M-F TS: I wanted to be a girl so bad, just like now, if I still felt the same way now as I did then about God, I would be doing the same thing regularly now. I was called a sissy.

Dr.: Why were you called a sissy?

M-F TS: Possibly the way I walked, or talked.

Dr.: Do you think you had effeminate mannerisms?

M-F TS: Yes, I did, because my brother used to always call me a sissy.

Dr.: What about your parents? They must have noticed the same thing.

M-F TS: No reaction at all that I can recall. If there was any reaction at all it was never brought to my attention.

Dr.: Why not?

M-F TS: I don't really know. Possibly just because they were my parents, and parents will often tend to look over the tops of their children's heads when something is going wrong, or think that they'll outgrow it.

Quite true, as will be seen in following chapters. One can speculate on the future development of this boy if his parents had not continued to play ostrich.

Dr.: What else do you remember about your mother?

M-F TS: You know how mothers are about little boys handling themselves where they shouldn't? Well, my mother was no exception. She threatened *to cut it off* if I didn't stop playing with it. Well, I thought that was a peachy keen idea!

Dr.: You remember this pretty clearly?

M-F TS: Oh, very clearly, because it was given to me as punishment.

Dr.: Do you remember what she would say?

M-F TS: "If you don't stop playing with it—your thing—I'm going to cut it off."

Dr.: Did she say "with your thing"?

M-F TS: She called it a "dirty thing." "If I see you handling that I'm going to cut it off."

(Hardly a way to promote positive regard for one's penis!)

M-F TS: Of course, my mind as young as it was was able to figure out that this would hurt, but I knew that there were other things that hurt. My older brother and sister were having teeth pulled, and they cried, and they got well, and people got sick and well, so I figured "OK, I'll get well," and I confided to my brother and I said, to him, "What would happen if she did? Do you think she would?" He said, "Sure she would," and he named some boy that he apparently knew where it had happened. I asked my brother what would happen and he said, "Well, you'd have to wear girl's clothes then because so-and-so's mother did it to him and now he is a girl."

Dr.: I wonder where he got this information.

M-F TS: I don't know. But I thought that was a very good idea. And when I found out she wasn't going to do that, then I got punished a lot less.

One is free to speculate on the extent to which this is childhood logic, defense against anxiety over possible castration, or a rational process erected during the passage of time.

M-F TS: Then when I was I surely must have been five or six anyway —I used to go in a closet in my sister's bedroom. I used to just like to sit in there and think. My mother had a bag of scraps like country women used to have for quilts, and she kept it right on the floor of the closet, and it made a nice little nest, and I'd sit back in it, close the door, and it was dark. I would sit in there and start musing. Dresses were hanging around me, and it was a very, very happy environment, and I would daydream out loud as to what I would get. I would go through a complete wardrobe that I was going to pick for myself when I grew up. I would say, "I'm going to get me some silk underwear. I'm going to get me a dress, some stockings, high heels, and I'll get a purse and a pretty hat with flowers on it."

He did, and was quite attractively dressed when interviewed.

Example 4-2

This male-to-female transsexual has lived as a woman for ten years and is married to a man; genital surgery is yet to be performed.

CHILDHOOD MEMORIES

Male-to-Female Transsexual: I remember that as a little girl [sic] I used to lie in bed at night with my penis between my legs and my ankles crossed real tight and play a silly game and say if I did this, in the morning when I'd wake up, it would be gone. This is very, very long ago.

Doctor: How long ago?

M-F TS: Definitely preschool. I don't know where I got this notion, but I just felt that it would go away by morning, and I was so disappointed because every morning I'd reach down there and there it was.

In Chapter 11, a mother reports similar behavior in her boy.

M-F TS: In kindergarten the kids used to make fun of me because I was girlish.

Dr.: How?

M-F TS: I used to like to play with girls. I never did like to play with boys. I wanted to play jacks. I wanted to jump rope and all those things.

The lady in the schoolyard used to always tell me to go play with the boys. I found it distasteful. I wanted to play with the girls. I wanted to play the girl games. I remember one day the teacher said, "If you play with the girls one more day, I am going to bring a dress to school and make you wear it all day long. How would you like that?" Well, I *would* have liked it.

Dr.: I am wondering if your parents were aware of anything unusual about you?

M-F TS: I talked with one aunt and asked her what did my mother ever say. And she said she was very worried, but she kept hoping that I would "outgrow" it.

Dr.: Do you remember your mom or your dad saying anything to you about your feminine interests?

M-F TS: They kept trying to make me a boy, and I resisted hard.

Dr.: How were they trying?

M-F TS: One time the kids were playing football out in the front of our house and my mother was determined that I was going to play football with the boys, and I resisted, and she literally kicked me out the door to play. . . . Also, the toys they bought me didn't appeal to me. These little cars and the bicycle which my father bought—I wanted the *girl's* bicycle when he went to the store. I was about seven, I guess, and I told them, "I'm not going to drive the bicycle you got me."

Dr.: Well, how about very early, like before school?

M-F TS: I know at Christmas I would get an endless supply of footballs, trucks, scooters, and I used to play like I was enthusiastic about all these. I said, "Oh, how marvelous." Then the day after Christmas I would go down to the basement and store them, and that would be the last I ever saw them. And of course my brother used to say, "Can I play with this?" I would say, "Go ahead," because I didn't care. I was very hurt inside because I wanted things my sister got. I wanted dolls and buggies. I wanted all this and my sister used to say, "Don't worry, I'll let you play with mine."

Unlike the subject of Example 4-1, this transsexual did not recall that her parents encouraged feminine behavior.

Dr.: What else do you remember from when you were little?

M-F TS: My sister and I used to dress up in our mother's clothes.

Dr.: How did that feel to you?

M-F TS: Natural. A game. We played acting grownup. Sometimes when we'd play doctor and nurse I'd get a piece of a curtain or something and put it over my head like it was a scarf. I always played the nurse. Or if we played husband and wife, I'd always be the wife.

Accounts of such female role-taking recur consistently in interviews with parents of feminine boys in Chapter 11.

Dr.: Was that sexually arousing to you?

M-F TS: No, it never was sexually arousing to me. I felt when I dressed in women's clothes from the very beginning, I felt very natural. This was the part that I know I should have felt: this is *strange* putting on nylons; this is *strange* putting on a slip. I didn't *feel* strange. When I put on male clothes it was abhorrent to me. I felt I was a fraud going out dressed as a man.

Absence of sexual arousal to wearing women's clothes has been cited as an essential criterion for the diagnosis of male-to-female transsexualism (Stoller, 1968).

EARLY SEXUAL FEELINGS

Dr.: When did you become aware of sexual feelings toward men?
M-F TS: When I was in the Cub Scouts. I was about nine, and I just knew I was different then, 'cause I got a crush on one of the boys.

Erotic arousal to males may begin very early.

Dr.: What did you think that meant?
M-F TS: I don't know. I just knew I liked him. I'd follow him all over the place.
Dr.: Lots of boys that age have buddies.
M-F TS: Oh, no. It wasn't good buddies.
Dr.: How was it different?
M-F TS: He was very good looking. I liked to be with him. I thought of him, I think now, as a little girl thinks of little boys. I know when my youngest aunt married this fellow I was very attracted to him, and I used to have these daydreams—he was going to run off with *me*. You know, the knight on the white horse.

The possible importance of analyzing childhood fantasies to predict subsequent sexual interests—hinted at here—is discussed more fully in Chapter 18.

Dr.: Did you think that there was something wrong with your having these thoughts?
M-F TS: You know, the first time that it dawned on me that I was abnormal—it was really weird—it was my sophomore year in high school. I could remember the exact day because I was in class, and just being seated the first day of school. Right next to me there was this kid standing there, and he was just the type I'm drawn to, very blond, very, very rugged, and I took a look at him and my whole heart seemed to go right in my throat. I felt like I must have blushed because I felt very warm and tingly. Every time he would look at me, it seemed, I'd just melt. And after school I went out to the beach. It was cold and foggy, and I sat there on the sand and these were the exact words I said to myself, "I started today. I've started something different. I don't know what it is, but I can't go back."
Dr.: Did you feel that you were homosexual?

M-F TS: Not *homosexual*. I felt that I was *drawn to men*. I could never think of myself as a man. I just couldn't.

Here is introduced the distinction transsexuals make between themselves and homosexuals.

PASSING AS A WOMAN

Dr.: Have any of your friends ever detected you without your first telling them?

M-F TS: Not that I know of. When I told one girlfriend she laughed. She thought I was putting her on. She said, "You're kidding," and I said, "No. You've heard about Christine Jorgensen? I'm like that." And she started laughing and thought it was so funny and said, "This is marvelous, tell me more." So I told her and said, "You know, I'm serious."

Dr.: How about the way you do things physically? Mannerisms.

M-F TS: A couple of people thought I was a lesbian, very masculine-type lesbian because of the way I dressed and the way I looked. It was sad.

Dr.: Confusing world, isn't it?

MARRIAGE

Further discussion on transsexual marital relationships is included in the following chapter.

Dr.: How long have you been married?

M-F TS: Altogether eight years.

Dr.: Were you dressing as a woman when you met your husband?

M-F TS: Off and on. I wasn't dressing when he met me. He was very drawn to me and he didn't know why because he likes girls and he didn't know why he was drawn to me 'cause I was dressed as a boy. He was pretty torn up in the beginning.

Dr.: What do you remember about that?

M-F TS: Just that when I told him he felt revolted by it. He wanted to get up and leave. And then we discussed it further and we began living together and he saw how feminine I was. He compared me with different girls he knew before, and he said I was just as feminine as any of them were in thinking, just not physically.

Dr.: What kind of sex have you found the most acceptable considering the limitations that you have?

M-F TS: Well, I prefer rectally because it is the closest to vaginal.

Dr.: Is that enjoyable?

M-F TS: It's enjoyable to him and to me too. He prefers not to see or touch those organs in front. But, nothing really arouses me terribly at this point. Mostly I find satisfaction in pleasing him and knowing that I am satisfying him the best I can.

Dr.: Do you have any kind of orgasm?

M-F TS: No.
Dr.: How do you feel about not having an orgasm?
M-F TS: Delighted. I wouldn't want to have a male orgasm.

Because this transsexual had not begun fully living as a woman when the relationship began, one would predict more of a homosexual component in the husband and perhaps more strain on the relationship as feminization progressed. This was in fact the case, as will be seen.

"I AM NOT A HOMOSEXUAL"

M-F TS: For a while I thought the homosexual life would be the answer, and it wasn't.
Dr.: Why wasn't it?
M-F TS: I found it revolting. To me the idea of two men in bed with each other is sickening. While a man and woman together is perfectly natural.
Dr.: How does that differ from the relationship you are in now?
M-F TS: I am a woman. I have a problem—a *growth*—but I'm a woman. I am in no way like a male.
Dr.: Except that you have a penis and testes, and you don't have a uterus, and you don't have ovaries.
M-F TS: Yes.
Dr.: So, anatomically—
M-F TS: Anatomically, I am female, with those things stuck on.
Dr.: But there are homosexual couples, for example, in which one does all the domestic chores and in effect functions as a wife, while the other member of the team goes out as the breadwinner and carries on the male role, socially, economically, and sexually. I am not sure I understand the difference you are making between that kind of a gay marriage and the kind of relationship you have with your husband.
M-F TS: Well, I've met gay couples and their way of life, and they don't act like husband and wife. Their idea of marriage—many of them play around outside of the marriage.
Dr.: Heterosexual couples do too.
M-F TS: That's true.
Dr.: In what other ways don't you feel that gay couples have a real marriage?
M-F TS: Well, in the eyes of God, for one thing. God didn't create a man for men. He created a woman for man. The male natures don't go together. And for another thing, when homosexuals have sex with each other they are both men and they think of themselves as male. When I had relations with men before I met my husband, I never thought of myself as a male, and I didn't want them to touch me down there. I wanted to be a woman to them very much. If any man showed any desire to orally copulate with me, that would do it.

Self-concept of being a woman during sexual relations and refusal to permit one's genitals to be attended to by the partner are important diagnostic considerations for transsexualism.

"I AM NOT A TRANSVESTITE"

Dr.: Have you known any male homosexuals who have felt the same way?

M-F TS: No. I've met transvestites though. They are quite different from transsexuals.

Dr.: How?

M-F TS: They enjoy their organs. They have a fetish toward clothes because certain clothes when they put them on they feel high or drunk. Well, I don't. When I put on the clothes I feel like I am just getting dressed.

This is another important diagnostic point.

Dr.: You mentioned before how different your brother was as a kid. What kind of a guy is your brother now?

M-F TS: He is quite a wolf, and was from way back.

Dr.: How do you explain the fact that two people growing up in the same family would wind up so different?

M-F TS: I am a girl and he is a boy.

Example 4-3

This male-to-female transsexual was interviewed before surgery and reports on the outcome of sex-change surgery in Chapter 6.

A TYPICAL TIME OF ONSET

Male-to-Female Transsexual: As far back as I can remember [emphasis added], I put on my mom's clothes. I would steal them.

Doctor: How far back is that?

M-F TS: I can remember even before I started school in the first grade, before I was five years old. Christmas or Hallowe'en I would always dress up in my mom's clothes and Daddy always frowned on it. He said, "Why can't you do what your brother does?" I always danced for my father. I still remember him spanking me for dancing for him in my mother's dresses.

Dr.: Were you dressing in girl's clothing at other times?

M-F TS: Oh, yes. My mother would always catch me. I had lots of beautiful material, and I was always making dresses for myself. I learned how to sew very young because mother was a good seamstress. Ever since I can remember, I just helped my mother. Later, when I graduated from junior high school, we had school plays and I always played the part of a girl. In fact, I had such a high soprano voice that many times the teacher would let me put on a blonde wig and come on and sing. Nobody in the audience even knew.

In contrast to the father's strong objection to his son's dressing as a girl, the mother assisted.

M-F TS: She thought it was a stage I was going through, a stage *I never got over*. Pretty soon she'd help me dress up. "This doesn't go with that" and "That shouldn't go with this," she'd tell me, and she just said there was no hope, so she said to my father, "We just can't stop him from doing it."
Dr.: When you were older, how did your family react to your dressing as a woman?
M-F TS: My father said had he known this was going to happen he would have died young. My mother has always been easygoing with me but she also frowned on it. She said, "Why can't you be like your brother who is getting married?"

The father considered that there was something physically wrong with his son.

M-F TS: I remember a couple of times when I was about eight. He made me sit up on the table so he could examine me, and wondered why I wasn't developing like my brother. I was so embarrassed when he used to make me do this everytime I would come out from my bath.
Dr.: He didn't think you were developing?
M-F TS: No, and he told my mother, "I had a dream last night that the youngest one lost his masculinity," and then I remember him putting me up on the kitchen table and examining me and questioning me constantly and having talks with me.

Her early sexual experiences were minimal. Homosexuals were repulsive to her, though she had had sexual fantasies about males.

M-F TS: I can truthfully say I never, ever had an affair with anybody of any kind. I was scared to. I never mingled in any homosexual company because I never felt that I was in the bracket. And to this day homosexuals revolt me, you know, the ones that are—what's the word for it—flamboyant?
Dr.: What were the kinds of things that would be sexually stimulating to you?
M-F TS: When I was in high school, I used to have a crush on somebody all the time. I used to go to the beach, and I'd see him down at the beach, and I would go just crazy, and I'd wind up with an erection. 'Course it wouldn't do me any good.
Dr.: What picture would you have in mind?
M-F TS: Well, I never had sex with anybody, so I never knew. I mean, just what you read in books, and, of course, I'd see the erotic magazines. There were pictures of nude men, and I went through a period of masturbation.

This is more typical of a male pattern of sexual release. Women less commonly utilize photographs for masturbation.

Dr.: What would you think about?

M-F TS: Of intercourse, I guess, anal and oral. When I first began dressing as a female, I always used to love to go and kiss as many men as I could. Then when I was older, I'd get them all frustrated, and I'd have to sneak out the back door the best I could. This is when I started consulting doctors.

Dr.: Would you ever masturbate to the idea of having a sexual relationship with a woman?

M-F TS: Gosh, no. Never.

Dr.: It never has been sexually interesting to you?

M-F TS: Never, never. I've always had girls for playmates when I was very, very young, and I just grew up together as *one of them*, and then since I've been dressing as a female, all my *best friends* are girls, really. They come over to the house and we do our hair, and this and that and the other, sew and cook, have parties and everything. They've always been my best friends, but never, *never* any sexual desire whatever.

Parents of feminine boys not wanting a homosexual son are sometimes falsely reassured about subsequent development of their son's sexual interest by his companionship with girls during preadolescent years. They fail to see that this reflects his *identity* and is more likely to be associated with a later sexual interest in males. This is pointed out in Chapter 16 in a group therapy session with mothers of feminine boys.

LATER EXPERIENCES

This transsexual had been living as a woman for the past eight years, since graduating from high school.

M-F TS: The day I graduated I left home, and I mean, it was just like that, and I've never, ever, ever gone back to anything else.

Dr.: How long have you been taking estrogens?

M-F TS: Nine years.

Dr.: What changes have they brought about?

M-F TS: It's been so gradual over such a long period of years. However, I do have pictures of myself, and as I go back I can see facial changes and body changes and skin texture. Oh, I mean, just everything changed.

Dr.: What body changes have developed?

M-F TS: Well, the loss of all hair, I guess, is one, and development, of course, of the breasts. Then, of course, loss completely of—what do they call it—"libido"?

Dr.: How gradual a loss was that?

M-F TS: Over about three years. It went down to absolutely zero.

Self-concept in her fantasy life, awake and asleep, is female.

Dr.: What are you in your dreams?

M-F TS: A girl, always, and if I'm not, then I wake up. If I'm in boy's clothes and I see somebody I know, like my boss, I say to myself, "What am I doing here?" If something is wrong, I just toss and turn until my husband wakes me up and says, "What's the matter with you? Are you dreaming?" And I say, "Yes," but I'd never tell him then what I was dreaming about. I mean, that was just part of the past, and I try so hard to forget that. The only time it occurs and I even think about it is in my dreams, or if I'm consulting with a doctor like you. I'll have dreams about it for a week or so after the consultation, and then it goes away. I hate to have those dreams.

MARRIAGE

Though still with male genitalia, she is married to a male.

Dr.: How did you meet your husband?

M-F TS: I was working as a secretary; we met and we went on a group bus ride. He didn't know anything about my background or anything. He had no idea I was a transsexual patient. He was just the kind of guy that wouldn't give up, and I said, "What am I going to do to get rid of him? It's gone too far, and he just can't figure out why he can't have anything to do with me sexually." And yet he thought I was the greatest person in the world, and I thought he was too. He was so persistent and said, "You're the girl for me." One evening I invited him up to my apartment, and I said, "There is something I want to discuss with you," and to that day I had never told a soul.

Because this transsexual's boyfriend, for the first part of their relationship, did not know the true anatomic status of his girlfriend, one would predict less of a homosexual component in his makeup than the husband described in Example 4-2 and no diminution in attraction as his wife becomes increasingly feminine with surgery. This proved to be the case.

M-F TS: I just went ahead and told him, and I was prepared to leave town because I figured this was what it was going to come to.

Dr.: How did you tell him?

M-F TS: Well, he asked me to marry him and kept asking me why I wouldn't, and he just assumed I was the original virgin type and never really tried to lay a hand on me because he had such high respect for me. And I said, "I don't know what impression I've made or what deep thoughts you have about why I have never had any relations with you. I'm a transsexual patient." And he said, "What in the world is *that?*" And I said, "Do you want me to *show* you, or do you want me to *tell* you?" He had seen me in bikinis and everything on the beach and he thought I had a fabulous figure, and I said, "You've never seen me with my bottom off my bikini, because, if you look at me, I look just like you." And he said, "Oh, is somebody dreaming this?" and he said "Oh, my gosh" and just left. The next day he called me on the phone and asked if I'd go out to dinner, and so I said, "Why don't you come up to my apartment for dinner? You probably want to talk." And he said, "Yes, really, I don't want you to leave town. I don't want you to do anything else. I'm so crazy about you, no matter what."

Dr.: How is the marriage going?

M-F TS: We just have a great time together, and all the couples that we know, that we mingle with and everything, they are always envious of us. They say that we two are just really made for each other, but nobody knows or has any idea about me.

Example 4-4

Interviews with a parent or a sibling of an adult transsexual are valuable in attempting to validate the patient's story. Questions are directed toward discovering early evidence of cross-sexed interests. Both the sister and the mother of this male-to-female transsexual, who is now a hairdresser, confirm an early interest in hair styling. Another feminine boy with a keen interest in hair styling is described in Chapter 11.

Sister: He seemed to be more with girls than with boys. He preferred to play with the girls more than with the boys.

Doctor: Beginning when?

Sister: Oh, I can remember back from when I was around five and he was about six. He would have much rather played with me and my dolls and my games and comb my hair, or play with my hair, than play with his older brothers. We've always been closer, him and I have always been closer than he and my brothers have. He always went more for the female. When he was twelve and I was eleven, he got a job downtown working in my aunt's dress shop, sweeping the floor, and he was around women. Instead of spending his money on himself he'd go out and buy some clothes for me. He'd buy me things and ask me to dress as though he would dress the same way. He made a lady out of me. I wish I had *his* poise. He's got a lot more female features than I have.

Dr.: In what way?

Sister: Oh, just his attitude toward thinking, his outlook on life, his outlook toward men. I think he would make a better wife than I would! He's got the outstanding points of making a good wife. When we were kids and we would play, he'd play the part of the female.

Dr.: How old was he?

Sister: Seven or eight. My doll clothes, my buggy—I'd find him playing with my dolls where a little girl would play with her dolls and her toys.

He would drop his toys and just play with mine. And it's been like that all through our life.

Dr.: Would your older brothers dress up as girls?

Sister: No, they'd dress up as pirates or ghosts, but he'd dress up like a girl every year. He took dancing lessons. He took piano lessons, singing lessons. He got along better with the female teachers than with the male. When you talk to him it's just like talking to a girl. When we were playing with our dolls or tea sets or something, there he would be right in the middle of it.

Dr.: Nobody objected?

Sister: No. I don't think anyone even took notice. I know I didn't take notice until he was about thirteen

Dr.: Looking back now at his early boyhood and knowing what's developed since then, when do you think one could have first noticed that he was different?

Sister: I'd say between seven and nine. He was constantly either alone or with the female. Even when he was playing with the female, and he could have played the part of a boy, he'd rather play the part of a girl. If I knew what I was looking for, those would be the points that I would take notice of first.

In this case, a grown sister corroborated her transsexual brother's story, providing support for utilizing the histories given by adults in the search for the pretranssexual boy. She also provides clues about the relationship of the pretranssexual boy and his mother.

Dr.: Do you know whether your mom and dad, after they had had two boys, wanted their next child to be a girl?

Sister: They wanted a girl very, very bad.

Dr.: When he came along?

Sister: Yes.

Dr.: How do you know this?

Sister: Because they told me.

Dr.: Do you feel, in any way, this wish to have a girl may have influenced his behavior?

Sister: I think if it's true what they say that when a baby is inside the womb that it's affected by the mother's feelings and actions, I think that just the thought of having a girl . . . for my mother—

Dr.: I'm not sure that thoughts while the baby is *inside* the mother would influence it, but I think how the mother treats the boy *after* he's born certainly could. I think mothers tend to treat little infant girls and little infant boys differently.

Sister: Yes, maybe my mother was just overloving with him the same as I was. I felt he needed me.

Dr.: Do you feel your mother treated him differently than the other boys?

Sister: My mom favored him quite a bit.

The mother's memory of her son's childhood confirms the sister's assessment and adds further details to the story.

Mother: Every since he's been a child, he's had feminine ways about him. We tried to break them, but it didn't do any good.

Doctor: How far back can you remember his feminine ways?

Mother: Well, he always wanted to stay in the house. He always wanted to play with his sister's hair and his sister's dolls. No matter how we scolded him, he was always right back at it again. Things like that ever since, I would say, he was about four or five. You see, he also was a sick boy, and we tried not to spank him like we did his older brother because of his condition.

Dr.: What was wrong?

Mother: We still don't know. He was very close to death as an infant. I'd say his first year of life, he was in the hospital ten months out of the year. I don't know what they did with him in the hospital when he was there, but every time I went to visit they were making over him. They were either brushing his hair or petting him.

Dr.: During the year after he had been in the hospital did you notice anything unusual about his behavior?

Mother: Well, he didn't like to be dirty. He didn't like soiled clothes on him, and I just took it that he smelled that sour milk so much from throwing up that he couldn't take it, so I tried to keep him clean. Later, though boys four and five usually play in the dirt and make mud pies, he wouldn't. You could put a suit on him, and it would be clean for a week.

A detail that may have contributed to subsequent alienation from other young boys.

Dr.: With whom did he play?

Mother: His *sister* mostly. He'd always be brushing her hair, and they'd sit and talk for hours, or they'd play house. He didn't like to go out and play.

Dr.: When he was younger, did you have any awareness of his interest in wearing women's clothing?

Mother: Yes.

Dr.: How far back?

Mother: Well, it went way back. It would start with my slippers when I wasn't home. I'd come home unexpected from the market, and he'd have my slippers on, or he'd have my apron on, playing house.

Dr.: How did you feel when you first became aware of it?

Mother: Well, I asked him what was he doing with my slippers on, so he says, "I was cleaning the house, so I thought I'd put your slippers on," and I just passed it off as a *joke.*

Dr.: Were you already aware by that time that he had some feminine traits?

Mother: Yes. It was seen all over him.

Dr.: How?

Mother: Well, the way he walked, the way he talked, the way he'd act with his sister's hair, and the way he'd like to set his aunt's hair, to fix his aunt's hair, or he'd watch when you'd put makeup on.

Dr.: What interests in his sister's hair did he have?

Mother: Setting it constantly, or I'd brush it with curls, and he'd turn around and the first thing I'd know, she'd have her hair going every which way, in different directions, and I'd ask, "Who did it?" and she said, "He did because he didn't like it the way I fixed it."

Dr.: Did anybody think that it was bad for him to be doing that?

Mother: No, I really didn't put too much thought behind it. I just figured he didn't have nothing to do, so he played with his sister's hair.

Example 4-5

In rare cases, evidence of transsexualism does not manifest itself in childhood. This man did not feel a strong urge toward feminine expression until his fourth decade. Further study of such cases is necessary before we can even begin to understand such a fundamental personality shift.

Male-to-Female Transsexual: I've been a transvestite for about twenty years, and it's with a leaning toward transsexualism for the last five years.

Doctor: How old are you?

M-F TS: Fifty-seven.

Dr.: So in your thirties you began cross-dressing?

M-F TS: Yes.

Dr.: Had you dressed before that?

M-F TS: No.

Dr.: Had you had any interest in dressing in women's clothing prior to that?

M-F TS: None whatever.

Dr.: How do you explain this sudden emergence of an interest in cross-dressing?

M-F TS: I have no idea, not in the slightest! I can even remember when it started: I was one day looking at one of the girlie magazines showing nude women, and I had seen quite a number of them before, and to my astonishment, it came over me not how it would be to be *in bed* with one of these, but how it would be to be *like* that, to be one of these people.

Dr.: To actually be a woman, or to be dressed as one?

M-F TS: *To be a woman.* I was astonished at my own reaction, and this continued and got stronger and stronger over a period of years.

Dr.: The first time you thought what it would be like to be one of these people, was that thought sexually exciting to you?

M-F TS: I believe it might have been, yes.

One would predict, on the basis of early masculine identifications, that cross-dressing at its outset would be sexually arousing (Stoller, 1968).

M-F TS: Then I gradually bought a few articles of women's clothing, stockings and then a negligee, a wig and cosmetics. And, strange enough, at the time I had a girlfriend, and for about twelve years I saw her almost every week. She had no idea.

Dr.: Did your dressing as a woman play any part in your sexual relationship with your girlfriend?

M-F TS: No. She was entirely unaware of my condition.

Dr.: Were you having sexual intercourse with her?

M-F TS: Yes, not real frequently, about twice a month. She was really the aggressor.

Dr.: Is that the reason you didn't have intercourse more often? You weren't that interested?

M-F TS: I think so, and previous to that time, women had shown very little interest in me, so I had seen prostitutes quite a bit because it was so easy.

Dr.: Would you masturbate?

M-F TS: Yes.

Dr.: Can you tell me the kinds of pictures that you would imagine in your mind when you were masturbating?

M-F TS: At that time, I imagined myself with a beautiful woman. Engaging in sexual intercourse.

Dr.: There was no fantasy of being dressed up?

M-F TS: None whatever.

Dr.: Then, lo and behold, one day in your thirties, you found yourself interested in being a woman, or dressing as one?

M-F TS: Of being a woman, and of course to advance that feeling and make myself feel that I was, I purchased some clothing.

Dr.: Was putting on women's clothing sexually exciting to you?

M-F TS: Yes.

Dr.: Would you masturbate when you put on the clothing?

M-F TS: Yes, at times.

Dr.: How often would you dress?

M-F TS: At first, a couple of times a week and within a space of two years I began doing it every night, applying cosmetics in the evening and a wig.

Dr.: Is dressing up as a woman still sexually exciting to you?

M-F TS: No.

Dr.: When did it stop being so?

M-F TS: Gradually. It gradually stopped being sexually exciting, and it began to feel perfectly *normal*.

The diminution in sexually arousing properties of women's clothing to the previously fetishistic cross-dresser requires further study. Is the change a function of a shifting identity (toward femaleness)? Does a shift in identity result in loss of sexual attractiveness of the garments? Is it related to the phenomenon that many objects (spouses included) having sexually arousing potential may also lose some or all of that potential with the passage of time?

Dr.: When you masturbate now, what thoughts do you have in your mind?
M-F TS: Now a different fantasy. It's of me as a *woman* having intercourse with a *man*
Dr.: Were you ever tempted to experiment with homosexuality?
M-F TS: Never. I just have a feeling that were I transformed magically overnight into a woman, my attitude then would be entirely different.
Dr.: Can you imagine yourself the way you are now having sexual relations with a man?
M-F TS: No. But equipped as a woman, yes.
Dr.: Do you have aspirations to be equipped as a woman?
M-F TS: Yes. I mean, I haven't formed a strong determination to do it, but the idea is very attractive to me. I must say that I have no explanation for this sudden change.

Example 4-6

At age seven, this male-to-female transsexual had been examined because of his feminine behavior and trouble in school. Ten years later, he and his father sought further consultation.

Doctor: Perhaps you could fill me in a bit on why your son was seen here ten years ago?
Father: He had a lot of problems. He was getting into a lot of trouble in school.
Dr.: What sort of trouble?
Father: We were getting continual complaints from teachers. At first I wrote it off as being a cranky teacher that couldn't handle kids. But it occurred that every grade he went into he had the same problems. One grade he was in the teacher accused him of lighting a fire in the trash can. . . . And, of course, he had a lot of these feminine traits. Which at that time didn't bother me overly because *all* boys go through periods of acting like girls.

Here, the father was more concerned about the boy's disciplinary problems in school than about his feminine behavior. As will be seen in later cases, fathers, more so than mothers, tend to dismiss the significance of feminine behavior in their sons.

Dr.: What sort of feminine traits did he have?

Father: Well, I don't remember that much detail, but he just acted like a girl.

Dr.: Beginning at what age?

Father: I guess maybe five, six, seven years old.

Dr.: Do you remember what he would do?

Father: No, I don't remember the details; it's too far back. It didn't bother me too much. I remember the doctor at the time specifically asked me, "Doesn't this bother you?" And I said, "I'm not overly concerned because I feel that in a few years he'll just grow out of it."

Dr.: How about his mother? How did she feel about the feminine behavior?

Father: She always took a position of protecting him. No matter what kind of discipline I wanted to give him, she always stepped in between. She's a very dominant type of woman, and I have a continual battle just to stay on top, otherwise she'd just crush me to the ground.

Wife-husband roles and their importance for the feminine boy are discussed in greater detail in Chapter 15.

Dr.: Was she concerned about the feminine behavior? Or did she feel the way you did?

Father: I don't think she was as much aware of it as I was. However, I say I was willing to accept it at that age because I felt he'd grow out of it. Subsequent events have proven that he hasn't.

Dr.: Yes.

Father: It's just gotten worse. I came into the house one day almost a year ago and caught him in all his sister's clothes. From head to toe, undergarments, everything.

The boy's story reveals an early desire to be a girl and a continuing interest in physically changing sex.

Dr.: You were seen here some years ago when you were a young boy. Why were you seen then?

M-F TS: Because my dad thought I was peculiar. I acted different from other kids. I was mean and I was quiet, and I wasn't really close to anybody but my mother. And she used to protect me a lot.

Dr.: Were you behaving femininely then?

M-F TS: Yeah. I used to not like to hang around boys. I didn't like them. I used to hang around with girls. And then all their junk rubbed off on me.

Dr.: Would you ever make believe you were a girl?

M-F TS: Oh, yeah, a lot of times. I'd go into the bathroom and put soap all over my face and make believe it was a commercial.

Dr.: Did the soap make you a girl?

M-F TS: You know these commercials, and they go, "Wow, my skin's soft" and this kind of thing.

Dr.: How old were you then?

M-F TS: About, oh, God, let me see, about seven. Then they had this dairy farm down the street from us. I used to go over there all by myself and play house with dishes. When I was about eight. I remember some kids; they weren't talking about me; they were talking about Christine Jorgensen. I was listening to them and one of the kids turned around and called me a big old sissy and then "Oh, you should have the operation done, just like her." And then he goes, "You even look like a girl."

Dr.: How old were you when you first felt you were sexually attracted to guys?

M-F TS: It goes so far back. I guess I always was. But then, you know, I was, I guess, too afraid to come out and say that. So I kept it to myself. Since I was about eight you know I thought, "Well, it would be better if I did have the operation done."

Dr.: Did you really think about having a sex change at eight?

M-F TS: I thought about it. I used to go, "Oh, gee, I wish I was a girl instead of a boy." I thought I'd be a lot better off. And then when I was about eleven I thought more about it.

Dr.: Why?

M-F TS: I just didn't have no feelings for girls. I didn't really like 'em. You know, I liked 'em to hang around, and talk to, and stuff like that. But as far as having sex with them, I don't think I could. . . . I want female hormones.

Dr.: What would hormones do for you?

M-F TS: Well, first, they'd kill all this ugly hair. Kill the hair roots and make peach fuzz grow back. And then they'd start filling out my calves and thighs.

Dr.: Why would you like that?

M-F TS: I guess so I'd look more like a woman.

Dr.: What if someone were to say to you, now at seventeen, "OK, you can have a sex-change operation"?

M-F TS: I would take it.

Dr.: Why?

M-F TS: Because I think I'd be more happier that way, because right now I know people talk about me.

Dr.: What do they say?

M-F TS: Oh, they go, oh, I'm a big old queer and "Oh, you faggot." And then they do, "You should have been a girl."

Dr.: So if you had the surgery what would that do?

M-F TS: Well, I wouldn't have to—to be ashamed of myself, try to hide that I am a homosexual. Because I wouldn't be no more, right?

Dr.: What would you be?

M-F TS: I'd be a woman, I guess.

One motivation for sex-change surgery is avoidance of the label "homosexual." However, this boy's statement does not necessarily mean he wants to be a woman solely as a "cop-out" to avoid that designation. He may be credited with being unsophisticated in terminology and using the only language available to him. His lifelong feminine orientation and avoidance of the use of his penis during sexual relations point to transsexualism.

M-F TS: I mean, I'd have everything a woman has except for organs, the sex organs. I wouldn't be able to have kids, but, big deal, I don't want any. I guess it would just make things better for me.

Dr:. You think you could live as a woman?

M-F TS: Yeah.

Dr.: How do you feel dressed as a woman?

M-F TS: I don't feel so self-conscious. I don't feel afraid. I just walk out there normally.

Dr.: When you're having sex with a guy, when you're being screwed, how do you see yourself?

M-F TS: As a woman. They treat you like a woman; you know, they're real gentle with you. They don't push you around, and they do it very soft. They don't slam it in! I just see myself with boobs and everything. These thoughts are going through my head but when I look at myself I can see myself as a boy.

Dr.: Do you come?

M-F TS: No. Because I don't play with myself when they're doing it.

Dr.: Do they play with you?

M-F TS: No.

Dr.: And they don't jerk you off when they're screwing you?

M-F TS: It's not jerk, it's jack.

Dr.: OK, they don't jack you off while they're screwing you?

M-F TS: Uh uh.

Dr.: Would you like them to?

M-F TS: No, not really. No, I really don't get no sensation out of it. It's too dry. I mean, if you spit on it, it still stinks.

Dr.: Do you ever screw them?

M-F TS: Uh uh. I never screwed a guy.

Dr.: Why?

M-F TS: Because I like to get screwed, I don't think of myself as a queer. I see myself in the mirror and I say that, you know, I really do look like a girl. I even put on makeup and everything.

Dr.: You wear makeup every day?

M-F TS: Yeah, every single day. I even pluck my eyebrows. Rat my hair, dye it. See, this is my natural color. It's bleached out.

Dr.: You're wearing pancake makeup now?

M-F TS: Yes.

Dr.: You wear eye shadow too?

M-F TS: I wear everything, everything they do. I wear eyeliner, eye-shadow, and I put it on good, too. In fact, I can put it on better than some of those girls in school. And a lot of 'em know I wear it. They go, "Wow." And then, like every guy I go out with, they tell me how tough my eyes are.

Dr.: What would you like to see happen to you?

M-F TS: I'd like to check out of the school I'm going to. During the summer I'd like to go and have a sex change and check into a different school where nobody knows me and just start off on a different foot.

Figure 4–1 is a behavioral summary of "boyhood" as recalled by thirty adult males who requested sex change. Very few preferred boys' toys, even fewer preferred boys as playmates, and less than half preferred boys' clothes or had a clear conception of themselves as being boys.

These case histories illustrate that the early-life onset of feminine behavior in boys (if the stories are valid) is not necessarily a passing phase, but that parents may dismiss it as such. These recalled experiences point the way for identifying a population of preadolescent males at high risk for the later emergence of atypical gender behavior.

One way to help people who do not outgrow the kind of conflict described here is outlined in Chapter 6. A detailed study of young boys perhaps on their way to this adult picture is presented in Chapters 10–16.

FIGURE 4–1.

Recalled childhood behavioral features of thirty adult males who requested sex change to female status.

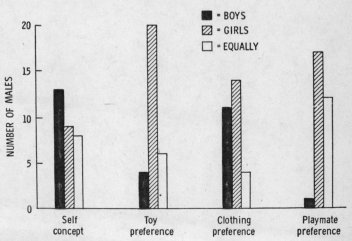

5

BOYFRIENDS AND HUSBANDS OF MALE-TO-FEMALE TRANSSEXUALS

The men who fall in love with and perhaps marry women who are themselves former males, by and large, have known their partners only as women. Their prior sexual experiences have been only with females. They consider themselves heterosexual and their relationships heterosexual. To varying degrees they are consciously and unconsciously aware of the biologic status of their partners, but it would be simplistic and would furthermore blur generally accepted definitions to call these men homosexual. Rather they are men who respond to the considerable femininity of male-to-female transsexuals, ignoring the dissonant cues of masculinity. Surely there are other males, with more internal prohibitions against behavior suggestive of homosexuality, for whom such a response would be impossible. However, the purpose here is not to portray these consorts in full but rather, by the descriptions of their relationships, to supplement the self-portraits of femininity in the previous chapter.

Example 5-1

A man describes meeting his future wife. Unbeknownst to him, she was an anatomic male.

Husband: I'm very, very fond of her, and if the operation could ever come to pass, I'm all for her, whatever she wants and makes her happier. If it's not feasible, that would be all right too.

Doctor: How long have you known her?

Husband: Two and a half years. I was very much attracted to her when I met her. I was single, and, at the time, I had stopped going with a girl. I was right in between dates, you might say. She seemed like a very nice girl, and one thing led to another, and about a year later we were married.

Dr.: Can you tell me your initial impression of her?

Husband: Well, she was very outgoing. A lot of fun.

Dr.: When you first met her, did you have any idea that there was anything different about her?

Husband: Not in the slightest. It never entered my mind.

Dr.: Had you done any kind of necking, any kind of petting, during this period?

Husband: Yes.

Dr.: What was it like?

Husband: I did think it was unusual that she always wore a very tight girdle. . . .

Dr.: What would she say when you would comment on it? How would she fend it off?

Husband: She said she had some kind of surgery.

Dr.: You accepted that at the time?

Husband: It did seem a little unusual. I don't think I'd ever gone with a girl that long without getting better results. Maybe I was impressed by it, I don't know.

Dr.: It certainly didn't dissuade you?

Husband: Not before I knew, no.

Dr.: And how did the truth finally show itself?

Husband: One evening she tried to mentally prepare me and came out and told me.

Dr.: What did she say?

Husband: She said, "You'll probably hate me, but I have to tell you this." She thought maybe I already knew. I said, "I'm sorry, I can't guess it." And she told me. She used the term "I am part male." I was very shocked. In fact, I was thinking of going to a psychiatrist at that time. It really shocked me. I was in a daze for a couple of days. I still liked her, and to me I don't think you'll find a more feminine person.

Dr.: You say you were dazed?

Husband: She offered to show it to me, and I said, *"No, I believe you."*

I was a little bit confused for several days, and I just didn't know what to say. I just more or less resolved the situation in my own mind.

Dr.: How did you do that?

Husband: Well, as I said, I liked her in every way. We had always gotten along so well. It was, to get right down to the point, a few days later that I went to bed with her. It was a little awkward at first. I had never had any experience.

Dr.: How do you mean "awkward"?

Husband: I really didn't know how to go about it. . . . I wanted to talk to somebody, but I never did. I thought, well, I'm going to face it myself. I think that's the only way a person can keep their sense of balance.

Dr.: What had you found particularly attractive about her before this?

Husband: Well, she's a very good dancer. She's a good mixer. She's a very intelligent girl. Very vivacious, a lot of fun to go out with, and a wonderful cook, just a fantastic cook, really, and we just got along so great.

His wife had not told him the full extent of her maleness. The male-to-female transsexual had described it this way.

Doctor: What have you told him about yourself, about your anatomy?

Male-to-Female Transsexual: I told him I was born this way.

Dr.: What way?

M-F TS: A girl. That I've always looked this way, and he knows nothing about me ever taking one estrogen pill. He thinks I am going about getting corrective surgery, and this is all he knows.

Dr.: And he has no idea that you have had breast implants?

M-F TS: No, he hasn't the vaguest idea.

Dr.: He thinks that you were born—

M-F TS: And developed these things naturally.

Dr.: What have you told him about the penis and testicles?

M-F TS: Well, he's seen them.

Dr.: How did you explain them to him?

M-F TS: That there are hermaphrodites walking around that are born with both organs. I said that all I have to do is get rid of the male organ and everything will be fine from there on. So he's just waiting for me to get it done.

Dr.: Is one of the things you are worried about that he would think your relationship was homosexual?

M-F TS: Yes. Exactly, and to my knowledge I don't think he has any homosexual tendencies, really. I think he is just as much man as any of them. I wouldn't want anybody that has homosexual tendencies.

Dr.: You wouldn't?

M-F TS: No, definitely not. I abhor the thought. I know there are millions of them and everything, but still I personally have no interest in anyone who is one.

Dr.: If you were to have your surgery, does your husband feel that you could have children?

M-F TS: No, he doesn't. He knows I can't.

Dr.: How does he understand that?

M-F TS: He has asked me point blank, "Can you have children?" and I've told him no. He was a man who was expecting to have children, I know.

Dr.: Does he think that you have any female organs inside you?

M-F TS: It's been my fault if he does. I have said neither yes nor no, and I've said we can't really tell until I have surgery. Sometimes when we have sex I do bleed, and it's just from that he's hurt me, and he asks me, "What's the matter?" and I just say, "It's that time of the month," and I think he really thinks I do.

Dr.: You told him that you menstruate?

M-F TS: Yes, I have, because of the presence of blood sometimes, simply because I've been hurt. If he knew he had hurt me, we probably would never have sex again, so I just tell him that it's that time of the month and to lay off for a week or so then I'd be OK. He just thinks there is something inside that's wrong with me that has to be corrected. This is it, and he thinks surgery is going to correct it for me.

Example 5-2

A postoperative transsexual relates what she had told her fiancé about "her" past. This person, in addition to being extremely feminine since childhood, is also an example of Klinefelter's syndrome (Baker and Stoller, 1968).

Doctor: How long have you known your fiancé?

Male-to-Female Transsexual: Not really long, but as far as in my mind it's like I've known him for five years.

Dr.: And how much does he know about your past?

M-F TS: Everything. I told him everything. Of course, it was very difficult. You know, telling him anything. I didn't have to tell him about the surgery at all. But I told him that I did have surgery, and that I'm not able to have children, which he's very happy about because he doesn't want to have children.

Dr.: What did you tell him about the surgery?

M-F TS: I just said that as far as everyone was concerned, including myself, that I had always been female. So many percent female and the rest probably was male, and that my genes were predominantly female, and so today with the DNA structure they have a way of telling long before what would be the best for the baby to continue female or to continue male.

An acceptable explanation had been given this patient to permit accommodation to her cross-gender identity.

M-F TS: Then I said, "We won't go into that because I thoroughly, in my mind, I know what I am," and I said, "If you don't want to accept it, here's the door, because I've been through it and I don't want to hassle about it, and I don't have to make excuses for myself." If people don't like it, they won't accept it. To hell with them. I'm not going to let it bother me any more. I have my life to live.

Dr.: What was his reaction?

M-F TS: Well, he was very sympathetic, you know. He had never heard of anything like this, and he was astounded. I said, after I told him everything, I said, "Do you think you could live with me knowing all this?" And he said, "Let me tell you what I think of you first. Do you think you would feel secure married to me? Do you think married life would be something you would really enjoy?" I haven't told him anything about—I've led him to believe that I'm a virgin, but I'm not. I've had other affairs. I'm not going to tell him everything, you know, because if I tell him everything I won't have any little surprises.

Dr.: Have you been having intercourse with him?

M-F TS: Yes.

Dr.: How is that?

M-F TS: Well, he thinks—he's kind of hurt, I think, because I won't play with his genital area, you know, and I don't know why, but I sort of seem very shy about it with him. Maybe it's because I really truly love him and respect him, and I have a deeper feeling for him, and I think that I would rather do all of these things after we are married. Then I wouldn't feel so guilty about it. We've had intercourse a couple of times, only he can't enter me because I'm closed now. I was supposed to go for more surgery but I don't want to have surgery until we're married. I really don't. After we're married then it will have some bearing.

Dr.: Have you been able to have intercourse since your surgery?

M-F TS: Yes, I have had sex quite a bit. You name it and we did it.

Dr.: What did it feel like to you?

M-F TS: Wonderful.

Dr.: You enjoyed it?

M-F TS: I had an orgasm too, and I still do. I get them even closed up.

Dr.: Are you able to satisfy him?

M-F TS: I do.

Dr.: How?

M-F TS: Well, I'm on the bottom and he's on top, and it's just rubbing, but it's very normal, only he's not getting inside. But I refuse to have any sex play through the rectal area or orally.

Dr.: Why do you feel that way?

M-F TS: Because I don't want anything that would remind me of the past, although I have never had any homosexuality in the past before surgery.

Dr.: How does your fiancé feel about homosexuals?

M-F TS: He hates them.

Dr.: He hates them?

M-F TS: He despises them. . . . He says—he calls them—he says those SOBs. And I said, "You know that's really unfair, because—" He says,

"Well, why do you defend them?" I said, "Well, basically I had a penis at one time. Even though I wasn't considered male at home, but basically what the hell are you to call that? Maybe there was no testicles present, but—" He said, "It was just a dead piece of skin." I said, "Well, I considered it a dead piece." I said, "Even the butcher probably wouldn't buy it." He said, "You could never convince me in a hundred years that you looked anything but what you are now."

Her fiancé's story reveals him as a man who considers himself a typical heterosexual male and his fiancée an unusual female.

Fiancé: I'm thoroughly convinced that she's a woman. I think there was a mistake on the birth certificate.

Doctor: How do you see the mistake? What do you feel the mistake was, from your understanding?

Fiancé: Well, basically, the way I see it is that she was born with sort of a dual situation with an overriding on the female side, and I think that a lot of research went into it before any operations were taken, and I feel that the right steps have been taken so far.

Dr.: When you say there was an overriding of the female, are you talking in terms of—

Fiancé: Strictly physical.

Dr.: You're talking about physical, not personality?

Fiancé: Not mental or personality. The only psychological problem is that her father wanted a boy, and this caused the birth certificate situation, I guess. And a little psychological situation problem there too, but I think that's all over and done with now.

Dr.: What is your impression of the kind of operation that was performed?

Fiancé: Well, my understanding was the removal of the male characteristics of the situation took place. That's my understanding of it. Other than that I don't know.

Dr.: I think that's essentially so. Do you think her male characteristics were completely normal before surgery or that there was something unusual about them?

Fiancé: I feel that it was underdeveloped and incomplete, and that it was a minority situation as opposed to a majority situation. This is my impression.

No challenge to this man's impression would have been appropriate here. However, some further exploration of his feelings about the matter was pursued.

Dr.: This is essentially so. Let's make up a make-believe sort of thing for a moment. Let's presume, and it's not so, that your fiancée's genitals were perfectly normal male and there had been no basis whatsoever of femaleness, how would you then feel about that?

Fiancé: What, if she was a male? Well, in that case I wouldn't be in favor of associating with her under that circumstance.
Dr.: Can you say why?
Fiancé: Well, I don't know. I like girls.

Knowledge exists from interviewing his fiancée that vaginal intercourse is not possible.

Dr.: May I ask a little bit more about your current situation? I know from your fiancée's medical records that there has been some difficulty with the aftereffects of the surgery. There has been some closure of the vaginal opening. I am wondering, has this affected your relationship with her?
Fiancé: Well, no. She still enjoys sex relations. I guess if the operation were performed it would be a more normal act, but I'm happy with her the way she is, and I would probably be even happier after the operation.
Dr.: In what manner do you have sexual relations now?
Fiancé: Well, that's a pretty personal question. I'd like to pass that.
Dr.: Correct me if I'm wrong. At the present time, it's not possible to enter the vagina; that's closed down after the surgery?
Fiancé: Yes, but she does still receive a normal sexual sensation or fulfillment in the vaginal area through the way we do it, so this is a highly desirable situation.
Dr.: Are you satisfied with how the relationship is now?
Fiancé: It is enjoyable, yes. I don't know; it would probably be even better with the operation.
Dr.: Have you ever known anyone like her before? Anyone who has had this kind of medical-sex problem?
Fiancé: No, she's very original.
Dr.: Have you ever known any normal males who have wanted to become women and were looking for so-called sex-change surgery? Christine Jorgensen–type surgery?
Fiancé: No, I've never met those before.

Perhaps the word "before" hints at a deeper sense of awareness of his fiancée's status.

Dr.: How do you feel about men who are homosexual?
Fiancé: I don't know what their problem is, but they have a problem.
Dr.: Do you think it's some kind of a mental illness or do you think it's a biological preference over which they have no control?
Fiancé: I'd say it could be either *stupidity* or *biological* or *both*.
Dr.: As you know, there is a fair amount of controversy as to whether homosexual relations should be illegal or legal, that is, whether it should be a private matter between two people.
Fiancé: In my estimation they ought to throw them in jail.
Dr.: Why?
Fianceé: Because I think homosexual sexual relations are illegal according

to the statutes, and they are crimes against nature, and they are just not right.

Dr.: Have you ever had any homosexual interests yourself?

Fiancé: None whatsoever.

This man may well have had no experience with genital homosexuality, and perhaps never any conscious desire for this pattern of sexuality. However, because of the strength of his antihomosexual feelings, one suspects conflict at some level.

Example 5-3

This husband, whose wife is still preoperative, differs from the fiancé of Example 5-2 in the extent to which he can consciously acknowledge homosexual interests. In fact, as will be seen from the following interview with his wife, the closer she gets to feminizing surgery, the more distant he gets from her. An important difference between this man and the two consorts, Examples 5-1 and 5-2, is that when he first met his future wife, she was still living as a man.

Doctor: Do you remember your initial impressions of your wife?

Husband: The first time I ever remember was she was walking across the street, and one of the fellows I work with said, "Hey, that looks like a guy wearing capris."

Dr.: How did that strike you?

Husband: It just seemed to me to be sort of odd. I'd never seen a male who looked quite so feminine. Not effeminate. She never has been effeminate.

Dr.: How would you make the distinction?

Husband: Effeminancy is an application. You might call it a striving to be feminine but, of course, not being one as it is foreign to them. But to be feminine is to be graceful, and certainly no masculinity.

Dr.: So you felt that this person was feminine?

Husband: Yes.

Dr.: How did you feel the first time you spoke to your wife?

Husband: A little bit funny. I don't know how to describe it better than that. I never had seen a person like this before, seen a male who was quite so feminine, and it was a little bit puzzling. A little confusing too. Not mind boggling, but just a little bit unordinary. Different. That's the most I can say. It was a little bit awkward.

Dr.: Do you remember your sexual feelings?

Husband: Well, there was no immediate sexual thing. My first thing was a slight bit of curiosity, and she seemed to be a nice person. Very nice personality. I think this was the initial attraction, and I guess I have to admit there was a little curiosity too.

Dr.: How long did it take before you were aware of the fact that you did have some sexual feelings?

Husband: It was sort of a gradual progressive building up of feelings of affection and protection.

Dr.: Were you puzzled by the fact that you did develop sexual feelings?

Husband: No, because, as I say, the major part of it is personality complimenting personalities, and the sexual part of it is it more or less takes care of itself as long as you're compatible.

Dr.: Had you had some sexual experiences before this?

Husband: No, I actually hadn't. No.

Dr.: You were a virgin?

Husband: Right.

Dr.: What about masturbatory activity?

Husband: I engaged in that.

Dr.: Everybody has certain favorite themes they imagine when they masturbate, things which are most arousing. What kind of things were appealing to you?

Husband: Sort of a chieftain, if you will, or someone who has a responsibility, or protects, or he conquers, but he protects also a woman or women. Sort of benevolent chieftain or father. Less carnal than protective, a loving and caring person.

Dr.: Would you actually imagine yourself having sex with a woman during the time that you were masturbating?

Husband: Yes.

Dr.: Had you ever imagined yourself having sex with a man while masturbating?

Husband: It is a little bit erotic, the thought of it.

Dr.: Would you consider acting on it?

Husband: No, there is no need to.

Dr.: Because of your relationship?

Husband: Yes.

Dr.: How do you see the relationship you have in terms of what's happening sexually?

Husband: My wife is a woman with a *medical obstruction*, and our relationship now is the best compromise because of this. If she had the normal vagina that she should have, then there would be nothing different to distinguish her from normal, or what is considered male and female relationship.

His wife, however, is not so sure that their relationship is "the best compromise." She sees her husband's attitude changing as the time for her sex-change operation draws near.

Male-to-Female Transsexual: My marriage is not doing so good. It's not good because my husband more and more has turned to—now he's turned more and more to homosexuality. It's something I've found very difficult to live with. I could understand his turning to another woman, because of my position, but not another man. It really tears me up.

Doctor: Why is that more upsetting than if he turned to another woman?

M-F TS: Because I cannot give a heterosexual man the gratification that he may want. But to turn to a *man*, I don't know, it just irritates me.

Dr.: What did you think his sexual interests were when you married him?

M-F TS: I felt that he was heterosexual. Now I am disturbed over the lack of sexual relationship with him. He is completely impotent with me. It is ego deflating of me to be literally thrown out of his bed. I have come to the conclusion that I would have to find a sexual interest outside of the marriage. And the two men that I have met and had relationships with were just great guys.

Dr.: You're still planning on the operation?

M-F TS: Oh, yes.

Her husband appears to have delayed her genital surgery.

Dr.: How long have you actually been saving for this operation?

M-F TS: Oh, you wouldn't believe this. Since about the day my husband and I first got together, but there's always been something.

Dr.: What's come in the way?

M-F TS: Mostly him. We'd get about a thousand up and he would get suspended from his work.

Dr.: What would happen?

M-F TS: He'd goof up. Continual tardiness. He's always late, and just generally poor conduct at work.

Dr.: Would this affect the amount of money you'd have saved?

M-F TS: Exactly. It would all go right into it.

Dr.: Before the relationship got as bad as it is, how did he feel about your having surgery?

M-F TS: He said it meant a great deal to him.

Dr.: Do you have any question about that now?

M-F TS: Yes, I do, because we were closer before I started dressing as a woman regularly. The point was when I got my breast operation. It was one thing he did I didn't understand. It meant so much for me to get this operation, and when I did get it, he was very cold for about two months afterwards. He was very nasty to me.

Dr.: After you got the breasts?

M-F TS: And he told me that as time goes by I'm getting more womanly and more adjusted, and this is bugging him.

Dr.: Do you suspect now that he didn't want you as a woman? That he really wanted you as a man?

M-F TS: Yes, I do. I think that.

Example 5-4

This next young man describes his gradual accommodation to his girlfriend's maleness.

Boyfriend: I liked her very much when I met her. She was a lot of fun. And after dating her about three times I received a letter from her which explained her situation, and I called her and told her I'd like to talk to her about it.

Doctor: What did you think at first?

Boyfriend (laughing): I didn't believe it. It really shocked me. And, I mean, I was aware of people in this situation, but, I mean, I believed it after I overcame the shock, but, you know, it was kind of astonishing. You know, there had been a few things that hit me. A couple of times we got into little push fights, and she was much stronger than I would expect of a girl, but, nothing. It never crossed my mind. So I went down and talked to her, and I kind of decided since I had no intentions of going with a girl seriously at the time, I might as well keep seeing her.

Dr.: And when you made this decision that you'd like to stay with her and get to know her a bit better, did you foresee the prospect that the thing would become a sexual relationship?

Boyfriend: No, I really didn't. The thought crossed my mind, and I put it out of my mind. I mean, I didn't think I would get that involved. The first time we did have sexual relations, at the time it didn't bother me at all. I wasn't repulsed by the whole thing or anything but I felt a little bit repulsed, like "Well, I don't really want to do *that* again," but at the time it didn't bother me and it didn't bother me the *next* time we had a relationship.

Dr.: What have been your other sexual experiences?

Boyfriend: Intercourse when I was twenty, and I have had it with about four girls. I went with some girls, none to the point of being steady. I dated some. I guess there were four or five girls I dated.

Dr.: How about masturbation? Was that your primary sexual outlet?

Boyfriend: Yes.

Dr.: I've been impressed by the fact that people have all different kinds of fantasies when they masturbate. I am interested whether you remember during high school what some of yours were like.

Boyfriend: I suppose mostly it was *Playboy*-type things. Oh, yeah, there were times when there was a girl I would have liked to have, and I thought about her, but I don't think it was any more complex than that. As far as I know, I wasn't aware of any homosexual tendencies. In fact, I would say that the only thing that bothered me about sexual life was that I was a little reserved in approaching girls.

Dr.: I'm interested in how you felt the very first time you seriously considered having sex with Judy, not really having had any kind of sexual contact with a male previous to this.

Boyfriend: I don't know exactly why, but she was going to stay with me one weekend. It was two nights and we were doing something that weekend and this was, of course, after I already knew the situation. The first night she slept in my bed and I slept on a sleeping robe on the floor, and the second night she started crying during the night. She had a bad dream or something, and I was trying to talk to her, and after a long discussion, she was feeling a little bit better and she asked me to stay in bed, and so I joined her in the bed. I was clothed, and I was holding her, and we started kissing a little bit and after a few minutes she reached down and grabbed hold of my penis, and it bothered me a little bit at the time, and I wondered. I probably should have stopped it right there, but I guess maybe after talking to her about an hour after all this, I didn't.

Dr.: Did you begin having intercourse?

Boyfriend: Another time. I think it was two or three weeks later. I was seeing her fairly often during this time. I do remember the first time we had intercourse that I didn't feel like doing it again, and it must have been a couple of weeks or more before we had it a second time.

Dr.: How often do you have intercourse now?

Boyfriend: Once or twice a week. Twice a week.

Dr.: What is it like?

Boyfriend: It's enjoyable.

Dr.: What sort of position do you get into when you have intercourse?

Boyfriend: Mostly lying down with her legs over my shoulders so that she's on the bottom and I'm on the top. There have been times when I sat up and she pulled her legs around me. Those have been about the only two.

Dr.: When you're having intercourse with Judy, are you consciously aware of the fact that Judy has male genitals?

Boyfriend: Yeah, usually. I mean, it's pretty hard to overlook. But it's not on my mind. I mean, *there* every minute. In fact, it's on my mind a lot less than I expected it to be, after the first time we had intercourse.

Dr.: How do you see the relationship? Do you think to yourself "I'm having a homosexual relationship," or "I'm having a heterosexual one," or what?

Boyfriend: I don't think the homosexual aspect comes in a great deal or anything, because that word seems to have so many connotations. It is a relationship between two males as far as anatomy is concerned, and I would not be so presumptuous to say that I understand the psychology involved in it. You know, I really think to myself that she's a female. I mean I'm not trying to block out the fact that she's a male, but I usually think of her in terms of a female.

Dr.: She *looks* like a girl.

Boyfriend: Yes, which is probably a lot of it. And when I first met her, the first week or ten days that I knew her, I thought of her as a female, and I've always related to her as such except for certain sexual behavior.

First meetings are important, not only for consorts but also for investigators. It is more difficult for the interviewer to accommodate to a male's feminine appearance if earlier interviews were with the patient in male status.

Dr.: Where do you see your own plans heading now? How would you feel about marrying her with her history as it is?

Boyfriend: I think there are possibilities of it. You know, I can't form a definite opinion in my mind because I don't know what will happen. I'm faced with the problem of the draft now, and I don't know how that's going to change her relationship with me because I have no intentions of getting out of the draft by pleading homosexuality.

Thus, the extent to which adult males who want to become women are feminine is demonstrated by the attitudes of males who become their boyfriends and husbands. The consorts are masculine, a requirement of the male-to-female transsexual to complement her feelings of femininity and nonhomosexuality. For similar reasons she must believe that her consort has never experienced homosexual relations. A certain amount of deception may be practiced by the transsexual, enough to permit her partner to adjust to the situation without being overwhelmed by "homosexual" implications. By and large, these couples have heterosexual friends and assimilate unremarkably into society.

6

TREATMENT OF MEN WHO WANT TO BECOME WOMEN

The adult who wants to change sex can be exasperating, intriguing, and/or pathetic. He or she is at the nidus of one of the more controversial dilemmas of modern medicine. Few human phenomena engage such charged issues of morality, medical ethics, law, psychiatric theory, and the individual's right to self-determination. Attempts to resolve childhood sexual identity conflicts through psychiatric counseling are described in Chapter 16. By this means it may be possible to prevent the adult dilemma. What, though, is the answer for adults who still request sex change? How can these unhappy people be responsibly served?

In its most general sense, psychiatric management of a request for sex change consists of (1) understanding the patient's motivation, (2) facilitating a realistic appreciation of the limits of medical procedures, (3) management of difficulties experienced by the patient's family, (4) encouraging the patient to try reversible changes, during a trial period, prior to irreversible surgical steps, (5) lending support during the period of social transition into the new role, and (6) promoting a realistic anticipation of what the future may hold after sex reassignment. For those patients who undergo surgery, the psychiatrist's role extends to (7) assisting in postoperative adjustment.

DIAGNOSIS AND PREOPERATIVE COUNSELING

Typically, the patient recalls a lifelong history of behaving as someone of the opposite sex, as exemplified in Chapter 4. However, a request for sex change may also come from patients with other backgrounds, persons whose histories seem more typical of homosexuality or transvestism.

The differential labeling of transsexualism, transvestism, and homosexuality is not always clear-cut, although a few oversimplified distinctions can be made. The essential basis on which differentiation is made focuses on gender identity (a person's self-concept as a man or woman) and sexual object choice (whether the person is sexually attracted to males or females). Broadly stated, gender identity is contradictory to genital anatomy in transsexualism and in accord with anatomy in transvestism and homosexuality. In contrast to the transsexual's self-conception of being of the other sex, and feeling comfortable dressed in clothes usually worn by the other sex, transvestites are typically sexually aroused by cross-dressing, feel themselves to be men when not cross-dressed (and may, too, when cross-dressed), and are sexually attracted to females. Homosexuals typically consider themselves to be males, are sexually attracted to other males, and if they cross-dress (which is not typical) do so only to attract certain males, or to put on a show. These distinctions have been described in detail by Stoller (1968).

In practice, diagnostic distinctions may be blurred. Unequivocal categorization may be difficult. And, there are some persons whose past experiences seem more consistent with transvestism or homosexuality, but, when interviewed, make a better fit into the picture of transsexualism.

The practical significance of diagnostic distinctions lies in the extent of the patient's male identification and the pleasure derived from the use of his penis. Intuitively, it would appear that the more masculine a person, the more difficult would be the transition into living the role of a woman; and the more sexually gratifying has been penile sexuality, the more significant would be its loss through surgery.

Assessing the patient's gender identity takes into account childhood behavior and fantasies, adult body imagery, masturbatory fantasies, and sexual and social relations. Did the person experience conflict over gender behavior as a child? Have there been life periods in which he was adequately able to relate as a man? Can sexual arousal accompany imagery of himself with male genitalia? Has cross-dressing been sexually exciting? Does the person consider himself a man or a woman when dressed in men's or women's clothes? To what extent does he, by his physical behavior, convey an impression of femininity?

Example 6-1

Men who have enjoyed their penises and who have been sexually attracted to females may nevertheless desire sex change and seek the advice of a doctor. The therapeutic strategy with such patients is to stress the possible consequences.

Doctor. You've enjoyed the use of your penis. What do you feel would be your sexual arousability after surgery?

Male-to-Female Transsexual: Everything. I want everything with a man *except* a sexual relationship. Everything.

Dr.: So you need a vagina like you need a hole in the *head*. You've used your penis?

M-F TS: Yeah.

Dr.: And you've had pleasure from it?

M-F TS: Yes.

Dr.: And there's a reasonably good chance that, if you had surgery, you'd never have an orgasm or have any kind of sexual pleasure whatever.

M-F TS: That's right. That's right.

Dr.: So, I'm not sure how you can just sit there and say, "I'd be willing to do that."

M-F TS: Yes, but there are other things, like forty is my age.

Dr.: So, what does that have to do with it?

M-F TS: Well, I don't have any sexual drive right now, but I have a terrible need for close companionship. I have very, very little need for sexual satisfaction.

Dr.: Sitting here now, do you feel as though you're a man or a woman?

M-F TS: Woman. I'm definitely a woman.

Dr.: But in terms of feeling as a woman, you don't pick up the sexual part?

M-F TS   No.

Dr.: You would really separate gender and sex?

M-F TS: Yes. I wish I didn't.

Dr.: To go ahead and have your male genitals cut off doesn't to me make any sense.

M-F TS: Maybe my decision is based on some insecure—some feeling that really doesn't amount to anything. For instance, when I dress I can't wear *capris*. Now, if I had an operation, I've always said that the only reason I'd have the operation is so I can wear capris. Another thing, too, is when you—when I first started going to lesbian bars someone would go, "Pst, pst, pst. It's a guy." All these gay girls belong to this inseparable club. That's a very tight group. You just don't get in. There's no way for me to get in.

Dr.: I don't know what you'd accomplish by having surgery.

M-F TS: No.

Dr.: I mean if you were somebody who wanted to be screwed by guys—

M-F TS: Yeah.

Dr.: Then I could see some logic in it, but I don't see what the hell you'd accomplish.

M-F TS: No?

Dr.: I don't see any gain in it. There's a potential for regret too.

M-F TS: Yes, I suppose I don't disregard that.

Dr.: You've flip-flopped enough times in your life.

M-F TS: Uh huh.

Dr.: The potential of your flopping again in the other direction is always going to be there.

M-F TS: Right.

Dr.: And I think for you to take an irreversible step—

M-F TS: In other words, don't take it off until you know. Don't you think that after a period of time that the hormone castration would be chemically irreversible?

Dr.: No.

M-F TS: It wouldn't really?

Dr.: No.

M-F TS: That's wonderful.

Dr.: You should always keep the option open because sexually you're still a man.

M-F TS: Yeah.

Dr.: And I think for you to go into an irreversible procedure and castrate yourself would be a mistake.

M-F TS: Umm.

Dr.: You've got a lot of male identification.

M-F TS: Yes, I know I do.

Example 6-2

Some males, although they have some feminine identifications, see changing sex principally as a means of finding love from a male. This next person recalls a boyhood similar to many transsexuals but is primarily identified as a male. However, he is pessimistic about finding a meaningful emotional relationship in a homosexual union and sees greater promise in marrying a male if he were a woman. His story demonstrates one of the many motivations for sex change.

Patient: From childhood, as a young person, I think I started right off with a bend towards feminine interests—say, like dolls or paper cut-outs or something of this sort. Then I had a transvestite period, I call it, from about the age of nine, ten, eleven, up until early teen-age. The first homosexual experience I had, I was about six or seven—curiosity. Then I had some during and after the little transvestite period. Then I sort of became real ascetic with myself, disciplined myself. I was going to make something out of my life. I went to college. All of the overt sexual desires just didn't take place. It was all fantasy, and I found that to increase my—what shall I say? —my orgasmic pleasure, that imagining myself as a woman increased it rather than imagining a male-male homosexual relationship. Men turned me on.

Doctor: Do women turn you on?

Patient: Not in a long, long time.

Dr.: When did they?

Patient: I loved women, I think, when I was about seven years old. From about the age of seven up to puberty.

Dr.: Does the fantasy of having a wife and a family appeal to you at all as something you would like to see for yourself?

Patient: It was a wishful thought for me, yes. I mean, I imagined myself ending up normally, but I couldn't encourage it. I knew it was like a dream.

Dr.: What kind of sex do you enjoy?

Patient: Well, I can't say that I actually do enjoy it, for all the effort that's put into it.

Dr.: What do you mean?

Patient: Psychologically I enjoy it. Psychologically I do, but actually I don't. I like the idea of having this done to me, but, honestly, I can't say that it's a real good feeling.

Dr.: What do you like about it?

Patient: I'm being given something. I like the idea that it's a man, and that he's thrusting his penis into me, although physically I don't get any great thrill out of it.

Dr.: Do you get pleasure from your penis?

Patient: Some. I have orgasms.

Dr.: Having someone handle your penis is pleasurable?

Patient: Yes, it's pleasurable.

Dr.: Have you ever dressed up as a woman?

Patient: I did once last year. Outside of that, it hasn't been since about the age of fourteen or fifteen—just to see what it would be. I guess I feel a hunger for a love and an affection that I don't seem to be able to find in a homosexual.

Dr:. How do you expect to find it?

Patient: Changing my sex is, I guess, the way. Trying to become the love person to some man.

Dr.: Why? How would that be different from what you're doing now? Why would that be more permanent and more satisfying?

Patient: I don't know. There must be something better. This is no good. You know, like I said, I did envision a normal solution to becoming normal and a marriage and a happy ever after, but that hasn't been for a few years. It just doesn't seem to be working out. I don't know what I thought therapy would do for me, but it didn't change my feeling about being turned on by some men, so what are you going to say to yourself? Pretend that a woman is turning you on when she isn't turning you on? I say I'm being basically honest with myself.

Dr.: Can you imagine yourself living as a woman? The body of a woman? Living and dressing as one?

Patient: It has occurred to me, although I'm not taken with clothes. I want to be a woman because I want a man. I don't want to be a woman because I just want to sit around and have tea and put on a dress.

Dr.: What you want is a good, solid homosexual relationship?

Patient: I don't think this is possible.

Dr.: It happens. There are homosexual marriages that are as successful as heterosexual ones.

The issues that such a person must deal with include the need to be loved only by a man, the extent to which this is possible to achieve as a man, and problems that might arise for him, because of his masculine identifications, were he to pursue a course of sex reassignment.

Example 6-3

Some men decide on surgery without having had any experience living as women. Consider this person who has lived as a male fifty-eight years and has decided he will suddenly re-enter society as a woman.

Doctor: How much confidence could you have as a female?

Male-to-Female Transsexual: I think I would have a 'great deal more.

Dr.: Why?

M-F TS: I don't know. I just think I would.

Dr.: You never lived as a female. You're fifty-eight years old. That way you're going to emerge on the earth as a female with confidence? It's hard to know where your confidence comes from.

M-F TS: I don't know. I believe it would. I'm convinced it would. Maybe it's a matter of feeling, rather than reason or logic.

Dr.: Most people before surgery try living as a woman, first, just to see what it's like, before going ahead with an irreversible step.

M-F TS: Living as a woman? How can you do that?

Dr.: Just by dressing as one and working as one. To see what it's like.

M-F TS: But that wouldn't make you a woman.

Dr.: No. Neither does *cutting off your penis.* It can make you a man without a penis.

Example 6-4

The importance of a trial period of living as the other sex before undergoing genital surgery cannot be overestimated. This safeguard has been stressed by Benjamin (1966). An excerpt from an interview with the sister of a male requesting surgery is representative of advice given directly to patients.

Doctor: He's an unhappy person. I don't know whether he'd be happier living as a woman. That brings an awful lot of problems in itself.

Sister: But if he weren't happy living as a woman, why does he tend to do it now?

Dr.: Well, he's not living full-time as a woman. He's never worked as a woman. He hasn't lived fully as a woman. He's never been hired as a woman. My feeling is that before people go through with the irreversible surgery of changing sex, they ought to live and work as a woman for at least a year.

Sister: Well, do you really think that working as a woman or being hired as a woman, a full-time woman, would make a difference?

Dr.: I think he ought to find out what it's like while he could still change his mind about it. Once he has had the surgery, then that's it. If he changes his mind after the surgery, then it's too late to go back.

Sister: But even if it's too late to go back, even if he's not satisfied with being a full-time woman, he'll never be a complete man. As long as he'll never be one complete thing—

Dr.: He has to experiment a little to find out which is the more satisfying. He knows he's not satisfied living as a man, but he doesn't know yet whether he would be satisfied living as a woman. Right now he is straddling the fence. Surgery is very expensive and also irreversible, you know, and once your genitals are cut off, once his penis is gone, it's *gone*. And if he decides that "I made a mistake," you can't grow it back on again! And so our advice to people like your brother is to say, "OK, you feel you would be more adjusted living as a woman—go find out. Start dressing all the time as a woman, go out and try to get a job as a woman, see if you can pass successfully as a woman, see if you can support yourself as a woman."

Sister: What is the purpose? How come to have something like that done as bad as you want it, you have to see a psychiatrist?

Dr.: You don't *have* to. If you've got five thousand dollars you can go off and find yourself a surgeon that probably would do it.

Sister: You can't just go in, if you've got the money, you can't go in and just have it done?

Dr.: There are some surgeons who will do it. They don't care whether you've ever seen a psychiatrist. But my feeling is that people ought to have a fairly good feeling of what they're up to before.

Such advice is not idle.

Consider here two males who desperately wanted sex change when first interviewed but who changed their minds during trial periods on female hormones. Their reasons for abandoning the goal of surgery differ. One met and fell in love with a teen-age girl, and the other married a woman who herself had been sex-changed from being a man.

Example 6-5

The first, masculine in appearance, experienced an abrupt end to his desire of becoming a woman as he became infatuated with a girl half his age. Previously he had also experienced remission from his transsexual desire when he felt a woman loved him. Of especial interest are two dreams that took place during this transition. In them are revealed some of the "behind-the-scenes" work involved in this change of heart.

Doctor: How are you today?
Patient: Beautiful.
Dr.: What has made life so great?
Patient: I hate to admit it. I think I've fallen in love.
Dr.: With *what?*
Patient: A *girl!* I decided to try a little experiment and get involved with females, and I did. I feel lighthearted, happy. I don't think there is anything I wouldn't do for her. I'm happy when I'm with her. Is this good or bad?
Dr.: Well, how does it feel?
Patient: I feel good. Although, it does bother me seriously. I have had a philosophy for a long time. I've had a feeling that no person, no woman especially, could move me. But now one has, so it has wrecked my way of life. Not that I'm objecting. I think of nothing but her.
Dr.: You've had involvements with women in the past?
Patient: Oh yes, but none like this.
Dr.: What has been different about those?
Patient: I would get a feeling of maybe closeness for a while, but then I would get back in my old routine again.
Dr.: Your old routine being?
Patient: The way I was living before, doing women's things. The relationship wouldn't last for long. It wouldn't last a week. But now I've been feeling very comfortable. I've been feeling like a man.
Dr.: What do you mean "feeling like a man"?
Patient: OK, the man takes the dominant part. I've been feeling that way. I've had more confidence the past three or four weeks. I don't care

to dress up anymore. I haven't—I started feeling a little something when I first met her, but I was suppressing it. I was really suppressing it because I wanted this thing to come off.

Dr.: This thing being what?

Patient: The sex-change operation.

Dr.: At that time you thought there was a real chance that you would have surgery?

Patient: Yes, and I think after the first time I saw you I had some doubts in my mind,

Dr.: When you were here the first time you said you didn't feel like a man. You enjoyed doing women's things, housework, sewing, and cooking, and so on.

Patient: I still like to cook.

Dr.: That's what I said the first time. A lot of men like to cook.

Patient: That's right. So what's the big deal? There is no big deal. I like to cook. I'll probably always like to cook.

Dr.: A month ago you felt that was an indication of femininity.

Patient: Right. Right. I was narrow-minded. I had one way of thinking.

Dr.: What about the feelings of wanting to cross-dress?

Patient: I haven't had any. You know, I've had dreams constantly. One provocative dream that really got my interest. We went horseback riding a couple of weeks ago; she loves horses, and so do I. In the dream I was sitting on one of those corral fences, and this black horse, this beautiful black horse comes trotting down the road. And as soon as it got in front of me *its tail fell off*. All it was was like a broomstick with a tail glued to it, and the tail fell on the ground, so I jumped off the fence and I picked up the tail, and the horse was still going away, and I tried to catch the horse and put it back on, and I couldn't reach it, and I woke up.

Dr.: What do you make of that one?

Patient: OK, for one thing she has long hair, and I think I would probably lose some of myself if she lost that hair for any reason or other.

Dr.: Do you feel that the hair there and the hair on the horse's tail could signify anything else? What else would you feel concerned about if it were lost?

Patient: The horse's tail would be a part of the horse, and it fell off, but the horse didn't even know it. It didn't realize that it was gone, and I tried to get it back, and I couldn't do anything.

Dr.: It was too late. What comes to mind about that?

Patient: Wait a minute. You said that sex-change was irrevocable.

Dr.: And what kind of surgery were you asking about?

Patient: Genital surgery. Having my penis cut off. And I couldn't put it back, right? Oh, that's fantastic!

Dr.: It sounds like this became a real concern to you, the fact that it was an irreversible procedure, and this aroused anxiety in you.

Patient: Well, I think I knew that it was irrevocable even when I asked, really.

Dr.: What other dream?

Patient: There was a wide open space, very wide like a desert, and there was a motor scooter behind me like the mail carriers have, only this was a policewoman. I think that she was actually the metermaid that I often encounter. I'm running frantically down this desert, and she's behind me in this scooter, and she's trying to catch me, and she's gaining on me. I keep looking back and she's still coming. A man reaches into his suit pocket and gives me a piece of paper. And I said, "Give me one more hour please, just one more hour." At this time he says, "Just one hour." She gets out of the scooter and grabs my hand. I grab her hand and we start running, and she said, "Come on, we'll make it," and we're running and running.

Dr.: What thoughts come to mind?

Patient: I have no interpretation at all for that one.

Dr.: Just start talking about it.

Patient: Maybe he is you, and he says—and I wanted some more time for some reason or other. I wanted an hour. Then he grants me one more hour.

Dr.: When did you have that dream?

Patient: This morning. This very morning.

Dr.: Do you think that the one hour in the dream could have anything to do with the one more hour *here?*

Patient: He granted me one hour.

Dr.: Essentially that's what I did. I said, "Come back for another hour."

Patient: Then she grabbed my arm, and we left together, and she said, "We'll make it."

Dr.: What does that bring to mind?

Patient: She was chasing me; she was behind me; she was after me; and I was running away from her. But then I'm granted another hour. Then we're together. She and I are together. Male and female together. That means I could live with myself.

Dr.: You mean even with the feminine part of you?

Patient: Yes.

Dr.: Are you saying that even if all the feminine things don't go away, like your interest in cooking, or whatever, it's still OK, you can still be you?

Patient: I've overlooked those things already.

Dr.: I guess my feeling the first time you were here and the second was that you had a lot of masculine identifications, a lot of maleness in you. And I think you have demonstrated that you do have quite a capacity for being a guy.

Patient: I've felt more like a guy. I've been feeling more like a guy. I've been feeling more like acting like a guy.

Example 6-6

The other male who changed his mind had been taking female hormones for a year, was undergoing electrolysis for the removal of facial hair, and had had his nose and "Adam's apple" surgically modified to appear more feminine. Enter a beautiful girl, herself a former male.

Patient: I won't need you any more. I've solved all my problems.
Doctor: Tell me how.
Patient: Well, I'm going to drop the transsexual bit and be a happy normal guy and marry a "sex change." How's that?
Dr.: Tell me about it.
Patient: We have a lot in common. Everytime I would be around her for any length of time and not see her I would go away really depressed. The last time we had a pretty decent talk. That was the first time I realized that I was in love with her. I've now got two issues, namely my feminine self and this girl. If I'm choosing the wrong one, I would always be depressed, right? I decided that what it really must be is that she is most important for my happiness. She knows what my big hang-up is, and she knows what the odds are. It doesn't bother her, and it doesn't bother me.
Dr.: Well, what are you going to do? You're taking female hormones, cross-dressing.
Patient: Well, we had a long talk about that, and I think that I'll probably stop taking hormones. It's important if I'm going to function with her sexually. Frankly, I have no doubts about that.
Dr.: It will be a while before you're potent.
Patient: Yeah, a day or two!
Dr.: More than that.
Patient: Yeah. Just teasing.
Dr.: You probably have pretty shrunken testes.
Patient: Yeah, maybe half or something. So, basically, that's what we'll do. I'll see her and spend a lot of time with her, and if I still dig her and we function sexually and I still feel the same way, then there's no problem.
Dr.: Will you consider getting married?
Patient: Oh, definitely.
Dr.: Did she have a legal sex change?
Patient: Yes. It's going to be a great relationship, that's for sure. There's no doubt about that as long as I'm not hung up over transsexualism. As I see it, that's about the only problem.
Dr.: There might remain some residual in your fantasy life.
Patient: Well, I don't know. I really don't know. It's not that I don't want to be a girl. It's just that I would rather have *her* than be a girl. I don't know if I would ever dress occasionally or not. I really don't know because I don't know how I'll feel. Maybe it would even be wise if I have a slight urge to go ahead and dress once a month or once in a while, as opposed to never doing it one time if it comes back. But just dressing occasionally should be no problem, you know. It's this transsexual problem, the hormones and all that.
Dr.: What about her is so appealing?
Patient: I don't know. I really don't know. She really has it for me. We're

really just great friends, you know, and that's really important. On top of that I am attracted to her.

Dr.: How does she compare with other women you've known?

Patient: Well, personality-wise, of course, I don't know a lot of women really well. I have known maybe seven or eight women in my life and I think I like her a lot better.

Dr.: How is she different?

Patient: Well, most women, even the ones that I didn't like, there is just this little bit of phoniness or an over-concern of what-the-neighbors-are-thinking type of thing. She doesn't do that. That's not many good reasons, I guess, but that's the way it is. I don't know what it is, but it must be *something* to convince me that I don't want to have surgery! I tend to think as far as sex itself is concerned I am basically bisexual. Well, I *know* I am. I'm positive of that. I think if I had met some guy that would accept me as a woman the same thing would have happened, but I genuinely do dig this girl. I don't have to hide a thing, which has never been true with any other girl. I don't know. Perhaps with other girls I go out with, and don't tell about my transsexual problem, I've got just enough guilt or something holding me back that I can't function sexually.

Dr.: Do you have any misgivings about the *nose* surgery you had done?

Patient: No, that's water under the *bridge*. The only misgivings I might have would be all the money I've blown on electrolysis. Not that I'm bothered that I don't have a beard.

Dr.: It sounds like you're feeling much better.

Patient: I've made a lot of big discoveries. It's nice to be at peace. I've never been so relaxed in all my life. It's been the best week of my life from the standpoint that my problem has gone away. See, you *cured* a patient. Chalk one up!

He did, in fact, function sexually. The couple was married and a year later reported a successful marital adjustment. Transsexual desires had not returned. It may be that the patient was able to channel these wishes by identifying with the extraordinary success with which his wife had accomplished that same task. What better solution, too—short of marrying a true hermaphrodite—for channeling bisexual drives?

POSTOPERATIVE COUNSELING

Emotional problems during the postoperative period need be anticipated. Many transsexuals have led lonely, isolated lives before surgery. They optimistically look forward to sex reassignment as a rebirth. Unrealistic expectations of an immediately blissful life, exciting and romance-filled may be harbored. They may profess the belief of shortly meeting the man of their dreams and settling into a happy family life. Unrealistic expectations can lead only to disappointment. Tempering should take place *prior* to surgery.

Preoperative patients should know the limits of medicine and surgery. The male beard will not be eliminated by female hormones. An expensive, extensive, and uncomfortable procedure, electrolysis, is necessary. The masculine vocal pitch will not be raised by female hormones. The thickening of the cords that takes place during the male puberty is irreversible. Males should not expect a rapid transformation into idealized female proportions. Many believe that breast size is a function of how much female hormone is poured into the system. They overlook the dismaying fact that many females, exposed to female hormones since puberty, have but limited breast development. The limit in the system appears to be the genetically determined responsivity of the tissue.

With respect to surgery, cosmetic and functional results of genital surgery vary widely. Vaginal function especially is highly unpredictable. Many patients are plagued by slow healing of internal suture lines and by canal closure. Even with vaginal patency, the canal may be insensitive and the capacity for orgasm lost. The postoperative woman will be sterile.

Example 6-7

The subject of the following interview is the same as in Example 4-3. She is now interviewed six months after surgery.

Male-to-Female Transsexual: It seems to be fine. I'm still wearing the form, and I guess inside seems to be doing all right.

Doctor: Has there been any problem with closure or stricturing down, getting narrow or—

M-F TS: I know a couple of times I just got so tired of wearing that big, horrible mold that I just said, "I'm going to leave it out today." And I went to work thinking it might improve on the healing if I'd leave it out while I was at work, but trying to get it back in was just almost impossible, so—

Dr.: If you do leave it out it starts to shrink down?

M-F TS: Yes, and so the longest I've ever left it out is about eight hours, and it took me the whole evening to get it back in.

Dr.: Do you have feeling inside of you? Do you feel things there? Pressure or touch? Anything?

M-F TS: I'm sure I do, because I can feel the form in, and when it's out I can feel it going in, yes, so I'm sure there's some kind of feeling there. It's not just dead.

Dr.: Is there any sexual feeling?

M-F TS: No, I don't think so.

Dr.: It's more like the feel of skin anywhere?

M-F TS: Yes. It starts to itch way up inside of there, and you have to scratch, and there's no way of doing it.

Dr.: But there's no real sexual feeling on the inside like the tip of the penis or something? Not that kind of feeling?

M-F TS: No.

Dr.: What about during love-making with your husband?

M-F TS: We haven't been doing very much of that. In fact, just a couple of times, because it hurts so bad.

Dr.: You haven't been having intercourse?

M-F TS: Just a couple of times, and the last time I came to see the doctor down here, he said definitely not, so that blew that.

Dr.: How's your husband taking that?

M-F TS: I don't know. He's going to start looking pretty soon if I don't get better.

Dr.: Do you have any kind of sexual contact without intercourse?

M-F TS: No, none at all.

Dr.: How many times have you had intercourse since you've had your vagina?

M-F TS: Not more than half a dozen, if that many. I'd say half a dozen.

Dr.: It was painful to you?

M-F TS: Well, if he's real, real, real careful, then it's OK, but then that spoils it for him. You know, he has to get—if he puts all his weight on me there's not enough room for him, you know, deep—depth, and if he takes it real easy, then it's OK, but nothing strong or physical.

Dr.: What does he do, take cold showers?

M-F TS: Yeah, he *does* take cold showers. He wakes up in the morning and says, "My gosh, I'll have to take a cold shower, thanks to you," but that's about it.

Dr.: Would you consider the possiblity of resuming anal intercourse?

M-F TS: No, it never even entered my mind. I don't want to do that again.

Dr.: What's your feeling about the cosmetic appearance of it?

M-F TS: Fine. Everything's fine.

Dr.: You're satisfied?

M-F TS: Yes, I'm quite happy with it.

Dr.: And he?

M-F TS: He's happy with it.

Dr.: I am wondering how you would describe the thoughts you have about it now, six months later.

M-F TS: I was just thinking of that on the way down to work today.

I can almost forget that I've ever had surgery. It's like I've been like this all the time. It is quite pleasing to me. I have never, never regretted going through with the surgery. I have always been happy, even at the worst moments when I'm fighting to get a form in or something, or bleeding or running down to see the doctor. I've never been sorry. It's been worth all I've gone through.

Three years later the patient remains delighted with the surgery and her marital relationship remains compatible.

Example 6-8

Another patient compares sexual climax as a woman with previous orgasms as a male.

Male-to-Female Transsexual: I had sex fourteen days after my operation.
Doctor: Can you describe what it was like the first time?
M-F TS: I was petrified the first time. I was still quite swollen, and the first time was more or less like a growing-up child would do, experimenting with something new, and it was really nothing. I couldn't reach a climax, or do anything. But it still was a sensation of some form, and the second time that I had a climax, it just wouldn't stop, I really, and then I started, at first I started to climax with a regular flow, and then it started bleeding, and I was petrified.
Dr.: You said you started to flow. What do you mean?
M-F TS: Well, with my sperm or semen. It was clear. Any coloration had been eliminated before surgery.
Dr.: How would you compare how the climax felt then with how it felt before surgery?
M-F TS: It's much more. It lasts much longer, and now I climax over and over. And before, in fact, I used to—my only form of sex was masturbation maybe once or twice a week, and now I can climax four or five times right after another.
Dr.: During how long a period of time?
M-F TS: Oh, I could keep it up all night, if I could find some man that could do it.
Dr.: What is the quickest you can climax twice, what is the shortest interval in between?
M-F TS: Oh, just a few minutes.
Dr.: And is the kind of climax the same as you had previously experienced as a male?
M-F TS: No, I can't say that. It's a different feeling completely.
Dr.: In what way?
M-F TS: You still have this sensitivity and everything that you had as a male, so, of course, I have to be emotionally aroused a lot, and my breasts are my big factor as far as sex goes. I love to have my breasts fondled. I know many times, the first time I don't even know I've done it, but then I

continue throughout the night, and it just builds, and builds, and builds until I'm just really exhausted.

Dr.: But are they real climaxes as in the previous sense?

M-F TS: Yes.

Dr.: Or are you describing feeling constantly excited?

M-F TS: Well, I've been told this, and I don't know if it's true or not, but I don't always have a flowage. Now I will, once or twice, maybe three times, but I have had my sensations five times in one evening, right after another. I mean, we'd just quit, and work each other up again, and continue.

Dr.: And when you have your climax, are there involuntary movements of the pelvis which you experienced as a male before your surgery? Do you go beyond the point where you can control it?

M-F TS: No, I can always control it.

Dr.: Could you stop a climax in the middle?

M-F TS: I have. My boyfriend used to get so mad at me because the first couple of times he would try to please me I would get so worked up and I would get the sensation feeling. It was just like there was something built up inside of me, and I would be afraid to continue with it. So one night, he really got mad, and he said, "If it takes us all night, I'm not going to stop until you've reached your climax." Then that was the night I did. It just ran right down my legs. It was something else.

FAMILY COUNSELING

What should a patient tell family members when he wants to change sex? When the patient is married and has children the situation requires delicate handling.

Example 6-9

To this family, the wife as well as the children, the husband's desire to become a woman came as a great surprise. The father's explanation to his sons about what was happening to him left something to be desired.

Wife: It was really quite a shock to me. He kept it a complete secret from everybody, and he chose first to inform the boys.

Doctor: Were you aware of his feminine interests prior to that?

Wife: I have been aware of, to a small degree, that there was some kind of a problem. When we first got married he was wearing men's shorts, and very shortly thereafter he began to wear women's underpanties. Always with an explanation that he had hemorrhoids, and the smooth material was better. So I didn't think much of it.

Dr.: Did you think there was anything unusual about the explanation?

Wife: I didn't think too much of it because *I'd never had hemorrhoids.* So far as I knew it, he was perfectly normal. Then other things came up. He had to wear women's loafers because his ankles were so narrow he couldn't keep a man's shoe on.

Dr.: Did you believe that?

Wife: After a while I began to get really irritated about it, because he made such a point over it. I should have realized now what was bothering him.

Dr.: Has he told the children something about what he is doing?

Wife: Yes. The way he tells it to me is that they noticed that he was developing breasts and they questioned him about it. He said, "I'm turning into a woman." He says, "Mother Nature is turning me into a woman." The younger one was a little concerned about it. What do you suggest I do? I'm interested in their future health. I feel they should not be around this influence.

Dr.: I certainly appreciate your concern. I think what one has to do is weigh two things against each other. One is the admittedly confusing influence of being around a man who has strong womanly identifications. And the other aspect of it is "What does it mean to the boys to be irrevocably alienated from the only person in the whole world who's really their father?" Both of these are very, very important influences in one's life. I don't think it's an "either/or" thing.

Wife: Well, this is, of course, what makes it very difficult. A very difficult situation, because I don't want to hurt them.

Dr.: Both are artificial circumstances. Certainly, saying to two boys who are eight and ten "You can never see your dad, even though he lives in the same city" is an artificial thing. I think that it in itself can be detrimental to boys. I think they're both very difficult. It would appear from what you say that the boys are already aware of what your husband is doing.

Wife: Well, he told them.

Dr.: So it's not a question of "Let's try and keep this incredible secret from them." The cat's out of the bag. As far as the great shock and the damage from the initial disclosure is concerned, it's been done. They know.

Wife: Although I do feel that if they are constantly repeating the experience of observing and being around him, that it is going to perpetuate the emotional problem for them.

Dr.: Well, I think that it could also be looked at from the standpoint that the reason that they repeated the talk about it is that that's the way they have of handling their confusion over it. To just put it in the back of their mind somewhere would be a very difficult thing for them to do. I think by talking about it and joking about it is their way, as eight- and ten-year-old boys, of coming to accept the fact that this is going on.

Wife: Well, but don't you think that if they are not around the problem, that it will recede from their minds and not trouble them?

Dr.: No, it will never recede from their minds. Because they know about it, and because it's happening to the only person in the world who's ever been and ever will be their father. You see, it's not a stranger.

Wife: I see.

Dr.: Does your ex-husband dress as a woman when your children visit him?

Wife: He said that he did once or twice to show them what he was talking about. I called in the older boy and questioned him about it, and asked him, "Has your father told you that he's turning into a—what did he tell you about him—the change in him?" "Well, he said, 'Mother Nature is turning him into a woman.' "

Dr.: I guess I object to his saying it that way. If I do have a chance to talk with them, I would like to explain it in a somewhat different way. This way it sounds like it's coming out of the sky.

Wife: I said, "Don't ever get the idea that all of a sudden a person starts changing. This is something that your father thought up and is doing himself. This is *his* choice." I don't want them to get the idea that—

Dr.: I would underscore what you've said. That this just doesn't *happen* to people. That if your daddy's body is changing it's because he's getting *special medicine* for it, that this will *not* happen to you. It might make more of an impression if it comes from a doctor.

Wife: I felt like before I brought them down I would like to know from you what your attitude is on how you would explain it to them.

Dr.: I would first need to know what they think is going on. And then I would see whatever misconceptions they have and try to straighten them out. And I would eventually say that there are people who feel that from very early in their life they'd rather be girls. Obviously these boys *don't* feel that way so they immediately know it's *not them.* And that sometimes as these people grow up they don't grow out of it, and they decide that sometime in their life they're going to see what they can do about pursuing life as a woman. And that's a very unusual thing. And just because your dad was like that doesn't mean *you'll* be like that. He's still your dad, and if you talk to him about it, I think you should try to understand everybody's a little bit different. Your dad's a little bit different, but obviously most men aren't like that, and you're not going to be that way either when you grow up.

Considerable supportive therapy may be necessary for wives of men going through the anguish of deliberating over sex reassignment. One wife condemned herself for having failed in her role as a woman. She benefited from reassurance that her husband's atypical gender identity existed prior to their relationship and that it was highly unlikely that anything she could have done would have altered it. Other wives, if angry at their husbands, may benefit from knowing that their marriages were not sinister tricks or frauds perpetrated on them, but that their spouses initially hoped the marriage would work.

Truthful explanations to very young children can be more confusing than helpful. The concept of sex change is bewildering enough for adults. It is better if children are told that their parents are divorcing, that their father will be living far away, and that he will probably be unable to see them. They need assurance that he still loves them and that the separation is not their fault. At best this will be difficult. At a later time they can be told the truth, if the mother wishes. Older children are in a better position to understand.

Parents of transsexuals, too, may need help in assimilating the change. They may feel responsible and guilty for their child's behavioral anomaly. Regardless of one's idea of the role parents may play in the etiology of transsexualism, little will be gained by indictments at this stage. Parents need support and help in understanding the pervasiveness of their child's sexual identity conflict.

Observing the parents furnishes the psychiatrist with impressions of the family settings in which his patients have matured. Meetings with parents also afford a psychiatrist opportunities to pick up additional details of the transsexual's early years, in order to contrast them with what has been previously reported by the patient. Such meetings can further provide some extraordinary information about the parents. In one case, following a family interview, the mother acknowledged to her transsexual son that she herself had been through an extensive period in which she had wanted to become a man. The son had not previously known this.

It is clearly not possible for the psychiatrist to be sufficiently objective in the treatment of the person seeking sex reassignment if he has strong emotional feelings against it, believing that under no circumstances may a person be helped by such procedures and that under no circumstances is it a legitimate course for the patient to follow. Nor can a psychiatrist be sufficiently objective if he feels reassignment should be freely granted to all who request it. Rather, it is preferable to maintain a position of objective open-mindedness until more hard research data are available. This wait-and-see attitude, together with an interest in gender-role adoption and a desire to assist another human being toward the resolution of a profound conflict, can make such patient management uniquely rewarding.

7

WOMEN
WHO WANT TO
BECOME MEN

Females who want to live as men seem to be fewer in number than their male counterparts. Estimates are that in the United States they are only one-third to one-sixth as common, that is, only one female wants to become male for every three to six males who want to become female.

A number of theories have been offered to explain this disparity. (1) Neuroendocrinologists point to the increased likelihood of errors in the psychosexual development of males in consequence of the additional component necessary for masculinization, gonadal hormone (see Chapter 3). (2) The more sociologically oriented point to the greater latitude our society affords the female with respect to cross-gender behavior, which makes it less necessary to seek radical means of disguise. (3) Psychologists and psychiatrists point out that the first person with whom a child identifies is a female, its mother, and that a subsequent shift in identity is required only of males. And (4) the surgically trained underscore the technical limitations inherent in procedures designed to metamorphose females into males. They suggest that since, as one surgeon quipped, "It's easier to make a hole than a pole," fewer females will seek a surgical solution.

Whatever may be the reasons for fewer females than males requesting sex change, the fact remains that many females do feel that they are essentially male, wish to become male in the eyes of society, and seek medical help. These women face the same dilemma as do their more numerous male counterparts.

As in Chapter 4, the purpose here is not to debate the ethical issues surrounding the transsexual's dilemma, but rather to indicate, through excerpts from four case histories, the pervasiveness of cross-sexed identity in adult females. The childhood memories of these females who want to become male reflect mirror images of the early memories of males who want to become female. Typically, they were "tomboys." They roughhoused, enjoyed sports, and liked wearing the clothes of boys. They remember wanting to *be* boys.

Again, as with males who want to become female, caution must temper total acceptance of the accuracy of the patients' memories; present desire can, all too often, obscure past fact. Nevertheless, such adult histories provide a valuable background for studies of sexual identity conflict in children as well as a potential aid in resolving it. In the excerpts from interviews given here as Examples 7-1–7-4, females who desperately want to become male describe their current dilemma and recall their "girlhoods." Their stories are offered as first approximations of what to look for in girls who are on their way toward extensive adult masculinity.

Example 7-1

This attractive, feminine-appearing young lady looks as though she were applying for a job as receptionist or secretary. Yet behind this feminine appearance is a strong, hidden drive toward maleness. This drive has been present since childhood.

Female-to-Male Transsexual: I've never talked to anybody about it before. This is the first time.

Doctor: What kind of talk do you feel you need?

F-M TS: Well, I want to be a man very much because I feel like it, and I think most of the time I think more like a man than a woman. It is possible to do it, which I didn't know until one month ago. I understand you can give hormones and perform surgery when someone wants to change their sex.

Most people have heard of sex change from male to female; fewer are aware of procedures in the opposite direction.

Dr.: You say you've never spoken to anyone about this before?
F-M TS: No.
Dr.: How have you managed to keep it to yourself so long?
F-M TS: Partly it's something you don't go around talking about, and also some people are kind of narrow-minded about it. I don't consider myself homosexual. I think that's one thing people would think of automatically. I just feel like the opposite sex.
Dr.: To what extent?
F-M TS: Everything I do I feel very unnatural. Wearing woman's clothing. Things I like to do, usually sports, outdoors, swimming. I don't know how to explain it. There are a lot of little things. I have wanted to be a boy ever since I can remember, but there are no logical reasons for what I feel inside.

Like male-to-female transsexuals, females who want to be men deny any interest in homosexuality and affirm a cross-gender orientation "as far back as they can remember."

CHILDHOOD MEMORIES

Dr.: When you were a kid you felt like this?
F-M TS: Yes. Part of the time it used to be if you were a boy you could do more things. It was just sort of the way I felt. I used to like playing football. I didn't like being a girl and doing things girls do, and lately, it's gotten more so. I feel very awkward being dressed up and going places as a girl.
Dr.: To what extent is your family aware of your feelings?
F-M TS: They knew it very much. They always considered me a tomboy. My mother used to always try to get me to play with dolls and everything, and I wouldn't do it. I played cowboys and Indians with the boys, climbed trees and rode horses, went hunting and fishing with my brothers. I was always out wrestling with the boys. I wasn't doing what she thought I should be doing, but she kind of got used to it, I guess. I never really did change much.

Here no blame is put on the parents. While they may not in fact have encouraged boyish behavior, it is also possible that they did but that the patient has forgotten.

Dr.: When you were small did you feel that you were a boy or a girl that liked to do boyish things?
F-M TS: I'm not sure it was just wanting to do boyish things. I don't know how to separate my feelings of doing these things.
Dr.: Have you ever felt that you were a boy or a man?

F-M TS: Well, I know I'm not, so it's kind of hard. I think I feel like one most of the time. It's a little bit hard to really distinguish what you really feel like when unconsciously you know it's not.

Dr.: Do you think you were more tomboyish as a kid than anybody else?

F-M TS: I didn't know any girls that liked to do the things I did. I remember when I was little I always used to wish I were a boy. I don't think I played with girls too often. Sometimes I'd play games, but I never played the part of the girl in the games. I always pretended like I was a boy.

Again, as with male-to-female transsexuals, fantasy expression during role-taking games appears to be an important early clue. This may be a better reflector of masculine identity in girls than an interest in wearing jeans, climbing trees, or playing ball.

EARLY SEXUAL FEELINGS

Dr.: How far back did you find yourself sexually attracted to a woman?

F-M TS: High school. I'm not sure when I was actually sexually attracted to them. At the time I was dating boys—parties and that sort of thing—but when I got out of high school I felt uncomfortable.

Dr.: Had you had any romatic experiences with men?

F-M TS: More or less. Four or five years ago.

Dr.: Can you tell me a little bit about that?

F-M TS: Well, it didn't go far. I liked him a lot, more as a close friend or brother rather than somebody I'd want to marry. We had a lot of fun together—horseback riding and that sort of thing. At that time I realized that I wanted to be a man, and I figured it was hopeless so I talked myself out of it. We got close to having sex. He wanted to, but I just couldn't do it.

Dr.: Did you like him as a person?

F-M TS: Yes, I liked him very much. I know it would have been kind of foolish to have married him. I didn't love him, and I wouldn't feel like a wife. I guess that's when I really realized that I couldn't play the part of his wife.

Dr.: When did you start having girlfriends?

F-M TS: I guess the first one was when I was in junior college. There was one I really liked like a man likes a woman, not as a girl's friendship.

Dr.: Do you have any kind of sexual outlet now? Masturbation?

F-M TS: When I was younger, not now. It's something I figured was wrong.

Dr.: Can you tell me the kinds of thoughts or fantasies that you would masturbate to?

F-M TS: My being a boy. Sometimes there was television shows that I watched, and I catch myself still doing it, watching shows with nice-looking girls or something. I used to wish that I was in the man's place to try to pretend that I was playing their part.

AVERSION TO HOMOSEXUALITY

Dr.: Have you ever had a sexual relationship with a woman?
F-M TS: No.
Dr.: Have you thought about it?
F-M TS: Yes, I've thought about it. I've thought about it very much, but somehow or other I've never done it. Not as a girl I don't want to. It just bothers me, having sex. That's not what I want.
Dr.: Do you feel that if you could conduct a homosexual life, as many women do, and not feel guilty, this might make your life easier?
F-M TS: I don't really think so. Like even with my girlfriend I have to be careful, like opening doors or things like this. Maybe the way you look at somebody. You can't be free, and besides I don't think sexually that it would be satisfying. It's not meant to be.
Dr.: It's very common.
F-M TS: I know it's very common, but I don't see how they can be satisfied with it. I don't know. I don't think I would be. I definitely believe in God, and I have my own religious beliefs.

Religious inhibitions to homosexuality may be for some an important motivating force behind the desire for sex change, prior to instituting sexual relationships.

F-M TS: If I had another body I think I could feel free. I don't know what would happen with relations with girls. But even if it was possible you can't walk—you can't open doors for girls and things like this. It is more natural for me to do it, but I can't ever do it.
Dr.: What's to prevent you from doing a certain number of the things that men do now?
F-M TS: Well, I *do* do a lot of things they do, but it's still not the same. I still look like a girl. I am a girl. I just don't feel like the body and I fit together.

Example 7-2

This patient's story is similar, including memories of being a childhood tomboy, sexual attractions to females during childhood, and a strong aversion to homosexuality. Surgery was sought as the only solution to the dilemma of openly loving another female.

Female-to-Male Transsexual: I would like a transsexual operation.
Doctor: That's pretty much to the point. Tell me a little bit more about yourself.
F-M TS: I have a problem in that as a little child I always dressed more as a male than as a female.
Dr.: More so than many other girls?
F-M TS: Definitely.

Dr.: From how little?

F-M TS: Five years old.

Dr.: What else do you remember?

F-M TS: I was a tomboy. Although I don't think I was a tomboy as much as I was a loner. My grandparents had a lot to do with my upbringing. My grandfather was a carpenter, so I picked up that instead of playing with other children. I went through a period where I went to a lot of movies, and I was associating myself with being the *actor*. When I was very young I saw a lot of cowboy movies.

Dr.: During those preteen years, do you think your family was aware of how tomboyish you were?

F-M TS: No, not at all.

Dr.: How do you think they saw you?

F-M TS: Normal, you know, that I would overcome it.

There is more reason to believe that tomboys *will* overcome it. Their parents can be faulted less for their optimism than the parents of very feminine boys.

F-M TS: I've never discussed this with my parents. I've never discussed it with anyone. That's why it's pretty difficult. It's the first time I'm ever talking to anybody about it.

Dr.: When you were a little child, did you think you were a girl? Or did you think you were a boy?

F-M TS: I knew I was a girl biologically, but I never tried to fool myself in that respect. I didn't like it. I don't really like my body.

Dr.: Say more about that.

F-M TS: Well, the first thing, I don't like the breasts.

Dr.: How old were you when you started to develop breasts?

F-M TS: Eleven or twelve. I disliked it immensely.

Dr.: Were there any comments made about your breast development?

F-M TS: No. I wasn't teased or anything like that, but I was very self-conscious.

Romantic feelings toward females began during childhood.

F-M TS: I would say I was always attracted to females. Back to when I was a small kid. I would say it went back to about five or six. I always had dreams about females.

Dr.: Such as?

F-M TS: There was always just some kind of attraction. I found them more exciting. Attraction in that I would like to be around them. As a little kid I can remember that always.

Dr.: Do you remember having any crushes when you were a kid?

F-M TS: Yes. It was always on an older female. I always thought of them as being very beautiful.

Dr.: This is how old?

F-M TS: I would say seven or eight.

Analysis of childhood fantasies such as these may help identify tomboys (and perhaps feminine girls) who are on their way to homosexuality.

Dr.: What about in your early teens? Did you have any kind of fantasies about kissing or hugging?

F-M TS: Yes, the physical, the kissing. But that was more in dreams. I would be kissing another female, the female that I had a crush on.

Dr.: When were you first aware of adult-type sexual feelings? Genital types of feelings?

F-M TS: Very late. I would say when I was a teenager, around sixteen or seventeen.

Dr.: What do you daydream now?

F-M TS: That I will be a male kissing another female I was attracted to.

Dr.: How would your life be changed now if you were to be living as a man?

F-M TS: I would be dating, for one thing.

Dr.: You would be *dating*? Why not now? It wouldn't be the first time in history that two women have dated.

F-M TS: I would have a homosexual hang-up. I don't know. I don't think I would feel right in doing this. And I think that would also be true of the other person. In other words, society frowns upon this, and I don't want to seem different. I also think that if I wanted to have a lasting relationship with someone, I wouldn't want to start it now. I would prefer to have the operation and *then* start.

The implication here is that the desired consort be someone who would not have responded to femaleness, that is, a nonhomosexual female. The idea of being attractive to a heterosexual female is necessary to support the self-concept of manliness.

F-M TS: I would be very honest with the person. I would just rather have it come more natural.

Dr.: Will you explain that to me further, your being able to do something you can't do now because of breasts, and no facial hair?

F-M TS: I don't think I could do it. I just couldn't do it. Not now.

Dr.: Why would you be able to do it if your breasts weren't there?

F-M TS: Because the desire, wanting to do it, is there. But I just have too much of a hang-up this way, a psychological hang-up!

Example 7-3

This female-to-male transsexual lived through seventeen years of a heterosexual marriage and raised three daughters while feeling she was a man.

Female-to-Male Transsexual: I'm interested in sex reassignment. I have never spoken to a doctor or a psychiatrist about it. I'm forty-one now.

Doctor: How is it that you haven't spoken to any doctor before now?

F-M TS: I was raising some daughters. I think that's one reason. Although I dress this way [mannishly] all the time, I'm no different when I'm with them. When I was raising them, I just didn't follow this desire through.

Dr.: Did anybody know about it?

F-M TS: Oh yes. I have some very wonderful friends that I went to college with that I've known through the years, and they thought I should have done it sooner. They're glad I'm seeing about it now. These are straight people, married, with families.

MARRIAGE TO A MAN

Dr.: Are you still married?

F-M TS: No. I haven't been married for years.

Dr.: How long were you married?

F-M TS: Seventeen years.

Dr.: You describe a situation that sounds like from its inception was rather impossible and yet—

F-M TS: But he was on the road. He traveled.

Dr.: For *seventeen years?*

F-M TS: Yes, he traveled all the time. Sometimes he'd come in on weekends to see the kids. You see, I was brought up in a very strict religious home, and I didn't believe in divorce. And with the children I thought it best to keep the home together, under any circumstances. Just give of yourself. This was the way I was raised.

Dr.: How much about this problem did your husband know when he married you?

F-M TS: He didn't know anything about it. That was a case of getting married to get away from home, but he was on the road all the time, so it wasn't too much strain except when he'd come back. He knew something was wrong. And then, of course, well, he knew how I would dress, but he thought I was just tailored or very athletic. I used to wear my brother's clothing when I was little, used to wear my husband's clothes when I was married, and always bought men's clothes. I grew up in sports. I played professional ball. But then after we got married he knew what was wrong. He wasn't a bit understanding about it.

Dr.: How did he realize something was wrong?

F-M TS: Well, I didn't want sex with him, so there was a fight all the time. Of course, I was a wreck from it, and I'd end up going out with a woman. It was a lot of trouble. It has hard for him. It was hard for me.

RAISING CHILDREN

Dr.: Can you tell me how it was bringing the children up?

F-M TS: It was quite a struggle. We were very close. Maybe because of this, but I had a struggle all the time. I didn't feel I was fit for anything like this.

Dr.: Do you remember how you felt when you first learned you were pregnant?

F-M TS: Not exactly, because I was very apprehensive. I knew how I felt, and yet I knew how I loved children, and I'd take any child and raise it, but I didn't actually myself want to bear a child. I wouldn't let the baby nurse or any of these things. I just don't have this kind of feeling. I refused things like this.

Dr.: How about during the time you were carrying the baby?

F-M TS: Well, I still wore masculine clothes like this because I didn't show much anyhow. And I just wouldn't, I just wouldn't put on maternity clothes.

Psychological concepts of the origin of excessive nausea during pregnancy (*hyperemesis gravidarum*) stress the antimaternal nature of this reaction with an unconscious desire to expel the fetus orally. Adherents to this theory would therefore predict that a pregnant female, psychologically identified as a man, would experience a difficult pregnancy.

Dr.: How was your health during pregnancy?

F-M TS: I had morning sickness for nine months. I was constantly sick to my stomach. Morning, noon, and night. . . . I never felt anything like a mother, but I love the children. I love them dearly. And all three have turned out to be ideal human beings.

Dr.: How did it affect your raising them? This conflict that you describe?

F-M TS: Well, I ran from it a couple of times, thinking that they'd be better off. But they weren't, and, of course, they were pleased that I came back, and I'm glad I did because I finished raising them these past six years all by myself.

CHILDHOOD MEMORIES

F-M TS: I don't understand enough about it. I cannot believe that this is all psychological. I just feel that it is part biological. You can't just feel this way all your life—just something in your mind. Just can't feel this. How does the mind of a *child* perceive something like this?

Dr.: How far back are you talking about now?

F-M TS: As far as I can remember. Three years old.

Dr.: What do you remember?

F-M TS: I remember wanting to be a boy. Wearing boy's clothes and wanting to do all the things boys do.

Dr.: You remember this at *three*?

F-M TS: I remember it, and I remember my mother as I was growing up saying, "Are you ever going to be a lady? Are you ever going to wear women's clothing?" These kind of things as far back as I can remember.

AWAKENING SEXUAL FEELINGS

F-M TS: I can remember as I got a little older always looking at women, always wanting a woman.

Dr.: Now you're talking about what age?

F-M TS: Fifteen and sixteen, but I was so busy in sports that I didn't let myself until I was about eighteen years old, because, like I say, I was brought up very religiously, and it scared me. I didn't know why I felt like this. Why didn't I feel like other girls?

Dr.: Do you consider yourself homosexual?

F-M TS: Well, I must be. I'm a woman and I love women, and yet I cannot call myself one, because I don't feel like one. I feel like a man, and I feel like my loving a woman is perfectly normal.

A diagnostic distinction may be made here between female-to-male transsexuals and female homosexuals, even those who are masculine or "butch." The latter for the most part consider themselves female even if they don the trappings of masculinity including a short haircut, a leather jacket, and jeans.

Dr.: What does it mean to feel like a male?

F-M TS: I just feel like a male. I never felt like a woman, like a female. It's just the way I work, the way I live, and the way I raise children. I don't feel like a woman.

PASSING AS A MAN

Dr.: What kind of work have you had?

F-M TS: Well, I worked in a factory. I was an apartment manager for about a year. Now I'm working as a man.

Dr.: The people at work, do they know?

F-M TS: Well, they didn't. Until they saw my driver's license. See, I had to show my papers and everything. And they all thought that I was a man.

The driver's license in our society has become a primary source of civil identification. Transsexuals passing as members of the other sex are unable to execute routine procedures such as cashing a check because the name and appearance (in some states) on the driver's license boldly contradicts the appearance of the holder. Some Motor Vehicle personnel have been extremely cooperative with medical centers and have issued new driver's licenses to transsexuals upon psychiatric recommendation.

F-M TS: They were very, very shocked, but they were wonderful, because I do my job, and I respect them, and I don't bother anybody. Naturally they all refer to me as "he." One time I went out with a senior worker —to teach me the job, and he was close enough to see that I didn't shave, plus he talked to me long enough, you know, and so he came back and spread it around that I had to be a woman. So they called downtown and found out, but they never showed a sign. They were just wonderful, because I had done a good job.

Dr.: How do you feel about working as a man?

F-M TS: How do I feel? Wonderful. I really do. Because I feel myself.

Dr.: How do you feel knowing that the other people working with you know you're a female?

F-M TS: Well, they're wonderful. They just call me one of the "fellas," and I remember when I left the station to go down for my training my boss kind of grinned and he said, "Wherever you go, you'll do a good job. You're a good *man,*" and then he smiled and he shook my hand. They've been very understanding.

Dr.: What sort of difficulties have you run into?

F-M TS: Well, in stores for one thing. I've tried going in dressing rooms with my daughter, and I've been told to get out. Men weren't allowed in there. Rest rooms, same thing, you know. I've had people walk in a store and ask me if I was a man, and I've asked them if I really bother them that much. Before I matured, I used to get pretty hateful. I'd get a chip on my shoulder, and thought it was none of their business.

Dr.: You mentioned public restrooms. What kind do you use when you are out?

F-M TS: Well, I've used both. Just like the other day I went to the restroom. Well, now the workers all know me, and we work back in the workroom floor. So, I opened the door and walked in the women's restroom. I didn't think anybody would be in there. I always pick a certain time when there are no breaks, see. And a woman came in from somewhere else. I thought she was going to flip. She thought I was a guy in there. And I just said "Hi" and walked out. I didn't want her to be embarrassed, but I watched her then when she walked out and walked on the other side where she worked, and she was just gathering up a storm with everybody and pointing.

THE PATIENT'S GOALS

Dr.: How can we help you?

F-M TS: I'm going with a woman now.

Dr.: What does this entail?

F-M TS: It entails just about everything.

Dr.: Do you live with her?

F-M TS: Not yet, but we want to. She has two children, and we'd like to see if anything can be done. That we can go out into society and not have to raise these children the way I've had to raise mine. We are sort of waiting to see if anything can be done for myself so that we can go out into society legally . . . because there are two little girls. I do love them and they love me, but I'd like to be able to raise them with our heads up, be accepted in society. Treatment is important because I'd like the relationship to be completely legal, and I'd like to be all the way male. If I could go out into the world as a male, my papers as a male, maybe my voice a little deeper, and maybe hair on my face so that I could shave; I could do without a penis, but it would be a wonderful experience for me if I could have it.

Dr.: In you sexual relationship do you ever use an appliance, a substitute for a penis?

F-M TS: No, I never have.

Dr.: Has this idea occurred to you?

F-M TS: Yes, but I won't.

Dr.: Why?

F-M TS: To me, it's either real or it isn't. It's either me or it isn't.

After sex-change surgery, this transsexual married as a man. His wife is interviewed in the following chapter, Example 8-3.

Example 7-4

The parents of a sixteen-year-old female-to-male transsexual describe their daughter's earlier tomboyishness and current insistence on living as a boy.

Mother: My daughter has told me that she is a transsexual, and since then she's been wearing boy's clothing and says she wants to be a boy and nobody can change her mind. This is what she wants. She told me that since her ninth year she had said something to me and that I ignored her. Since she was about four and a half, when my husband left, she used to like to wear cowboy boots and guns. People say now, "Couldn't you recognize problems?" I said no, because my sister was twelve before she got out of cowboy boots.

Father: I thought the same thing. She'll grow out of it. She's just in the cowboy stage.

Mother: She liked short hair. She was always good at building blocks and putting things together.

Doctor: Beginning at what age?

Mother: At a very young age, I would say three. Two or three years old, doing puzzles. She was very fast at putting puzzles together. Even today at puzzles, she's very fast.

Dr:. And the years before kindergarten, did she play with girls or boys?

Mother: There were three boys up the street. She associated with them. There was also little girls. There was quite a few on the street.

Father: There's one thing sticks in my mind. This is going up to the fourth or fifth grade. I feel like I should throw this in. When I took her to school one day and this was prior to school starting, she ran out in the playground to play with the kiddies and the girls were all in a circle and she went up there to play ball with them—she couldn't have been more than six or seven—and one of the girls yelled at her, "If you want to act like a boy, go play with the boys." It didn't bother her at all. She went right over to the boys. That sort of hurt me. I didn't think too much about it. Maybe I should have.

Mother: She's always admired her broad shoulders which I thought was after her father.

Dr.: What kind of clothes did she like to wear when she was five, six, or seven?

Mother: Her father bought her very nice clothes. He bought her nice dresses, frilly dresses.

Dr.: Did she wear them?

Mother: No. She liked to wear pants and things. At times I thought maybe I forced her to wear them, but I felt she was a girl and should dress like one and to look pretty for her father. I tried to tell her that. Oh, when she was seven or eight, one time she wore perfume, and she balled me out. And I said, "Well, your father's coming, and I'm sure he wants his girl to look nice and smell nice." She said, "Ugh, take that stuff off me. That smelly stuff!"

Dr.: Was she considered a tomboy when she was young?

Mother: Yes.

Father: Definitely.

Mother: In fact her school records in, I think it was, her sixth year, they had her write in her score for throwing a ball. She had thrown the furthest. She's very good with her outdoor activities, but if it doesn't go her way, if it's too slow, she gets angry.

Dr.: What kind of relationship did she have with you before you left the family?

Father: Oh, very good. As far as I can remember it was always quite close.

Female-to-male transsexuals report being emotionally close to their fathers, in contrast to adult males who wish to become female.

Father: But I got to say this: nearly all the times that I came to see her I very seldom came to call when she was dressed as a girl.

Mother: I'm not going to slam you, but one time I had her in frills and everything, and she says, "My dad doesn't like me this way." This is what she told me, and she says, "He wants me to go with him and be comfortable, so we can enjoy ourselves."

Father: All right.

Fathers' encouragement of masculinity in their daughters is discussed in Chapter 17, a more direct look at masculine girls.

Mother: I think that's the time I put the perfume on and she really got after me. I do recall you came through the door and said, "Let her dress the way she wants."

Father: Well, if she was raising a fuss about it, I probably said that.

Dr.: What does your daughter want now?

Mother: She doesn't want to finish school as a girl. She wants to finish eleventh year as a boy, but if she can't do that, she's going to move out. And, if not, she's going to kill herself.

The sixteen-year-old tells her story.

Female-to-Male Transsexual: I'd say the farthest back I remember is about three years old. I recognized that I was more male than female. I mean, I didn't like dresses or girls' toys or things like that.
Doctor: Not at all? Not ever?
F-M TS: No. I think I had one or two dolls, and I had a few stuffed monkeys, but that's about it, and I always preferred male companions to female. As I grew up, especially around puberty, I began to realize that—at first I thought I was a homosexual.
Dr.: What made you think you were homosexual?
F-M TS: At thirteen, fourteen, fifteen—somewhere around there—I started being attracted to females and this—I was shocked. Maybe I expected it. So I thought, "Well, what else is there? I must be a homo." So I got literature on that and read up, and I couldn't—it just didn't fit! So I looked for other things.
Dr.: Why didn't it fit?
F-M TS: Because I didn't think of myself as a female, so a relationship with a girl to me would be normal. So after I decided I wasn't a homo, I tried to find under "hermaphrodite" as I figured, "Well, there must be something internally wrong with me that caused this," but my doctors over the years had never found anything so there was no reason for me to believe that, even though I would much rather that had been the case. It still may be. So I finally found information on transsexualism. I thought, "Well, that's the closest description I've read so far regarding what I feel."

In their sexual identity conflict, transsexuals may search for years for a label that comfortably fits.

Dr.: Let's come back a little now. You talked about some of your interests when you were three or four.
F-M TS: Well, very young, in my third year, I noticed I couldn't play with a girl because, you know, they noticed there was something boyish about me, so I played with boys. I just felt isolated as I grew older. I remember in the second grade I was angry at having to wear dresses at school. I thought of myself as a fellow, so why did I have to wear dresses? You know, I didn't know the differences in sex much at that young age. So I figured, "Well, all my playmates are male, all my interests, everything," so I wanted to be as much male as I could.

An exclusive preference for boy playmates by a girl, while potentially helpful in diagnosis of extreme tomboyishness, is not nearly so diagnostic as an overriding preference for girl playmates by a boy.

Dr.: How old were you then?

F-M TS: It was second grade.

Dr.: You say you didn't know too much about the difference between boys and girls?

F-M TS: Well, I knew there was male and female and all, but I didn't really know the looks of the genitals or anything like that of either sex. I figured, "Well," you know, "I'm a guy! Why do I have to have people refer to me as 'her' and a girl's name and everything." It really bugged me. "Superman" was my favorite comic strip.

Again, a hint at current and future identity from favored fantasy figures.

Dr.: Did you have any interests in sports when you were young?

F-M TS: Baseball for quite a while. Now I more or less lean towards football.

Dr.: And you played with girls or with boys?

F-M TS: When I was young I preferred playing with boys, because girls, they wanted to play dolls and sit around, prissy attitude and everything, and I wanted to go out where it was rough-and-tumble and wrestle and climb trees.

Dr.: What would you like now?

F-M TS: I'd like to get started on hormones. At least make a start. I

FIGURE 7–1.

Recalled childhood behavioral features of eleven adult females who requested sex change to male status.

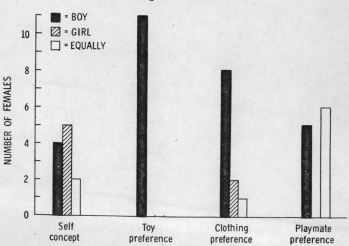

understand that if you're in your late teens possibly the breast size will diminish. Maybe not, but I thought it might help. If not, there's nothing to lose. We could try it. And if not, I guess I'll have to bind them, but that's something I kind of hate to do, because I'm still growing.

Figure 7-1 is a behavioral summary of "girlhood" as recalled by eleven adult females who requested sex change. None preferred girls' toys, most preferred boys' clothes, none preferred girls as playmates, and less than half conceived of themselves as being girls. These recollections provide a beginning toward identifying those tomboys who are on their way to adult masculinity.

The women who love and marry such females, after they have become men, describe their relationships in Chapter 8. One way to help people with the kind of conflict described here is outlined in Chapter 9. And, a look at some young girls, perhaps on their way to this adult picture, is found in Chapter 17.

8

GIRLFRIENDS AND WIVES OF FEMALE-TO-MALE TRANSSEXUALS

As with the consorts of women who were born male, the females who love and perhaps marry men who were born female have been primarily heterosexual in their prior experiences. Most of their experiences, however, seem to have been less than ecstatic, for they typically have not been brought to orgasm by heterosexual intercourse. Usually, they have become orgastic for the first time with a man who was formerly living as a woman, *a penisless man*. Such women consider themselves heterosexual and their relationship heterosexual. They want a husband and a family. To call them homosexual would be both an oversimplification and a misuse of the term. They differ from the usual homosexual female, even those attracted to masculine, "butch" women. They want a relationship with all the trappings of a conventional heterosexual union. They want it, however, with a "man" who lacks a penis.

The psychodynamics of such women will not be explored here. Consider, rather, the following descriptions of their current relationships and their past sexual experiences as characteristic views of women who are consorts of female-to-male transsexuals. Consider also the extent to which their descriptions underscore the extent of masculinity in females who become men.

Example 8-1

This woman's sexual relations with males had been less than fully satisfying. Then she met, grew to love, and formed a satisfactory union with a female-to-male transsexual.

Doctor: Tell me how you met Lou.

Girlfriend: At the roller games with some friends of mine. First when I met him I didn't know that he was a girl or anything.

Dr.: You didn't?

Girlfriend: Not really, offhand. I mean, I knew about the kids I was running around with.

Dr.: What kind of kids were they?

Girlfriend: Homosexuals.

Dr.: When you said you didn't think Lou was a girl, you sort of hedged on that. I was wondering what—

Girlfriend: I wasn't sure until after, this friend of ours said something about it, that Lou was a girl, and I said, "Oh, really?" And then, after that, I didn't see Lou for quite a while, and every time I'd shut my eyes I'd see his face or hear the name, and it just kept bugging me, you know. I couldn't get it out of my mind, and I couldn't really understand it at first.

Dr.: What did you feel?

Girlfriend: Well, relieved, good, relaxed, anyway to have someone, I don't know, there was just something about after we first met that just drew us together. I needed someone I could lean on. Pretty soon I got so that when we weren't together, I just felt lost. It was as though only part of me was there. And soon after that we started living together. And I can say I've never really been happier. You are probably wondering whether Lou is the first one. True, Lou is the first girl I've gone with, but when I say "girl," the reason I hesitate is that I can't think of Lou as a girl, because to think of Lou and try to think of the way a girl would react, there isn't any reaction as far as I'm concerned. It's hard for me to think of him this way.

Dr.: Did you go out with men before?

Girlfriend: I went out with a few of them, and I'd gone to bed with a few of them, which I will admit. As far as homosexuality goes, I figure if a person is happy in what they're doing, I don't think it's wrong. It's better to be happy than to be miserable.

Dr.: Do you consider yourself homosexual?

Girlfriend: Not completely. I think that if Lou and I, just saying "if," anything ever happened to us and we broke up or something, I can't see myself going with another girl. I don't think of Lou as a girl in any way. My feelings toward Lou is that of a male because I can't think of Lou as a female.

Dr.: What about when you are in bed?

Girlfriend: I still cannot think of Lou as a female, even during sex. I don't know whether it's psychologically working on my mind or what, but even in sex I feel that Lou is a male. The way he goes about it. We both feel there is a penis, or something.

Dr.: Can you describe what you mean by that?

Girlfriend: In intercourse as a heterosexual would have it, with the man on top, a feeling of that when I contract, a feeling of something being there to contract with. Sometimes I'll contract and Lou will jump.

Dr.: What do you mean when you "contract"?

Girlfriend: Tighten my muscles.

Dr.: Of your vagina?

Girlfriend: Yes, and I could just swear there's something there. Something. We'll both say to each other, "It can't be true, but how can anything be so real and not true?" And so far as being sexy or anything else, I just can't picture Lou as a girl.

Dr.: Do you find the presence of breasts on Lou at all incongruous with this "something"?

Girlfriend: There isn't that much. I have seen a lot of males, or have been to bed with a lot of males that have that much breast as Lou has. I don't even notice them to tell the truth.

She then goes on to discuss previous sexual relations with males. Penis-in-vagina sex had been less satisfying than alternate techniques.

Dr.: Were you out with many men that you had sex with?

Girlfriend: That I actually went all the way with? Four.

Dr.: Four?

Girlfriend: Four or five, I can't remember exactly. Quite a few. I'd take them to a point and then I'd get a mental block and I'd say, "Forget it, buddy." I almost got my head knocked off a couple of times for that. I don't blame them.

Dr.: Up to what point would you take them?

Girlfriend: To just about the point of intercourse, and then I'd tighten my muscles of my vagina up so tight that they couldn't get in, and then I'd wiggle so that they couldn't, except for a couple of times when I was drunk.

Dr.: Did you enjoy intercourse with men?

Girlfriend: A little bit.

Dr.: Did you have orgasm?

Girlfriend: Yeah, but it was mainly through oral manipulation. They started with petting and then it worked on to that, and after that I could relax.

Dr.: You say you had orgasm with oral-genital contact. Did you ever have orgasm with a penis inside you?

Girlfriend: No.

Dr.: Never?

Girlfriend: No.

Dr.: Do you think you're capable of that?

Girlfriend: I really don't know. I've gone all the way with Lou and a couple other guys since then, but none that I really relaxed with and tried to enjoy it. A couple of times I tried, and I didn't.

Reference is made here to "Lou and a couple *other* guys," again displaying her basic view of him as male.

Dr.: Do you have orgasm with Lou?

Girlfriend: Yes.

Dr.: How?

Girlfriend: Well, we'll be making love as a heterosexual couple would with Lou on top, legs spread, and mine, and we reach a climax together. How I don't really understand myself, or don't know.

Dr.: Why are you baffled?

Girlfriend: It's impossible if you don't have a penis or something like this, but like I said, we felt, I feel as if there is a penis. But if there is something there we've never seen it.

Dr.: Do you manipulate Lou?

Girlfriend: No.

Dr.: Why?

Girlfriend: Lou doesn't care for it for one thing, and too, I just don't feel the inclination, if that's the word I want. When I first started going with him I felt tempted, but it just didn't interest me at all.

Female-to-male transsexuals, like their male counterparts, do not want their genitals manipulated by their partners, as this would interfere with their self-concept.

Dr.: What are your plans for the future?

Girlfriend: That depends as far as Lou is concerned—as far as an operation—sex change. And if this were to work out, and Lou could be classified as a male, then we probably would get married. Not probably, we *would*. This is the first time I have ever been happy in my life.

Dr.: How do you see the future beyond that?

Girlfriend: If possible, we would like to adopt, which I don't know how that would work out. I've heard of cases where it was done, and continue to live as a heterosexual couple.

A follow-up on this couple, with details of their child adoption, is given in the next chapter.

Example 8-2

In previous sexual encounters with males, this woman had been unable to allow a penis to enter her vagina. After meeting and becoming the girlfriend of a female-to-male transsexual, however, she was able to accommodate an artificial phallus used by him. Their relationship had begun before he had received any masculinizing treatments. His girlfriend nevertheless generally regarded him as a man, except when disturbing anatomic insignia would shatter the illusion.

Girlfriend: I'm not particularly happy living with a woman, and she's not particularly happy being one.
Doctor: Why are you unhappy about living with a woman?
Girlfriend: I like men better. It doesn't disturb me too much in that I regard her as a man most of the time, but there are times when you can't avoid regarding her as a woman.
Dr.: Uh huh.
Girlfriend: And those times are a bit disturbing to me. The only reason I guess I see a future in us is because of what she wants to have done.
Dr.: What do you think is possible to be done?
Girlfriend: I understand that there are certain injections and operations to remove the breasts and give her the physical aspects of a man. As far as the penis is concerned, I understand it's still in research right now.
Dr.: Yes.
Girlfriend: We've been working sexually OK with an artificial one. At least if she could have the physical outside look of a man it would relieve a lot of things.
Dr.: Such as what?
Girlfriend: Such as when she undresses, her breasts dropping down.
Dr.: What does that do to you?
Girlfriend: I usually don't look. She just turns her back.
Dr.: That disturbs you to see that?
Girlfriend: Um hum.
Dr.: And what about the absence of a natural penis?
Girlfriend: That was disturbing at first. It wasn't normal. It wasn't. But now I'm so used to it. It disturbs me sometimes, I've got to admit, but I guess when we make love I have to put myself in a certain mood, and a certain idea that there is a man there.

She then goes on to discuss her previous difficulties while engaging in sexual relations with men and the transition to her transsexual lover.

Girlfriend: I've been married, but I never had sex with my husband for a long time.
Dr.: How long were you married?
Girlfriend: Two years. He was away for a year and a half. I had a problem there, which is why I went to a psychiatrist for almost two years.
Dr.: Can you describe the nature of the problem?
Girlfriend: Yes, maybe I can pull it down to a few sentences, I don't know. My father was a very overpowering man, this is the explanation I

got through therapy. And he told me sex would hurt. Anyway, I developed some sort of muscle spasm in my vagina which was controlled by something beyond me.

Dr.: Um hum.

Girlfriend: My father and I, we'd discuss sex, and he had pointed out in a very subtle way always that it would be very, very harmful for me to have intercourse at a young age. I was about eighteen, I think, at the time.

Dr.: What did he say would be harmful about it?

Girlfriend: He said it would ruin my life. He said I was too young. He said it would hurt. I felt very guilty about that. I met my husband to be. We tried sleeping together, but it didn't work.

Dr.: I see.

Girlfriend: And the doctor helped me a lot with that. Before I went to a gynecologist and wouldn't even let him go in. And my husband left for a year, and we'd never slept together, and she's the first one I've slept with.

Dr.: You said you had intercourse with your husband though, before the separation.

Girlfriend: When he came back, yes, about four or five times, I'd say.

Dr.: How did you find that experience?

Girlfriend: The first time was very unpleasant because I had to pretend it was a first time. Now I had been with Jackie (the transsexual) while he was gone. I didn't feel right about it. I didn't feel right about thinking about maybe I was a lesbian. I had a lot of feeling about that.

Dr.: You had intercourse with Jackie with an artificial penis?

Girlfriend: That's right.

Dr.: And that was the first time you had anything in your vagina.

Girlfriend: That's right.

Dr.: How did you find that?

Girlfriend: Beautiful. I was so happy because it was like I didn't have a problem any more. I was so happy that *anything* would have gone in there.

Dr.: What understanding do you have of why it was Jackie first with an artificial penis rather than some other man?

Girlfriend: For one thing I was in love with Jackie then. For two, I think that my doctor got me to the point whereby the problem was somewhat resolved.

Dr.: Do you feel you could've had intercourse with a man rather than with Jackie?

Girlfriend: Oh, definitely, definitely.

Dr.: But it was Jackie.

Girlfriend: Right.

One can only speculate whether her marriage would have lasted if her husband had been first. At any rate, the masculinity of Jackie was sufficient.

Dr.: Did you have orgasm with your husband?

Girlfriend: No.

Dr.: By that time had you with Jackie, using an artificial penis?
Girlfriend: Not really.
Dr.: Have you since?
Girlfriend: Yes.
Dr.: At the time before your sexual involvement began, were you considering Jackie essentially as a man or as a woman?
Girlfriend: Essentially as a man. To live with and to be around. If you can say that there are masculine reactions and feminine reactions in attitude and so forth, she was mainly masculine in anything she did.

Her attractions are primarily heterosexual.

Dr.: Do you feel you're capable of being involved with a person who is clearly a woman?
Girlfriend: Involved like I am involved with Jackie?
Dr.: In a romantic way, loving someone who's a woman who would be feminine?
Girlfriend: Not the relationship I have with Jackie, no.
Dr.: How about in your fantasies, do you ever see some women you know that you think about later on in a sexual way?
Girlfriend: No, not with women. With men, *yes.*
Dr.: Do you see this relationship remaining pretty much of a permanent one?
Girlfriend: If she can have this operation, yes. If she can to the extent that it is possible, if she can have everything possible done.
Dr.: OK, let's say there's no penis construction. Would that be adequate, do you think, to sustain a permanent relationship?
Girlfriend: I think it would. I think it would. I'd like to get married. I'd like to have children.

Example 8-3

Divorced from her first husband, this woman, the mother of two children, married a female-to-male transsexual, the mother of three children. Her present husband is the subject of Example 7-3. The wife was most drawn to her new husband by his masculinity.

Wife: [During intercourse prior to my present marriage] I always seemed like I was acting. I always had guilt complexes about it. My religion and everything. I came from a very strong religious background. I think I almost felt like I shouldn't be enjoying it. I can remember getting the urge for sex, and I can remember even on a couple of occasions being aggressive, to make the man feel this way, and then it would always seem like—I would think of the church. It would leave me cold. Or, I would think of my mother.
Doctor: Did you have a climax?

Wife: No, not during my marriage.

Dr.: Did you have any homosexual relationship before your marriage?

Wife: I can remember being violently in love with a couple of teachers.

Dr.: How old were you then?

Wife: I would say ten. I can remember having some physical relationship with a girlfriend when I was about fourteen, but that was it.

Dr.: You find Tony [the transsexual] very appealing to you?

Wife: Yes, I do. She is strong and domineering, and kind of takes the responsibility of everything, you know. She takes over and she runs me. I don't know why, but for some reason or other I always believed the man should be head of the household, and this has always appealed to me in men, this type of person, and I think this is probably one of the main things.

Dr.: But Tony isn't a man.

Wife: No.

Dr.: So, you are talking about male-type characteristics.

Wife: Well, to me she's male, really. I look at her as the head of the house—male, you know. In a way I don't know whether she seems to be any sex, whether I really consciously think about it. I never think of her as being one thing or another. I think she's very handsome. I look at her as a man when she dresses and buys clothes, you know. I have two children, and we did a lot together with Tony and Tony's daughter, and the children's reaction to Tony is that Tony is a man, as they would react to a man.

Dr.: How old are your children?

Wife: Four and ten.

Dr.: What do they know about Tony?

Wife: Well, nothing. The little one doesn't know anything. I can remember the first time she met her, she asked her if she were a boy, and Tony kind of looked at her and she said, "Look, I'm just me, and we will leave it at that," and they did. I think children have a talent for taking people at face value.

Dr.: Do you have any worries at all about what influence this will have on your daughters?

Wife: No, I don't. Tony has three terrific kids. I hope mine will grow up as fine. I believe she was always honest with her children, and it certainly hasn't affected them, and I just don't have any fears. In fact, I believe that both of us together can do a much better job than I could do alone.

Dr.: Some parents might be concerned about the model of the relationship, the marital relationship being set here for the children, that they would grow up thinking that this was the way *everybody* is.

Wife: But I think in a way they must realize, in a way, that everybody is different. We must set our own moral codes. Again, I think they have to be brought up with tolerance of any type of situation in life.

Dr.: What clicked about Tony which hadn't clicked about men?

Wife: The odd part was her *masculinity.*

Dr.: Do you find the physical relationship with Tony satisfactory?

Wife: Yes. She makes me feel really like a woman. She has a tremendous appreciation for a female body. She knows how to make love, and it's just always satisfying. She really makes you feel beautiful, and very glad that you are a woman. It's kind of a feeling I get that I'm glad that I'm real feminine, and I'm glad that I am able to satisfy her this way.

Dr.: How do you satisfy each other?

Wife: Well, I think that Tony gets more satisfaction from loving me. Once in a while there is a mutual physical—what's the word I'm looking for? Well, Tony, in a way, is very inhibited, really, about her body. She won't undress or anything, and yet I know she gets pleasure from being touched.

Dr.: Where?

Wife: She avoids—she doesn't like you to touch her at all with the breasts.

Dr.: How do you feel about that?

Wife: I like chests. I like *men's* chests. I like *hairy* chests.

Dr.: How about female chests?

Wife: I don't find that very appealing. I think I want to only touch her body is because it's her. I like to be able to lie next to her. She won't do this. You have to respect the way she feels.

Dr.: In what way do you get your satisfaction?

Wife: I would say oral, but I know there are occasions I don't know how to explain it to you—there have been a great number of occasions where—when we were making love that I really wanted something there.

Dr.: A penis?

Wife: Yes, rather than this oral. There has been a tremendous urge, you know, to the point where I have actually asked Tony to do something with her hands inside, and it has felt very good. I think there is a different kind of satisfaction from it.

Some women describe an orgasm from vaginal stimulation as different from orgasm with clitoral stimulation only. Laboratory research fails to provide any demonstrable difference, however, in the physiologic pattern of response during masturbation focusing on the clitoris or with vaginal penetration (Masters and Johnson, 1966).

Dr.: Can you describe how it is?

Wife: Yeah, I think it is that the orgasm is much stronger, and it is much more prolonged. And the oral—it's funny, I feel—I feel funny like with climax, I don't want any part of anybody. I can't explain it. It seems like it's too much. Well, like I want to be alone, and Tony doesn't know that I feel this way, that immediately after a climax I don't feel anything. I seem all empty, whereas the other way, it's much warmer, and a different feeling of satisfaction from it, and there isn't that alone feeling. It's more like there's two people participating. Sometimes the other way I feel like it's almost like masturbating.

Example 8-4

The marriage described in the following interview is unusual, even here, among studies of atypical behavior. The husband is a middle-aged female-to-male transsexual and the wife is his former grade-school teacher. The wife describes their relationship as female student and female teacher, forty years before their marriage; her sexual affairs with men during the intervening years; and the emotional impact of seeing her former female student emerge as a male.

Wife: Well, it's a very strange thing, really. It certainly is, and it's amazing to me as well as anyone else who might know the situation. It began when I taught school. You know, I don't know now whether to say "he" or "she" because it's perfectly natural now. I never think of anything but "he."

Doctor: Yes.

Wife: But at that time, of course, it was "she." I thought she had a crush on me, and I thought that's what it was.

Dr.: What gave you that idea?

Wife: Well, attentions for instance. Anything that could annoy me was done to get attention, and misbehavior in class. And then she got this, what I thought was, a school girl crush, you know, as girls do.

Dr.: Um hum.

Wife: And yet I realized all the time there was something there that wasn't there in the other students. I think as I look back now I felt some attraction, but I pushed it all away because I felt that it was just some crush. So he graduated, and I think I saw him once or twice, and then I was married for several years, and there was no contact other than maybe an occasional letter. After the marriage broke up, we saw each other, I don't know how many times, maybe five or six times in all that period of years.

Dr.: I see.

Wife: And I had no particular interest. Well, then I was out here a few years ago. I was going to spend a few days, so I just thought, "Well—it was Doris then—I'll just tell Doris that I'm here and I'll see her at that time," so I did, and we had a very nice time.

Dr.: When you saw her four years ago, did you feel any kind of sexual feelings at the time?

Wife: I think there was. I could feel it, but, as I say, I always would resist it, because I couldn't understand it, and I certainly never felt that I had any homosexual tendencies whatsoever. Any sex feelings I ever had were toward a man. I just couldn't understand that I could have any toward a woman. I know that when I was visiting there she came into my room one night and when she went out, she kissed me on the cheek. Well, I didn't respond whatsoever. It really meant nothing to me. And then I guess it was a year after that that all this started. I'll change to masculine gender now. "He" wrote, I think, to a number of friends asking would he be accepted after an identity change, that he was receiving male hormone injections.

Dr.: Were you surprised by the question?

Wife: Uh, no, I don't think so. I knew that there was a very masculine trait there. It showed up to me all the time. At one time when she was working in this factory, her hair was cut real short like a man's hair, and you just wouldn't know it wasn't a man. Every movement was a masculine movement.

Dr.: Yes.

Wife: And then it was the next spring that I came out here.

Dr.: What did you think? First glance when you saw your friend as a man?

Wife: Well, I thought he had improved 200 percent as a masculine person. He was what he was supposed to be, because of all those masculine attributes that made him unattractive as a female were natural then.

Dr.: How was it in the beginning? The relationship was beginning to be defined in a different way.

Wife: The first night I had stayed at a motel. I didn't really see why I couldn't stay at his house, 'cause I had stayed with my students, but then I felt, "After all, he's just newly masculine, and I just better go along with it," so I stayed at the motel.

Dr.: Uh huh.

Wife: But it was awfully noisy. It was real bad. So then, next morning I just said I was going to be here one more night—I just said, "I'm staying at your house." And then after we went on a picnic, I guess I expounded at great length about how I was not interested in a man, how I had lost all interest in sex, how I had a life of my own, and how I had no interest at all in marriage. Yet I felt an attraction to him all that time.

Dr.: Yes.

Wife: That night we went to a show, and I said, "I'm gonna hold your hand," and I began holding his hand, and, of course, he was thrilled when I did. That night when we started to go to bed, I said, "Kiss me goodnight," and that was when it all started. I don't know why I said that.

Dr.: How did you feel?

Wife: I felt as though I were kissing a man. It was completely masculine, and I—to me now he is completely masculine. There is no femininity at all.

Dr.: That's certainly true in behavior and psychologically, but what about the body part? How would you reconcile that with your past experiences?

Like the consorts of male-to-female transsexuals, women attracted to men born female make a gradual accommodation to anatomic incongruities.

Wife: Well, it bothered me a little at first, but it doesn't any more. Of course, you know, the sex relationship is not complete because he doesn't have that much of a phallus, but he is very patient, and I enjoy it as much as I have with any other man that I've had relationships with, and I've had them with quite a few.

Dr.: What kind of sexual adjustment have you worked out? I understand there's been some hypertrophy of the clitoris from the androgen injections.

Wife: Yeah, quite a little bit. Quite a little bit, I'd say. He doesn't really enter the vagina, but there's a definite feeling there at the entrance.

Dr.: And what about the breast tissue, does that enter into the relationship?

Wife: No, not as far as he's concerned at all. It's completely ignored. We don't talk about it at all. At first he always wore an undershirt, and now it's got so he doesn't, and it bothered me a little at first, and I'm just accustomed to it now, and think nothing about it. After all, some men do have quite a bit of breast tissue. He has, of course, more than any man would have.

Dr.: When you were having intercourse with men in your earlier years, how responsive have you been?

Wife: I don't think I was very responsive.

Dr.: Have you been able to come to climax?

Wife: I can now; I didn't before.

Again, failure to achieve orgasm with a genital male.

Dr.: What is different? What are you describing now as an orgasm that didn't take place earlier?

Wife: Well, I think it's the pulsating feeling I get that I don't think that I got before. I think I throw myself into the act now. He takes it slowly, and he has been able through his explanation, and his acts, to do that while other men didn't. It's a feeling that I don't think I had before. It's been more satisfying than what I've had in the past, which is, to me, strange, because, of course, he does not have the ability to satisfy a woman, I would say, because of the length of the phallus.

Dr.: Have you tried sexual relations with any kind of phallus substitute?

Wife: Yes, and I didn't like it.

Dr.: What was the problem?

Wife: Well, it was too big to begin with. And it was very uncomfortable. So he had a smaller one which he did use—and he has suggested it a number of times, because he felt that I wanted it—but I have said, "No, I didn't." I was better satisfied with what was naturally his than to use something that was artificial.

Dr.: How old are you now?

Wife: I'm sixty.

Dr.: How long prior to your present relationship had you been without any kind of an affair?

Wife: It had been about seven years ago. There must be quite a strong attraction for me to give up all that.

Dr.: What do you think it is? What is that special thing?

Wife: Well, I must love him. I guess I do.

Dr.: But there were other people you've seen since you were thirty years of age when your marriage was beginning to fall apart. Why now, after thirty years, does this person have this particularly special—

Wife: Maybe it was a carryover from way back. When I think back— even though the body might have been feminine—when I think back, I can still see all that masculine trait.

The degree to which female-to-male transsexuals are masculine is illustrated by how they are seen by their girlfriends and wives. These romantic relationships have so far proven very stable. Most result in marriage and adoption of any children from previous marriages. The couple then merges unnoticeably into the heterosexual community. Their stability is similar to "conventional" lesbian unions, in contrast to the greater fragility of male homosexual relationships (Hoffman, 1968). As a corollary of this finding, it is noteworthy that fewer male-to-female transsexuals in our experience appear to settle into stable, enduring marital relationships.

An important piece of follow-up research will be the psychosexual development of children raised by two female parents, one of whom appears to be a man. Of particular interest is the effect on a child of learning that Daddy has no penis.

9

TREATMENT OF WOMEN WHO WANT TO BECOME MEN

In general, the principles of treatment of females who want to become males are the same as those enumerated and demonstrated for their male counterparts in Chapter 6. Specifically, however, some differences exist with respect to surgical limitations and the effects of hormonal treatment.

The effects of administering androgens, or male hormones, to a female are striking. The voice deepens to a masculine resonance, facial hair grows in the male beard zone, and body hair may sprout on the chest. Within a few months, a female who cuts her hair in a masculine fashion, binds her breasts against her body, and wears men's clothes can effect a dramatic change. Although most hormonally induced changes in females are reversible, as they are in males, the voice deepening that accompanies androgen administration is permanent. Other effects of androgen include reversible cessation of menstruation, increased sex drive, and clitoral growth. The clitoris may increase to an inch or more, but will remain bound down at its underside.

In female-to-male surgery, the biggest technical limitation is construction of a phallus. This has been accomplished in some medical centers, albeit with only partial success. Multiple procedures are required; scarring occurs at tissue donor sites; and the final product cannot change from a flaccid to an erect posture in the manner of a normal penis. To produce erection, a splint must be either permanently or temporarily inserted. Lacking the necessary network of nerves, the graft is incapable of transmitting any sexual sensation, although the nerves at the base of the new phallus, where it apposes the clitoris, remain intact and can be stimulated by friction. If the phallus is additionally constructed, the patient can urinate through its end while standing. To increase the similarity to naturally formed male genitals, a scrotum can be simulated by inserting prosthetic testes into the labial skin folds, which are then sutured together. Still another technique has been recently described (Laub, 1971), by which a phallus can be constructed in four weekly outpatient visits. This technique utilizes abdominal skin that is folded into a hollow tube and grafted into the appropriate position. The phallus accepts a splint for intercourse, but does not allow for the passage of urine. Additionally, a compromise genital procedure is currently being investigated in which the clitoris, enlarged in consequence of hormone treatment, is freed at its underside, making it more protuberant as a small phallus. Then, the urethra is advanced to the clitoris, enabling the person to urinate while standing. Coupled with a prosthetic scrotum, this may prove to be satisfactory for many patients.* While such surgical procedures may be implemented, the resulting anatomic structures fall considerably short of normal in both appearance and function.

Because of the limits of such surgery, most female-to-male transsexuals are well advised not to pursue the uncertain procedures required for phalloplasty but to settle for removal of breast tissue and, if they wish, removal of the uterus and ovaries. For a man born female, being able to take off his shirt at the beach can be very gratifying, especially if he has hair growth, due to androgen, and is able to display a decidedly masculine chest.

The following interviews with both preoperative and postoperative female-to-male transsexuals are representative examples of both general and specific advice given to patients seeking treatment.

---

* W. Goodwin, personal communication, 1972.

Example 9-1

This patient desperately wanted medical and surgical intervention to allow her to live as a male.

Doctor: I suppose you ought to know some of the things that hormones can and cannot do, and some of the things surgery can and cannot do. It's possible to find doctors who will give you male hormones. What they'll do is essentially lower your voice, give you some growth of facial hair, stop your menstruation. It may increase sex drive a bit. It may also increase the size of your clitoris, but not to the size of a penis. It will be a little growth. That's really about it. That's really all the hormones will do. Surgery will be much harder to come by. Very few people are doing surgery. It's all on a private fee basis and fairly expensive. The kinds of surgery that can be done are masectomy, the removal of the breasts, and hysterectomy, removal of the uterus, and also the ovaries. As far as building a penis is concerned, that's pretty tough. It's really not a very well worked-out technical procedure. The best that's been done is not very adequate, and is not in any way at all a normal penis. It's not a sexual organ. It's not erectile as a normal penis might be and there are many stages to go through and months of surgery. It is really quite inadequate.

Female-to-Male Transsexual: But they still are working on making progress in those areas?

Dr.: If you are thinking that it's possible to construct male genitals that would look like normal male genitals, well, that's out. That's impossible. It's never going to look entirely normal, and it's never going to function normally. What some people who feel very compelled to live as men have done is to take male hormones and have their breasts removed and perhaps have the uterus taken out, although on male hormones there is no menstruation, and they live and work as men. The thing is that they are not normal men, and as far as sex is concerned, what they can do sexually with a woman isn't really much more than they were able to do before they had the male hormones and surgery. They don't have a penis. So one has to decide whether it is actually worth it.

F-M TS: I don't think that sex is one of the major issues of my life.

Dr.: There is nothing right now stopping you from living as a man. You can go out right now if you really wanted to live as a man and cut your hair, wear men's clothing, and bind your breasts. Whether or not you are taking male hormones isn't going to make that much difference.

F-M TS: It wouldn't be the same.

Dr.: My own feeling is that people ought to, before they do anything irreversible like taking surgical steps, experience what it's really like to live as a man. They ought to live full time, work and socialize as a man, and during this time, if they want, they can take male hormones. But they certainly shouldn't go and take some major irreversible step until they have more chance to really find out if this is what they want. In the meantime, I think they ought to have a psychiatrist with whom they can sit down and discuss the experience.

The next three examples are interviews with patients who went through trial periods living and working as men while taking male hormones. Two of them by the time of these interviews had had some surgery. All three report successful adjustments to masculine status, are employed as men, and have married as men. Two have adopted children.

Example 9-2

This patient is the same as in Example 7-3. After a trial period on androgen and of living as a man, surgery was performed, and the female-to-male transsexual remarried—this time in the role of husband. His wife's young children accept him as "Dad."

Doctor: Refresh my memory on what your wife's kids know about your past.

Female-to-Male Transsexual: Well, they all know everything except the little one. She knows nothing.

Dr.: The little one is how old?

F-M TS: Six.

Dr.: She knows nothing?

F-M TS: She knows nothing. I'm a daddy to her and that's it. We're very close, too.

Dr.: The other kids know?

F-M TS: Know everything.

Dr.: Do they talk about it?

F-M TS: Not anymore. It's becoming so matter of fact that I'm Dad and that's Mother. It's beautiful.

Dr.: What about your own children?

F-M TS: My daughter that's married has a new baby. Even though she had known all along how I had been, we didn't tell her anything about my surgery until we got married. I just wrote her and told her everything. So it was a blow to her at first because it all came at once, plus she was pregnant. She said she read the life of Christine Jorgensen and says, "I'm beginning to understand." In fact, they said it's better now.

Dr.: What did you tell the older child that you adopted? How did you explain it to her?

F-M TS: Well, it's been so long ago that I don't exactly know the language. We explained that some people were born in this life with problems, and this was one particular kind of problem where people were born with a dual nature, sometimes a dual sex, and they had found ways to correct this, or at least help make an adjustment, and that we were going to make an adjustment, and that we were going to get married. I remember her answer. She said, "It doesn't matter. If they don't like you like you are, they're the ones that are losers," and it's "Daddy" and that's it.

Dr.: Was there anytime after your surgery that you experienced any regret at having had the surgery?

F-M TS: Oh no, never.

Dr.: When you look down at yourself in the mirror and you look at your chest, have you had any feelings of regret?

F-M TS: No, just good feelings.

Dr.: You never thought, "This is part of my body that is gone"?

F-M TS: No. Just like a *deformity* is gone. Something that shouldn't have been there. Psychologically it has been wonderful. I've gone for a couple of physicals on the job, and they won't pass me because of the genitals. This has been embarrassing. I've lost a couple of good jobs.

Dr.: What have you told them?

F-M TS: I told them I was a transsexual. You have to use proper terms, you know, and one doctor had heard about it, and the other doctor was an old biddy. Made me feel like I was a no-good something or another. This has been a little trying. I could have had a good job.

In lieu of an "in-house" physical, some employers will accept a letter from an outside physician describing the special circumstances.

F-M TS: Another thing—we don't know the legality yet of this marriage. We'd like to talk to a lawyer, although we had no problem when we went to get our marriage certificate.

Dr.: How did you manage that?

F-M TS: We just went and applied for one, and we got it.

Dr.: What identification did they request?

F-M TS: Didn't ask us for any. We filled out the papers, got our certificate, had a beautiful wedding in a wedding chapel. Nobody ever questioned anything.

Dr.: I'm glad it worked out.

Female-to-male transsexuals need to be rid of all possible physical attributes of femaleness, even those not visible.

F-M TS: A hysterectomy and ovariectomy is something still I want done.

Dr.: Why?

F-M TS: Because I feel it's important.

Dr.: You're not menstruating.

F-M TS: No, I haven't in over a year since I started hormones.

Dr.: Clue me in. Why is it important? You don't menstruate. You can't see your uterus.

F-M TS: I don't *feel* it's there, but I *know* it's there. Of course, I do feel it is important if I could ever go on, if they ever do get the penis operation perfected. Then I would finish out a complete transition.

Dr.: Well, the presence or absence of a uterus wouldn't effect whether or not the surgeons try and construct a penis.

F-M TS: Well, I thought it had something to do with the way they connect and everything. They don't have to remove it to do that?

Dr.: No.

F-M TS: Well, then, it would just complete the whole circle. You just feel like it is not quite complete. Of course, it doesn't hurt our life or our sexual life that way. I think more so I would want it than anything. Of course, I have grown about an inch anyhow with the hormones.

Dr.: Your clitoris is about an inch long now?

F-M TS: Oh, yeah.

Dr.: Does it become more erect?

F-M TS: Yes, it does. It surprised her, but it didn't surprise me because you and the endocrinologist both told me this would probably happen.

Dr.: Does it feel different to you now than it has felt?

F-M TS: Oh, yeah, sure. You know you feel it there now, and everything there rubs, and you feel the friction of it.

Dr.: Have the two of you ever considered using an artificial penis?

F-M TS: We talked about it. I'm so free now. We were laying in the sun, I just had trunks on. We were saying how great it felt. I don't know why, we just started talking about this, and I was saying, "I wonder if I could get one. I know there are such things." Especially when you wear a pair of trunks, you can see the difference. I don't know why this became important to me, and she said, "No, I think that's wonderful that you've gotten to this point."

Dr.: An artificial penis wouldn't be entirely appropriate for bathing trunks because it is erect. What you could probably do there is buy an athletic supporter and fill it with something. You know, fill it with some foam or tissue paper so that it would form some contour.

F-M TS: I never thought of that. It doesn't bother me in trousers because you can't tell. These gals get these padded bras.

Dr.: All's fair in love and war! Would you be willing to use an artificial penis in sexual relations?

F-M TS: Yes.

Dr.: Well, they're pretty easy to come by.

F-M TS: I completely satisfy her. Regardless. I think it is more for me. It's just that I've got to that point, since I've had surgery and everything. I've worked as a man, and I've been in the community as a man. I'm a father now to these kids. Even my own daughter calls me Dad. I've even got hair all over my chest, which thrills my wife to death and which thrills the kids to death. The first time I could take my shirt off around the kids, that made me feel great. Now I can go around like a man does. I sure feel good about it. My wife does. The kids do. My daughter is always coming up to my chest and going, "Boy, that's neat," you know. She's a crazy kid. They're beautiful. Everything is beautiful but the *smog*.

Example 9-3

After two years on hormones, this female-to-male transsexual married as a man. His wife, whose interview is Example 8-4, had been his grade-school teacher nearly forty years before their marriage.

Doctor: You look more gray.
Female-to Male Transsexual: Yeah.
Dr.: And losing a little more hair from the hormones?
F-M TS: Very much.
Dr.: You see what *men* have to go through?
F-M TS: Yeah, but I would still go the trip to have an identity that I can associate with, even if I become all baldheaded.
Dr.: When did your hair start thinning?
F-M TS: Well, it's been a gradual thing. I think I can say from about the eighth or ninth month after the hormone treatments I noticed decided thinning.
Dr.: What else has been happening?
F-M TS: Oh, I've been very, very well. As I told you in the letter, I am married now.
Dr.: Tell me more about that.
F-M TS: Well, I knew this woman. I was her student in grade school. Now we were friends at that time as teacher and student. After I graduated, in 1938, at Christmas time we would exchange cards and maybe a little note, and in the years from 1938 I had seen her exactly four times in about thirty years. She was through here in '67 on a trip.
Dr.: Did you have any feelings back then like a romantic or crush-type feeling?
F-M TS: Well, looking back on it, I think I admired her terribly, and I thought she was just the greatest. And I have often told her in the years since, in any conversations that we have held about it, that I thought that if anything I ever did was worthwhile in my life I could lay it directly at her door.
Dr.: How was it when she came out here in '67? How were your feelings about her at that time?
F-M TS: Mm. The same.
Dr.: You hadn't begun living then as a man?
F-M TS: No.
Dr.: Did you feel any romantic or sexual attraction to her in '67?
F-M TS: None at all. None whatsoever.
Dr.: So, how did this present situation come about?
F-M TS: Well, she had known that I was taking this step, this gender identity step. Her comment was, "Well, in your case I think this is perhaps the right way to go." She says that back in those grade school years that she felt I was very masculine. She knew that I was female, but she felt that

I was very masculine, and it frightened her and worried her. It perplexed her, and she didn't know how to deal with it. When she came out here a couple of years ago again, I can't explain it to you how it really happened. We just knew that now we felt something different.

Example 9-4

This patient, after hormones and surgery, has made the transition to manhood to the extent of marrying as a man and adopting a child as a father. He describes the experience of legally adopting a child after securing legal status as a husband.

Female-to-Male Transsexual: I'm going to a technology school, taking electronic servicing, and that's an all-male school. So then just before I started school I went down and got a driver's license and it has "male" on it. They asked me for my other license, but I just told them I lost it. I told them I lost it because on it it had "female."

The procedure described in Chapter 7 (see Example 7-3) is preferable, that is, done with the full, open cooperation of a Department of Motor Vehicles. In some states, this patient's deception may be tantamount to fraud or perjury.

Doctor: Did you have any difficulty enrolling in school?
F-M TS: No, the counselor came out to the house and enrolled me in, so I just went through the enrollment procedure, and then I started school.
Dr.: Does anybody in the school have any idea that you're a female?
F-M TS: No.
Dr.: They didn't ask for any proof? Birth certificate or anything like that?
F-M TS: No. Plus I had to take out a federal student loan, which I did as fully male.
Dr.: And you've adopted a baby?
F-M TS: She has my legal last name, and we're both down on her birth certificate as her legal parents. This all came about so suddenly. My wife had heard about the baby, so she left me a note at home telling me to get ready because we had to meet with the lawyer at 5:15 that same day. When I got home and looked, and I had the note, I scratched my head, and said, "Gee whiz," you know, I wanted to adopt children but that was just so sudden I didn't know what to think. So I said, "Well, the best thing to do is just go ahead and see the lawyer and talk to him and see what we can do." We went to see the lawyer, and he said if we give a check which would cover the baby's hospital bill, why, we could bring it home the same night. Somehow we both felt like parents, just seeing the baby for the first time. And they dressed her, and before we knew it, were were taking the baby

home. On the way home, we just couldn't believe that we had a baby, and she was only four days.

Dr.: Can you describe the circumstances around your marriage, the legal problems that were involved and—

F-M TS: When we got the baby they said that they wanted a marriage certificate. They didn't ask for a birth certificate, but in the meantime, well, we figured we needed a marriage license to show them. We went down to Tijuana and got married there, but we didn't get the license until the next month. We didn't tell the agent that we had gotten married in Tijuana, but we wrote to another state asking them for a copy of our marriage license, which we *knew* we didn't have there. They sent us back a letter saying they "couldn't find our records." In the meantime we told the adoption agency that they couldn't find any records of our marriage. So they sent us two forms, which pertain to common-law persons being married in the church, where it didn't have to be recorded in the Hall of Records as long as it was recorded in the church. So she and I went to the church and got married in a simple ceremony there. Then we sent the copy to the adoption agency and they said that everything checked out fine and that she [an inspector from the agency] would make a visit the latter part of this year and see where the baby slept and the atmosphere within the house. And she came over and checked everything out, and then it was decreed that we were the legal parents, the adoptive parents for the baby.

The few female-to-male transsexuals who have completed their pre-operative evaluation period living as men, and have gone on to obtain surgery, have reported, as these excerpts demonstrate, good postoperative adjustments. They have settled into stable family relationships, and experience little difficulty in supporting their families and integrating into society as unremarkable men.

Whatever psychological intervention might have been possible during childhood to reorient such females as women, by the time they are seen as adults, they are typically not at all motivated to living as women. Females who are unhappy living as women, and who insist they can be happier as men, generally go on to prove it.

10

FEMININE BOYS:
BEHAVIORAL
OVERVIEW

Based on interviews with adults with profound sexual identity conflicts, a study of children experiencing analogous conflicts was initiated. From the adults' recollections of their childhood, a composite behavioral picture was drawn of young children currently behaving in a similar manner.

The study has focused primarily on young boys with an atypical sexual identity, rather than girls. There are several reasons for this. Masculinity (or tomboyishness) in girls is much more common than is femininity (or sissiness) in boys. These relative numbers stand in contrast to the picture in adulthood when more males appear to experience sexual identity conflict. Thus many girls whose adult sexuality will be culturally typical are tomboys in their earlier years but become feminine during adolescence. As the current stage of knowledge contributes fewer indicators for identifying those few tomboys who will remain decidedly male-identified, a study which would include a significant number of such women would require a very large number of tomboys. Additionally, tomboyishness is by and large accepted by the child's peer group, parents, and teachers. Thus, due to an absence of social conflict, little motivation exists for such families to seek help at a psychiatric facility.

By contrast, femininity in a young boy (the term "sissy" carries a far more negative connotation than "tomboy") causes him considerable social distress. Furthermore, from the available follow-up data on previously feminine boys, such behavior more often portends sexual identity conflict during adulthood.

For the above reasons, it was decided that a study of atypical sexual identity development in children would best begin with a population of very feminine boys and their families.

To generate the study sample, letters announcing a research program for boys showing an unusual degree of feminine behavior were sent to psychiatrists, clinical psychologists, and some family practitioners in Los Angeles. A few gross behavioral features of such boys were enumerated. These included frequent dressing in girls' clothing, preference for girls' activities, and statements indicating the desire to be a girl. The upper age limit for referral was set at the eleventh birthday to insure that the boys would be prepubertal when initially evaluated, since puberty, with its surge of genital sexuality, considerably increases the complexity of evaluating gender identity. Additionally, one of the questions asked in the research is which prepubertal, nongenital behaviors correlate with subsequent genital sexuality?

During the earlier phase of the research most of the boys referred for evaluation were at the upper end of the age range, seven to ten. With increasing awareness within the Los Angeles community of our project and increasing education of the professional and nonprofessional community concerning the potential significance of early cross-gender behavior, the boys being referred have tended to be younger. It is less common now, for example, for physicians and educators to tell

TABLE 10-1

Age at Initial Evaluation

YEARS	NUMBER OF BOYS
3 years, 6 months–4 years, 11 months	5
5 years–5 years, 11 months	6
6 years–6 years, 11 months	6
7 years–7 years, 11 months	5
8 years–8 years, 11 months	8
9 years–10 years, 11 months	8

the parents of a six-year-old feminine boy that his girlishness is a phase
he'll soon outgrow, only to refer the same boy to us at age eight. Thus
about half the boys in the study group are now in the lower age range,
four to seven. This age distribution is shown in Table 10–1.

AGE OF ONSET OF CROSS-DRESSING

All the boys in the study group began cross-dressing before their sixth
birthday; three-fourths began by their fourth birthday. The most frequent age of onset of an enduring interest in wearing girls' clothes
was between the second and third birthday (Figure 10–1). This is
significant with respect to the developmental timetable for sex-typed
behavior in typical boys and girls and perhaps also with regard to the
capacity of these boys to show behavioral change.

First, consider typical masculine-feminine behavioral differentiation.
During the same years that most boys and girls are showing culturally
typical gender-related preferences in clothing (as well as among toys,
activities, and playmates) the boys in this study also began to show

FIGURE 10–1.

Feminine Boys: Age of onset of cross-dressing.

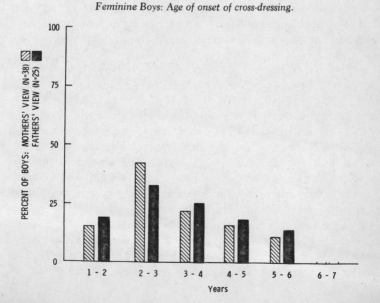

gender-related preferences—atypical ones. Thus, during the first two to four years of life, it appears that a child becomes capable of differentiating behavioral attributes that are gender-related, much in the way children become capable of acquiring language. Which specific language is adopted (or languages in the case of bilingual families) depends wholly on the culture. Whether gender-typing is equally dependent on culture is debatable, as suggested by studies of neuroendocrine factors and the behavior of nonhuman primates.

Research on the establishment of gender identity in anatomically intersexed children and attempts at subsequent gender-role reassignment may be relevant here with respect to the capacity for behavioral reorientation in very feminine boys. Those studies, cited in Chapter 2, point to the importance of the first four to five years in the establishment of a deeply engrained personality component—sexual identity. Thus when a child is unequivocally reared as a boy or a girl, efforts at subsequent reassignment are usually hazardous. However, the analogy here is clearly not perfect. The boys in the present study are not being reared unequivocally as girls. Besides, the most basic anatomic feature found to be influential in the establishment of sexual identity in intersexed children—genital configuration—is in feminine boys working in favor of *typical* development. Thus these boys may be more amenable to environmentally induced behavioral change initiated during later childhood. A remaining question will be the enduring influence (if any) of elements of a very early cross-gender identity on the adult male.

WOMEN'S ARTICLES UTILIZED

Cross-dressing is generally not restricted to a single article of women's clothing but includes a variety of garments. High-heeled shoes are the most frequently worn items of genuine women's apparel, and dresses are the most frequently improvised. Various articles are recruited to improvise dresses, including bathrobes, large towels, and T-shirts. Women's long hair may be improvised, when a wig is unavailable, from towels, mop heads, and hooded jackets.

Feminine boys may adorn themselves with costume jewelry, or necklaces, earrings, and bracelets may be improvised from paper clips, string, and a variety of other small articles. Cosmetics are often utilized, including eye makeup, lipstick, rouge, and nail polish. When these are unavailable, felt-tipped marking pens and crayons may be pressed into service.

These boys are attentive to the manner in which their mothers apply makeup and may become proficient themselves. They rarely, if ever, are attentive to the manner in which their fathers shave. Masculine boys in the same families are described as watching their fathers lather and shave, then simulating the activity with a bladeless razor.

SOCIAL RELATIONS WITH OTHER CHILDREN

Interpersonal relations with other boys are poor. Two-thirds are seen as being loners, either voluntarily or by the decree of other boys. Mothers, with more opportunity than fathers to witness their children's social interaction, rate only one-fourth as either "good mixers" or "leaders." Over 80 percent of the boys are seen as relating better to girls (Figure 10–2). This observation is similar to the childhood recollections of adult males who want to change sex (see Chapter 4). By contrast, nearly all masculine boys evaluated to date relate better to boys, and three-fourths are rated as "good mixers" or "leaders." The ease with which feminine boys relate to girls is frequently a signal of false reassurance to parents as to the developmental course on which their son is set. They feel he will be quite a "lady's man" when he grows up. What these parents fail to realize is that, during these years, playmate preference is more a reflection of peer-group identity than a predictor of later sexual preference. (This is pointed out during a group therapy session with mothers of feminine boys in Chapter 16.)

GENDER-ROLE PREFERENCE IN FANTASY GAMES

With respect to the role usually taken during mother-father or "house" games, half the feminine boys play the role of mother, and an additional quarter portray some other female (Figure 10–3).

By contrast, the majority of masculine boys so far surveyed (that is, of those who play house) take the role of father, and none typically plays the mother or another female. These are parental reports. Data presented in Chapter 13, collected in a laboratory setting, support the impression that feminine boys (as do typical girls) more often assume the role of a female in storytelling than do typically masculine boys.

FIGURE 10–2.

Social relations of feminine boys with other boys and girls.

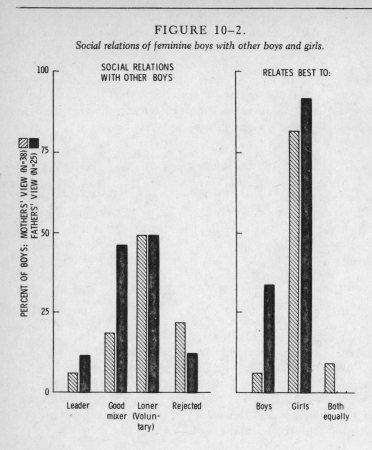

TOY PREFERENCES

Female dolls such as "Barbie" with many costume changes are the favorite toys of the feminine boy sample. These boys avoid the toys typical of boys their age such as cars and trucks. Should parents attempt to gradually shift the boy's interest from a female-type doll to a male one, such as Barbie's counterpart "Ken," the boy strongly resists. Observations of these boys in an experimental playroom stocked with culturally masculine and feminine toys are reported in Chapter 13.

FIGURE 10–3.

Preferred roles taken by feminine boys when playing house and extent of interest in playacting.

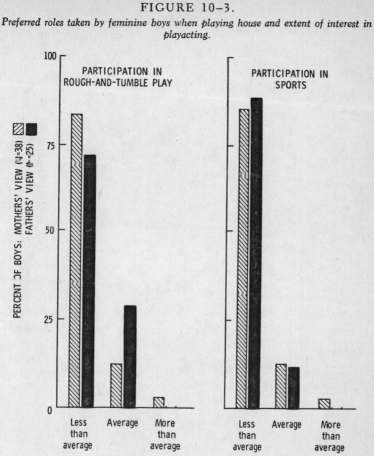

ROUGH-AND-TUMBLE PLAY AND SPORTS

Over 75 percent of the boys are seen as participating in rough-and-tumble play and sports to a lesser extent than the average boy (Figure 10–4). Thus, these boys, while showing feminine behavior, are not boys also capable of culturally typical masculinity. They are not boys who occasionally cross-dress or play at being a girl, only to be found the next hour climbing a tree, roughhousing, or throwing a ball.

FIGURE 10-4.

Participation by feminine boys in rough-and-tumble play and sports.

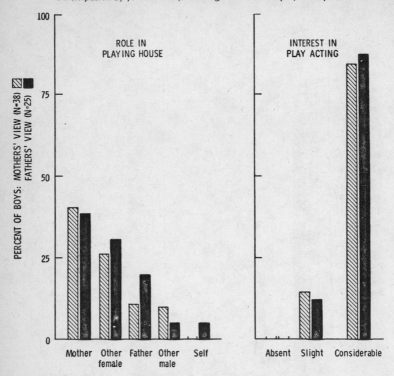

INTEREST IN PLAYACTING

Parents of the masculine boys so far evaluated have described their sons' interest in playacting in various degrees: 33 percent show no interest, 50 percent indicate only slight interest, and only 17 percent display a considerable interest. Of the feminine boys evaluated, however, more than 75 percent were described by their parents as showing a considerable interest in playacting, and none was said to be altogether devoid of this interest (Figure 10-3).

Further, the feminine boys were described as unusually *adept* at acting. Thus, an extraordinary talent and capacity for role-playing appears to be characteristic of feminine boys, a conclusion also reached in an earlier study (Green and Money, 1966). Perhaps this capacity "sets the stage" for their assuming feminine roles. The feminine boy is typically aware of the fact that he is a male. He *prefers* a female role, *wants* to be a girl, and *hopes* to become a woman, but still he *knows* he is a male. Even when he says, "I am a girl," it is usually within the context of make-believe, while cross-dressing or playing the mother in a "house" game.

A general overview of feminine boys' behavior bears considerable similarity to the childhood behavior described by adult male-to-female transsexuals in Chapter 4. The typically feminine boy, from the early years of life, cross-dresses, prefers girls as playmates, is rejected by boys, prefers girls' toys, avoids the rough-and-tumble games of boyhood, and takes a female role in fantasy games.

11

FEMININE BOYS:
PARENTAL
DESCRIPTIONS

Example 11-1

This mother's account of her son's behavior includes most of the elements of the general behavioral pattern of feminine boys. Cross-dressing began at three, fantasy characters portrayed are female, pictures drawn are female, mannerisms are feminine, preferred playmates are girls, and the boy states he wants to be a girl.

AGE OF ONSET

Mother: Well, I'd say about the time I separated from my husband my son started behaving strangely. He started running around with all kinds of hand movements, and dressing up in little girls' clothes. And I thought, "Well, maybe it's just a stage he's going into," and I didn't—
Doctor: How old was he?
Mother: A little over three. . . . I didn't think too much of it, and I asked my pediatrician, who is *no longer* my pediatrician, what I should do about it, and he said, "When he reaches puberty and he starts wearing dresses, then you *know* you've got a problem."

False reassurance is generally given by those inexperienced in the significance of early gender-role preferences in boys.

FANTASY CHARACTERS

Mother: His favorite characters are Cinderella, Snow White, and he loves *The Wizard of Oz* and copies the girl. Everything is girls this, girls that, and this psychologist told me that if he wanted to do those things, just to send him in another room. That didn't work.

Typically, the characters with whom the boy identifies are female.

Dr.: Does he draw pictures?
Mother: Yes, girls. Only girls. Practically refuses to draw pictures of boys. And if he ever does, I'm in the picture too. It's always me. He says, "I don't know how to draw a boy." I've showed him many times. "I can't do it! I can't do it!"

People in pictures drawn by feminine boys are usually female. In Draw-a-Person tests (see Chapter 13), these boys draw girls more often than boys. Masculine boys of the same age usually draw boys.

CROSS-DRESSING

Mother: He's always in with girls playing, and they've tried to get him away from the clothes, and even made him a sailor suit so that he would have something if he wants to dress up. And at home he's always putting on a blanket, you know, as a cape. He has put on my bathrobe, my nightgown, and things like that. I've caught him in a slip every once in a while— a half-slip that looks like a skirt. He puts on my shoes. I thought it was a little normal stage. A lot of kids like to dress up.

When no women's apparel is readily available, feminine boys will improvise, this boy utilizing a blanket.

Dr.: How often would he dress up?
Mother: He's got that cape on almost every day, in some way or another, and flies around the room. He's [being] the Wicked Witch of the West. It seems like every character that he plays is a girl. And I tell him, "If you've got a cape on, be Batman; be Robin." No, he's got to be the Cat Woman.
Dr.: When did he first begin dressing up?
Mother: I guess it's about two years now, when he was four.
Dr.: What was your feeling the first time you saw him dressed up?
Mother: I probably thought it was cute. I really don't remember the first time, but, you know, it's just one of the normal things kids do, and I probably didn't think too much of it. Of course, when I catch him in my clothes, you know, anything of mine, I tell him to take it off, it's *mine*. But, like with the cape and things like that, I probably didn't pay too much attention to it at first.

Her initial attitude—that such behavior is normal, and cute—is typical of mothers of feminine boys.

Dr.: Have you ever put your foot down and said, "No, you absolutely can *not* dress up"?
Mother: Yes.
Dr.: What happens then?
Mother: He does it behind my back. It's just something—a compulsion. He's got to dress up. One thing I did do a couple of weeks ago. I told him that if he promised to behave just like a good little boy is supposed to behave, that I might get him a puppy. The very next day he had on a skirt in school. I told him, "Look. You blew it. That's it. No puppy. You can't have it." And he told me, "You forgot to remind me that morning."

One way these boys show their strong need to cross-dress is their reaction when parents attempt to forbid it.

MANNERISMS

Dr.: What else concerns you?
Mother: The way he walks, swinging his hips, and to top it off, he has a slight lisp which drives me crazy.

Although he is only five, the boy's mannerisms are similar to those of an adult effeminate male.

GENDER-ROLE PREFERENCE

Dr.: Has he ever said to you, "I want to be a girl" or "I am a girl"?
Mother: He has more or less said that he would like to be a girl, and "I am a girl." I think it's usually when he's got the girls' clothes on. He hasn't said it too many times. Five, six times altogether. I just told him, "You're not a girl. You're a little boy." What else can I say to him?

When cross-dressed, these boys may insist, "I *am* a girl."

Mother: Usually he plays like a baby, or he says he plays a little boy. But I know from overhearing some of the games they're playing that he plays a sister, or he wants to be the mother. And the other kids tell him, "No, you're a boy. You're going to be the father or a brother," and he'll give in. But I have heard him says he wants to be the mother.

As with fantasy characters, the preferred roles of feminine boys in mother-father games are typically female.

PLAYMATE PREFERENCE

Dr.: With whom does he generally want to play house?
Mother: Well, there are quite a few kids in the building. He seems to pick

out the little girls to play with. There are some younger and some older. The older ones, he kind of clings to them a little bit more.

Dr.: Predominantly he plays with girls?

Mother: Yeah.

Girls are characteristically the favored playmates of feminine boys.

Mother: I told him, "Go out and play with the boys. Go ride your bike." And when he tries to go play with the boys, they tease him and make fun of him, and they don't want to play with him.

Dr.: Why do they tease him?

Mother: Oh, he says that they don't like the way he's playing the game, but I don't really think that's the reason. I think that they know that there's something just a little bit different with him, that he likes to play with the girls, and that he wants to do the girlish things.

Dr.: He doesn't like boys' games?

Mother: He doesn't like to rough-and-tumble. They've tried in school to get him to play softball, touch football, basketball, and he just absolutely refuses. He wants to either do the crafts or be inside watching television or playing with girls. He does like to swim. That he does, and he does well, but as far as the other sports, he just doesn't like them.

With the common exception of swimming, sports are avoided.

INTEREST IN PLAYACTING AND FEMALE ROLE-TAKING

Mother: He loves *The Wizard of Oz*. He knows every word to the entire story. He's always picked up the words and can sing all the songs ever since he's two years old. He's known words from any song he hears. Sometimes he'll throw in a little "Cinderella" or "Snow White," something like that. Only most of the time, it's *Wizard of Oz*, and he usually plays Dorothy or the Wicked Witch.

Dr.: Does he improvise costumes?

Mother: Yeah. He'll find a stick or a broom to be the Witch. Or he'll try to find a pair of my shoes that are like Dorothy's shoes—you know, her magic shoes that she has—and throw on a cape or find something that would look like girl's clothes while he's playing it.

Dr.: How would you compare the amount of playacting and role-taking this boy does compared to other kids his age?

Mother: He seems to spend an awful lot of time doing it, whereas most kids you see outside playing during the day, doing something. He seems to play at being somebody else besides himself more times than he is himself.

Example 11-2

The boy described here was four when his parents were interviewed. From the time he could walk, he has favored high-heeled shoes; since he was two he has wanted to be a mommy. Other details of his parents' story, including his talent for improvising girls' clothes, reveal the standard behavioral pattern.

Father: Well, most of it is that he still wears my wife's shoes to go to class, and he'll drag out all her shoes, and he wears them and he'll wear anything on his head, scarf or even a towel, and he'll wear her skirts and things like that. The other kids have done this when they were little, but they outgrew it. But he's still doing it. The baby got a set of these plastic keys on a ring, and he'll put it around his ears and wear them like earrings.

Mother: When he was two, you know how the other boys say, "What do you want to be when you grow up?" He will say he wants to grow up to be a mommy. We just kind of laughed at it at first . . . and he plays with the little girls all the time. He likes to play house, and he's the mama when he plays house. One day they were over playing and I said, "Why don't you be the daddy?" and he said, "No, I'll be the little sister."

Doctor: How long have you had these concerns?

Father: A year or so. It's been longer than that, but the other kids went through it, and we didn't think much of it until just recently.

Dr.: You say the other children have gone through something similar to this?

Father: Yes, you know, all dressed up in mother's clothes and high heels. They would clump around in them.

Mother (to father): None of them wore high heels, dear, *none* of them. He's the first one and it floored me when he did. One boy always wore *your* shoes, and the other two never wore shoes. He improvises a lot.

Mother: He's got a towel—it's a baby towel with a hood on it—and he puts that on his head, and he's Batgirl—he's not Bat*man*, he's Bat*girl*— and he's the Flying Nun, and he's Mary Poppins, and he runs around the house with it. And I have a size ten sweatshirt, and it zips up the front and it's short sleeved, and it's obviously quite large on him, and he puts it on to roller skate and it comes down to his knees. He wears it all the time. Because, I think, it feels like a girl's dress.

Dr.: Looking back at it now, what do you think was the earliest that your son showed any indication like this at all?

Mother: When he started with the high heels.

Dr.: How old was he then?

Mother: Thirteen months or maybe fourteen months, because I couldn't believe it because he was so little, that he could wear high heels. I couldn't believe it. I thought it was funny. I didn't think much of it. He could balance on them. He was only walking a few months when he did it.

Dr. (to father): Would he ever wear your shoes?

Father: I don't think he ever wore my shoes. I don't remember.

Dr. (to mother): But he really took to your shoes?

Mother: Oh, yes. He wears them all the time, and I didn't take them away from him because I didn't think anything of it. I just thought it was *funny*.

Dr.: Now, how often does he put on women's shoes?

Mother: Every day, if he can. The first shock of my life, last summer after the youngest was born, he was playing and came home one day with her dress on. I couldn't believe it. I didn't even know it was my boy.

Example 11-3

This mother's account of her six-year-old son contains details that point strongly to his concept of himself as female. Particularly indicative of this is his refusal to stand in line with other boys at school.

Mother: I'm concerned about the way he makes up behind my back whenever he can. And he plays with dolls. He doesn't like to play with boys. He likes girls. Like Christmas, he had gotten a plane and some other toys, and his sister, she had gotten a doll, and he was more concerned about the doll than the plane, and he really wanted to exchange gifts. When he first wore makeup, I didn't hit him or anything. I just talked with him, and I asked him why, and he couldn't tell me why. I was very upset. Recently, he came home late from school, and when he walked in the door he had all the makeup on—eyebrows, mascara, and nail polish. I didn't know what to do. The teacher told me he acted real feminine in school, that he won't get on the boy's line. He stays on the girl's line.
Doctor: Have other things concerned you?
Mother: He gets jealous of his baby sister, and he wished he was a girl instead of a boy.
Dr.: How do you know that?
Mother: He told me this. He said, "I wished I was Hannah [his younger sister]. I wish I was a little baby." And he would ask, "Mama, did you do the same thing for me?" and I said, "Of course I did."

Feminine boys who have been evaluated so far show a tendency to have younger rather than older sisters. See Chapter 15.

Dr.: What about television? What sort of interest does he show in that?
Mother: Oh, he likes "Family Affair." And he said the other night when he saw "The Flying Nun," he said he wants to be a nun.
Dr.: Does he imitate any male characters he sees on TV.
Mother: Flip Wilson.

Significantly, the only male television character the boy imitates is one who, himself, frequently impersonates a woman.

Example 11-4

This mother and father are the parents of a beautiful boy who is so pretty that "everyone says he should have been a girl." He apparently thinks so too. He is strongly identified with his mother.

Mother: He always says he wanted to be like me. He said, "When I grow up I wished I could be like you." I told him he couldn't grow up to be like me. I told him he was going to grow up to be a man. I told him he could be like Daddy.

Doctor: What did he say?

Mother: "I don't want to."

Dr.: What else?

Mother: He'd get mascara and try to put it on his lashes, but he would get it all over.

Dr.: How did you feel about that?

Mother: It made me mad, because he was ruining my makeup. One time he got my lipstick—and it was a brand new lipstick; I hadn't even used it—and he tried to use it, and instead of rolling it back down and putting the lid on it, he just shoved the lid on it, and it stuck on the top, and it really made me mad. I told him, "I haven't even used it! Couldn't you use an *old* one?"

The mother seemed to have communicated a "mixed message" to her son. By discouraging him not from using lipstick but only from using her new one, she may have given him her tacit approval.

Dr.: How would you compare his interest in playacting and role-taking with the other kids his age?

Mother: Well, that's all he wants to do all the time.

Dr.: Does he ever dress up in your clothes or show any interest in them?

Mother: When I was to the hospital last month for my operation, and I had to take my nightgowns, every time I called him on the phone, he said, "What nightgown are you wearing now, Mom? What color are you wearing?" He was obsessed with that. He had to know what color nightgown I was wearing, and he'd tell his daddy: "See what she's wearing, what colors."

Dr.: What was the reason for your being in the hospital?

Mother: I had my gall bladder removed.

Dr.: Had it been giving you some trouble for a period of time?

Mother: About three or four months. So now when we go downtown or do something he doesn't want to do, he's got a "stomach ache." Tuesday morning he got himself so worked up, and he said, "I'm going to get sick." And I said, "What's the matter?" And he said, "I'm going to throw up." So I carry a little litter bag, and I gave it to him, and I said, "OK, throw up in this."

Dr.: What kind of symptoms were you having with your gall bladder?

Mother: My stomach would hurt.

Dr.: Would you be nauseous and throw up?

Mother: Yes.

So strong is her son's identification with her that he even adopted the gall-bladder symptoms.

Dr.: Did you have a preference during this pregnancy for a boy or a girl?

Father: I wanted a boy.

Dr. (to mother): How about yourself?

Mother: I would have liked a girl. I had a boy already, and I actually wanted one of each.

Dr.: What did he look like as a baby?

Mother: He was always an extraordinary-looking child. He was pretty. You know, you don't associate "pretty" with a boy, but he was always a pretty baby. A very nice-looking baby, always smiling and happy.

Dr.: What about him gave you the impression he was pretty?

Mother: Just to look at him. His eyes. He had big, brown eyes and long lashes.

Stoller has observed that feminine boys frequently have unusually large, beautiful eyes.*

Father: Everybody commented.

Mother: Yeah, that was one thing. They all commented he was so pretty he should have been a girl. Some people still say it.

Father: Even sometimes in the store, they'll say how pretty he is.

Mother: His eyes. They'd say, "What beautiful eyes." It made me mad. But he *was* a pretty baby, and then when he got bigger, you know, it was obvious that he was a boy—we never dressed him like a girl or anything—they'd say right in front of him, "Oh, he is so pretty he should have been a girl." And I'd say, "Oh, he's a boy. He looks just like his daddy."

Dr.: How old was he when people would make those comments?

Mother: All the time. They still do. In fact, a couple of weeks ago we were here at the hospital, and a lady looked at him, and she said, "Oh, isn't he a nice-looking boy." And she started to say something about "He would have made a nice girl," and I just looked at her like "You idiot, why do you think we're here?"

Dr.: Has he shown a response to people's statements that he should have been a girl?

Mother: Yeah. He looks up at them and gives them a smile.

Example 11-5

These parents report that their son, at age two and a half, began showing an intense preoccupation with one item of women's attire—the classic fetish—high-heeled shoes.

Mother: Well, it started out he liked to play with high heels. I mean, a person would walk in the room with high heels on, and he'd about pull her down to take them off, and he kept on until he finally got them. He just wouldn't leave Grandmother alone because she had on high heels. Every

* Personal communication, 1972.

time she would step, he was there grabbing them. He always wanted my high heels. Eventually he got a pair somewhere. I don't remember whether he pulled hers off or he went and scrounged a pair somewhere because he ended up having a pair.

The boy's interest was extreme. It was more precisely focused on shoes than has been the case with any other feminine boy studied.

Mother. It was Christmas. And I've got a picture of him sitting on the floor, and he had on Grandma's high heels. I've got one where he is on the back porch, and he has a hat on and he has his apron tied up around—the strings themselves are made like straps. He's got a big old purse, and he has this pair of high heels on.

Parents of feminine boys often pose and photograph their sons dressed in women's clothes. Such special attention may serve to reinforce cross-dressing.

Doctor: How often would he play with high heels?
Mother: Whenever he could get a pair. I had to throw more high heels away. I'd finally break down and let him have them just to keep him quiet. He would go and sit down and play with them. And then, three years ago, this friend of ours gave him a pair of high heels which he really didn't wear much. He just wanted to handle them and to have them there.
Father: It was getting so nobody could walk in the house without his pulling high-heeled shoes off. And he just didn't want to wear high heels quite frequently, but *all* the time. And every woman that came in the house, he'd just pull their high heels off.
Mother: He just ruined I don't know how many pairs. It almost got to the point where you would dread having anybody come in if they had shoes on. Because he's going to be right there and pulling at them.

Although troubled by such behavior, the parents did not prohibit the boy's compulsive play with high-heeled shoes; the mother allowed it "to keep him quiet." Six years later, the parents reported that the boy, then eight and a half, still had a considerable attraction for high heels. Figure 11–1 shows a picture drawn by the boy at age eight and a half, which he identified as a male. Note that the picture, which depicts the male wearing high-heeled shoes, was drawn *before* shoes with elevated heels became fashionable for men.

Dr.: To what extent does he still show some interest in high-heeled shoes?
Mother: He wants to know if I'll wear them, but I don't know how long since he's asked if he could have a pair. Except, now, my husband's mother's got some little plastic ones that she fixes with flowers. He wants one of those. Oh, he's got a little doll high heel. A little tiny one, and he'll carry it around and put it on. On his finger.

FIGURE 11-1.

Male figure drawn by subject of Example 11-5 at age eight and a half.

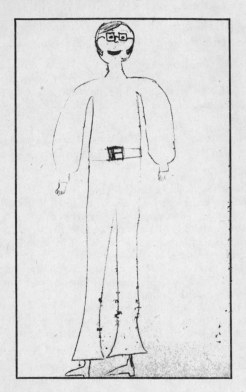

Father: He recognizes them in pictures quite a bit. Why, he'll say, like, "That lady has high heels." Or "How come that lady doesn't have high heels?"

Mother: A lady walked down the corridor a while ago, and he said, "Oh, she's got those old *fat* heels on."

Father: He still pays attention to them, but he doesn't ask to wear them anymore.

Mother: But three weeks ago, there's one little girl that lives up the street, and they were in the back yard. I had seen her, and I thought she had high heels, and she did, and he had them on. I made him take them off and give them back to her. And I heard him say, "I told you I couldn't wear them."

Dr.: What are his favorite toys?

Father: Barbie. . . . Anything feminine. Whether it be Betty Crocker

Bake Set up to the biggest doll he can get. He's got two G.I. Joes, and he doesn't play with them. He gets tired of them. We just bought him a new one at Christmas because it talked, but that really wasn't what he wanted.

A Barbie doll is the boy's preference. Its male counterparts have been rejected.

Mother: The dolls never really worried me for a while because I figured it was only natural. 'Cause I had heard a long time ago that if boys played with dolls when they were young, they made a better father, because they had the baby there. So, I said he would grow out of it. But now it bothers me more, because he's bigger and he visits around. And it's kind of embarrassing when he says, "I don't want to go there because they don't have any dolls."

Dr.: How far back does his interest go in doll playing?

Mother: Four years ago he had one baby doll, and that was all he had, and he didn't play with it much then. He started really playing with them when he would play with paper dolls when he went over to visit this woman's house because she had three little girls. And he started getting in with the dolls then.

Dr.: What was your feeling about it at that time?

Mother: I just went ahead and let him. There were no other boys over at this one lady's house, and she just had the one little girl, and so he played with her and played with dolls. So I figured, "Well, they didn't have any little boys' toys, so let him go ahead." It didn't really bother me until he got to the point there where that's all he wanted. He wanted a doll! He wanted a doll! And this friend of ours gave him a couple of them.

There is often a "helpful" friend who contributes a doll, or a dress, to the feminine boy.

Mother: When we first got here we lived by this little girl, and he wouldn't play with her unless she would bring her Barbies out.

Dr.: What was your feeling about the doll playing?

Father: Well, at first, I don't think I really paid any attention to it.

Mother: Also, he likes little cars, but they don't hold his attention that long. I think the only reason we buy the car is because we are forcing it upon him. He'd much rather, if he had the choice, between the doll or the car, the doll would come first. . . . I got kind of tired about people always saying something about it, so I don't really like him to do it.

Mothers of feminine boys are frequently driven to curbing cross-gender behavior or to seek professional consultation by the continuing comments of neighbors or teachers.

Mother: You see, at first I didn't mind him playing with dolls, but I didn't want him to have the shoes and things. I've never wanted him to have them. But then I would go ahead and let him have them.

These mothers are especially inconsistent in their approach to their son's feminine behavior.

Dr.: Does he draw pictures?
Father: Yeah. Usually girls. Most of the time he will either try to draw a woman or "That Girl," or somebody like that. Or else he'll draw girl stick-figures.
Mother: At school most of his were girls that he would draw, and the teacher said something about that one day.
Father: Yeah. Because they were told to draw a picture of *themselves,* and he drew a girl.

His drawing obviously reflects his sexual identity. When told to draw "a person" the majority of these feminine boys draw a female. So do girls. Masculine boys, by contrast, typically draw a male. These data are detailed in Chapter 13.

Example 11-6

These parents, a mother and a stepfather, disclose their ten-year-old son's early feminine behavior, his elaborate and creative improvisation of women's clothes, and his pronounced homosexual tendencies.

AGE OF ONSET

Mother: I noticed at two years old.
Doctor: What?
Mother: He liked to put things on his hair. Dish towels, anything that looked like hair. He would tie them with rubber bands. This was about two, two and a half, and he liked to do housework. He liked to follow me around, and he'd fold clothes—and little things you'd expect a little toddler to do. As far as his feminine actions and everything, he's been like this since he was a very small child.

IMPROVISATION OF WOMEN'S CLOTHES

Mother: He'll dig out any of my old garments, and he loves to make hairpieces out of things. He found two or three of my good wigs. Cutting and combing them and wearing them, and he's very ingenious. He can come up with a complete costume out of little or nothing. An old maternity smock, he'll belt and make a dress out of it. . . . He would even improvise his necklace to go into the hair.
Dr.: How did he do that?
Mother: Oh, he would pin them around with pins, and put them into his hair, and come up with some cute crown idea.
Dr.: How often would he do that?
Mother: Almost daily.

Stepfather: He has a habit of taking my T-shirts and, due to the fact that they are very large on him, they look like a dress or a smock. And I tell him not to do this, but he continually wears my T-shirts for nightgown purposes. And it's very agitating, because he'll act the role of the female when he wears them.

Dr.: What does he do?

Stepfather: Very passive-like. He sits down very dainty. Like a skirt he flares it out before he sits down, and he'll tuck it in. It just irks the hell out of me to see him stretch my T-shirts. I've told him constantly not to do this, but he'll go over my head and go to her and she'll say, "Well, don't do it next time."

Mother: I think he would prefer a real nightgown.

HOMOSEXUAL TENDENCIES

Stepfather: He's told me about occasions where he sees boys undressing, and he'll just go ape about it. He'd come in and say, "Wow, they've got groovy bodies," and what he'd like to do.

Dr.: What does he say he would like to do?

Stepfather: Go out and play with the guy and have the guy play with him, and just lay down and be close to each other. To hear a ten-year-old boy say this! You want to take it as he's just joking, but you can't with him. . . . He's even asked *me* to do it to him. He comes straight out and says, "Would you go to bed with me?" And, you know, for a kid to come up to his stepfather and say something like that, he ought to get his head cracked.

Miscellaneous Examples

The following examples, brief excerpts from interviews with various parents, re-emphasize some details of the six preceding examples and introduce other details that frequently occur in parental descriptions of feminine boys.

UNUSUAL TALENT FOR ROLE-TAKING

Mother: He is very imaginative in general, very imaginative in his play, and he has been since the time he was a little child, from the time he was under two. I was amazed at his ability to pretend and take on roles. He gets great pleasure from this. He is fantastic at accents, at languages. He is very inclined this way. He used to play a lot when he was little, and he usually was the woman.

Dr.: With whom would he play?

Mother: By himself. He would wear my shoes, and he would take my purse, and he would say, "Mommy going to the market." He had a very special relationship with my mother, and he had an imaginary playmate, and she is a grandmother. He created her with my mother. Teachers have begun telling him he has to be the father. He says, "I don't know what a daddy does." They said he has no idea what to do in that role.

EXTRAORDINARY PLAYACTING

Dr.: Does he playact or take on make-believe roles?

Stepmother: Yes. He's got a real knack for it. The little girl that lives up the street, he goes up there and plays in the back yard a lot. This other mother was telling about the shows they were putting on. In fact, she'd say her little boy—he's five—would get mad that he would hog the stage, and he wouldn't be allowed to get his two cents in.

Dr.: When you say he has a knack for this, do you feel he has more of a talent for role-taking and playacting than most boys?

Stepmother: Very definitely. I would say more than most children that I have observed. All of them I think have a certain knack built into them with their imaginations, but he in that sense seems to be able to transform himself into the role he's playing.

A UNIQUE IDENTITY

Mother: I'm concerned about his constant desire to play with girls, seeking out girls to play with, indicating that girls are softer than boys. He likes to play with dolls more than boys' toys, although he will play with boys' toys, but only for short periods of time. He states that he would like to have dolls bought for him and he's always asking if he's pretty. He says that he likes being a *tomgirl*. He doesn't care if they call him a sissy.

ECSTATIC CROSS-DRESSING

Dr.: What was the earliest thing that you noticed?

Mother: Wanting to put on a blouse of mine, a blouse which if he'd put it on would fit him like a dress. And he was very excited about the whole thing and leaped around and danced around the room. I didn't know how to handle it except I didn't like it, and I just told him to take it off and put it away. He kept asking for it. He wanted to wear that blouse again, and I said, "No, I'm sorry. That belongs to me, not you."

CONCEALING ONE'S PENIS

Dr.: Has he ever said, "I am a girl"?

Mother: Playing in front of the mirror, he'll undress for bed, and he's standing in front of the mirror, and he took his penis, and he folded it under, and he said, "Look, Mommy, I'm a girl."

Dr.: What did you say?

Mother: I said, "No, you're not. Stop doing that. You are a boy."

EXQUISITE SENSITIVITY

Mother: He is a very sensitive child in all respects, in terms of music and sounds and in terms of color. He listens to music and he says, "That sounds happy. That sounds sad." He is really turned on to so many things, and one of them is definitely touching. He loves to touch, and, for a while, that's how I looked at the dressing up he did at school, because they had silk and satin and ruffles, and all these beautiful textures and colors, and there are no men's clothes at nursery school either. There is a cowboy hat and a classic fireman's hat, but there is none of this richness in dressing up. For a long time I thought it was just that.

ATTENTION TO FEMININE FASHION

Dr.: Does he comment on your clothing?

Mother: Oh, yes. "Oh, Mommy, that is so pretty." If we're going to go out somewhere, he'll say, "Oh, Mommy, can I pick what I want you to wear?" Or he'll say, "Wear this," and he follows me from my bedroom to the bathroom, back to my bedroom, and "Comb your hair this way." He's always telling me what to wear. He always wants to pick my clothes, go in the closet. You can just tell by his eyes from looking that he is thinking, "I wish that was *me*."

MOTHER AS BEST FRIEND

Mother: I'm his idol. There's no doubt about it.

Dr.: Who's his best friend?

Mother: Me.

FEAR OF COMPETITION

Mother: Competitive sports are frightening to him. Yet I've seen him out there with a big rubber ball like a basketball socking it against the garage door and then catching it on his own. When there's no other person involved, the fear is eliminated, but when the other person's involved, the unsureness—whether they'll hurt him—comes through.

REASONS FOR WANTING TO BE A GIRL

Mother: He says: "I would like to be a girl. I don't like to be a boy. Boys are too rough. When I play boys' games, the ball hurts my legs. I don't want to go to school today because I'll have to play baseball. The boys will throw balls and hurt my legs." So he goes and plays gently with the girls.

Dr. (to second mother): What does he say?

Mother: "I wish I could be a girl because they get to wear makeup and wear jewelry and make my hair pretty."

Dr. (to third mother): What reason does he give?

Mother: He wants to be a grownup lady because they have more fun. They get to get dressed up and go places and go out to dinner.

ACCEPTANCE BY OTHER CHILDREN

Mother: He is getting laughter from the kids. The thing that disturbed teachers the most was that the children were drawing pictures of each other, and a girl drew a picture of him with a dress on and held it up proudly, and everybody and he was pleased. And all the other children were pleased, and nobody said, "But he has a dress on."

TEASING DURING LATER GRADES

Father: And the kids at school pull him down and pull his shirt off to see if he's got "chi-chis" or if he's built like a woman.

The teasing to which feminine boys are subjected often serves to motivate attempts by the child, the parents, and the therapist to modify their behavior. Treatment is described in Chapter 16.

12

FEMININE BOYS:
THEIR STORIES

In talking with boys who want to be girls, we obtain an idea of how they see their world, and catch glimpses of a fantasy life reflecting an unusual identity. However difficult it is to interview an adult to discover why he wants to be of the other sex, gleaning salient information from children is even more problematic. Although some clues come from play fantasies, even more telling clues appear, as in the following passages, during direct conversations with the boys. Here are four feminine boys who tell of their ideas about being boys and becoming girls.

Example 12-1

A five-year-old begins by describing doll play, dressing up dolls, and then his own dressing up.

Doctor: What kind of dolls do you have at home?
Boy: Barbie dolls.
Dr.: Are they your dolls or are they your sister's dolls?
Boy: They let me play with them, my big sister and my little sister. We nave some G.I. Joes that we can play with, but I only have one and lost it.

Dr.: Which do you like better, the G.I. Joe doll, or the Barbie doll?

Boy: The Barbie doll.

Dr.: Why do you like the Barbie doll better?

Boy: Oh, like if you want to play house, G.I. Joe has all the equipment stuff, and all the equipment stuff wouldn't look good just walking around the house forever. And Barbie dolls can change clothes and stuff like that.

Dr.: Do you like to play house?

Boy: Yes, I love it.

Dr.: Do you ever dress up?

Boy: I try different clothing. I was trying to dress myself. I use my grandmother's big robe. It goes down to there, and I dance.

Dr.: And who watches you dance?

Boy: Three of my aunt's friends. I forget their names.

Dr.: Were they ladies or men?

Boy: Girls.

Dr.: What did they think about your dancing around in your grandmother's robe?

Boy: They thought it was funny.

An example of the reinforcement that typically occurs when these boys initially exhibit feminine behavior. A positive response is evoked.

Dr.: Do you like making believe you are a girl?

Boy: Yes, it's fun.

Dr.: Is it? How?

Boy: Well, see, you turn into a girl instead of a boy. And my daddy said dolls are for girls, and I *want* to be a girl.

Dr.: You want to be a girl?

Boy: No, not no more, because I don't play with dolls most often.

Dr.: Did you used to want to be a girl?

Boy: Yes.

Dr.: When was that?

Boy: I wanted to be a girl the first time I started playing with dolls.

Dr.: Tell me, why did you want to be a girl?

Boy: Oh, because you're changing. My grandmother's robe is so fun. Sometimes I snap all the buttons except the top and twirl around. Sometimes I act like an old lady, you know, just walking around.

Dr.: Do you like doing that?

Boy: Yes.

Dr.: What's fun about that?

Boy: Well, I like her robe better than my robe.

Dr.: She lets you wear her robe?

Boy: Yes, every time I want to. See, she lets me do anything.

Dr.: Does she let you use any of her other clothing besides the robe?

Boy: Yes, high heels.

Dr.: Do you like wearing her high heels?

Boy: Yes.

Dr.: You do?

Boy: I put on her necklaces and rings.

Dr:. What do you like about that?

Boy: Oh, you see, like the necklaces are so pretty, and the high heels are so pretty.

Dr.: Who watches you do that?

Boy: Oh, my grandmother.

Dr.: Did you think you were a girl when you were wearing high heels and a necklace?

Boy: Everybody thought I was a girl because I wore dresses and earrings. I don't wear pierced earrings because I don't have pierced ears.

Dr.: Do you think it's possible for a little boy to turn into a girl?

Boy: No.

Dr.: Why?

Boy: Because there's no such thing as magic.

Dr.: Yes, that's right. Do you sometimes wish there could be magic and you could turn into a girl? Are you nodding your head yes? [Boy nods.] You do? Why do you want to be a girl? Tell me what the good things are about being a girl.

Boy: Well, you can do fancy hair-dos, like I tried to do this [twirling hair] every time I take a bath, and every time I do it, it just goes "eyak."

Though acknowledging that boys cannot turn into girls, he also acknowledges his wish to do so. Many such boys will soon hear the gossip of people who have "changed sex." For those who continue to harbor the wish, this awareness creates an additional conflict, as the impossible becomes remotely probable.

Example 12-2

Another five-year-old boy describes his feelings about cross-dressing and talks about why he would rather be a girl.

Doctor: Do you like to dress up like a girl or put on girls' makeup?

Boy: Yeah.

Dr.: What's fun about that?

Boy: 'Cause you dress up in makeup.

Dr.: Um hum.

Boy: 'Cause you dress in girls' dresses, which I like the best.

Dr.: Why do you like that so much?

Boy: Because every time I wear these clothes they get tight on me. I mean they get me hotter 'cause the pants go all the way around you and dresses just go out.

Dr.: Whose dresses do you get a chance to wear?

Boy: I never wear a dress, but I wear a bathrobe, and I wear a bath towel.

These two items, bathrobe and towel, are favorites of feminine boys in their improvisation of girls' clothes.

Dr.: I see. Is a bathrobe and a bath towel like a dress?
Boy: Yeah.
Dr.: Do you make believe it's a dress when you wear it?
Boy: Yeah.
Dr.: Do you get a chance to wear a real dress?
Boy: No.
Dr.: Why is that?
Boy: Mama doesn't let me.
Dr.: Why?
Boy: Because my sister's dresses are too little.
Dr.: What if your sister's dresses were not too little, but the same size? Would your mommy let you wear your sister's dresses then?
Boy: Yeah, but only if I was a girl.
Dr.: Only if you were a girl, not if you were a boy? Why is that?
Boy: Because boys don't wear dresses.
Dr.: They don't. Why not?
Boy: 'Cause they look funny in dresses.
Dr.: Um hum. They would look funny.
Boy: And because girls are supposed to wear dresses.
Dr.: If you had your choice and nobody would know about it, and you could do it in secret, all by yourself, would you rather wear dresses, or would you rather wear pants?
Boy: Dresses.
Dr.: What happens to little boys who wear dresses?
Boy: Their mothers get mad.

This boy does not report maternal (or paternal) encouragement of femininity.

Dr.: How about the fathers?
Boy: They get mad too.
Dr.: They do. Have you ever wished you'd been born a girl?
Boy: Yes.
Dr.: Why did you wish that?
Boy: Girls, they don't have to have a penis.

(An intriguing reason for wanting to be a girl.) Theoreticians who believe that castration fear is present in all young males may see this statement as one boy's mastery over the anxiety (that is, taking control of the fate one fears). This same interpretation may be made for the adult male transsexual's demand to have his penis amputated.

Dr.: They don't have to have a penis?
Boy: They can have babies, and because they—it doesn't tickle when you tickle them there.

Dr.: It doesn't tickle when you tickle them there? Where your penis is?
Boy: Yeah, 'cause they don't have a penis.
Dr.: They don't have a penis.
Boy: I wish I was a girl. You know what? I might be a girl.
Dr.: You might be a girl? Why do you think that?
Boy: Well, because if girls had penis and boys had, um—
Dr.: Vagina?
Boy: Um. It would be funny then, because you wouldn't know which was which, because girls have vaginas and boys have penis.
Dr.: Do you like to have a penis?
Boy: No.
Dr.: No?
Boy: 'Cause every time I'm in the wash, when I'm trying to soak my hair, to get the soap off, it tickles my penis.
Dr.: It tickles? Does it get big and stiff and stand up? [Boy nods.] It does? You like that? [Boy shakes head. No.] You don't like that? And if you were a girl that wouldn't happen? [Boy nods.]

Is it anxiety-evoking for some young boys to experience an erection? If so, why? Could it be the result of earlier prohibitions against playing with the penis in its erect state? Could an erection represent a distortion of body image accompanied by a concern that something is wrong? Could it evoke fantasies of a forbidden nature (the family romance or Oedipal themes)?

Dr.: How do you know it doesn't tickle a girl there?
Boy: It might, but it doesn't tickle as much as it tickles boys.
Dr.: Why do you think girls don't have a penis?
Boy: 'Cause they have to have babies.
Dr.: Um hum.
Boy: And babies can't come out of a penis.
Dr.: That's right.
Boy: Babies come out of vaginas.
Dr.: That's right. You think it's ever possible for a little boy to become a little girl?
Boy: No.
Dr.: That's right. How about a little girl becoming a boy? [Boy shakes head. No.] That's not possible either, that's right. Is there anything else about being a girl that's good?
Boy: There's nothing else I want to say.
Dr.: OK. You told me an awful lot. You told me how you feel about boy and girl things. You know, it's OK if it tickles down there.
Boy: It is?
Dr.: Yeah, sure. That's fine. If it gets big and stiff and tickles, that's perfectly OK.
Boy: But your penis doesn't go down for a long time.
Dr.: That's perfectly OK.

The cause of concern for this boy was not immediately attainable. Thus, in the remaining time that day, reassurance was given in an attempt to reinforce anatomic maleness.

Boy: But it hurts when it doesn't go down for a long time.
Dr.: But it does go down, and it doesn't *really* hurt. It just looks and feels a little bit different.
Boy: It tickles when it goes down.
Dr.: It's a nice feelings, isn't it? You're not scared of it when it gets big and stiff are you?
Boy: No.
Dr.: Good! It's supposed to do that when you tickle it. And you are lucky you have something like that, 'cause girls don't have that. That's one *big* advantage for being a boy, 'cause girls can't do that, you know.
Boy: Um hum.
Dr.: Sure they can have babies, but only boys can have a penis stand up like that.

Hopefully, female readers will see behind these apparently sexist statements an attempt to meet this boy where he is, at the core of his anxiety and dissatisfaction. It was an attempt to enable him to accommodate to the facts of anatomic inevitability.

Boy: I wish that boys could have boy babies and girls could have girl babies.
Dr.: Well, you know, boys help girls get babies.

The wish by males to bear children is probably more common than publicly admitted or consciously acknowledged. Here an attempt is made to accommodate part of this wish while continuing to support the boy's anatomic maleness.

Boy: How?
Dr.: Well, for every little child there's a father and a mother, right?
Boy: Yeah.
Dr.: So, you'll have something to do with the girl having a baby when you grow up and get married.
Boy: You mean making the baby?
Dr.: Sure, you'll help make the baby.
Boy: How?

This question led to an early lesson in sex education, designed to provide anticipation of an adult male role.

Dr.: Have your mommy and daddy told you how that happens?
Boy: No.
Dr.: Well, the boy gives the food for the seed inside the girl, and then the baby grows inside the mommy's belly like in a nest.

Boy: How can the food for the seed go inside the mother's belly?

Dr.: It goes into the vagina from the daddy.

Boy: You buy the food at the store?

Dr.: No, the daddy makes it inside his body, and then he puts it inside the mommy's body.

Boy: You mean it comes outside his tushie?

Dr.: No, it comes out his penis. That's what makes the penis a very special thing. See, the mommy has the seed inside her belly in her baby nest, and the daddy has the food that makes the seed grow. It's food for the seed, and that food comes from the daddy's penis and goes into the mommy's vagina, and that makes the seed start to grow and the little baby grows from the seed.

Boy: You mean the little baby is a seed?

Dr.: It begins from a little, tiny seed just like a plant seed. It's called an egg, but it's just like a little tiny seed.

Boy: You mean the baby's in a seed?

Dr.: Yeah.

Boy: How can a baby be in a seed?

(Our language is not always as graphic as we would hope.)

Dr.: Well, have you ever seen, like, a little seed grow into a flower? [Boy nods.] It's the same thing. It starts real little, and it gets fed by the mommy and daddy, and it grows and grows to make a tiny baby.

Boy: Oh.

Dr.: So, when you become married and you become a daddy, you'll help the mommy have a little baby. And that's why it's good to be a boy. And that's why it's good to have a penis. So you can help the mommy. She *needs* you.

Example 12-3

The following report is extraordinary. A five-year-old boy describes penile erection as a reaction to putting on girls' clothes.

Doctor: Who's your best friend?

Boy: Well, mostly my friends in school I play with. Let's see. Kathy is one. And Susan is another one.

Dr.: Who's more fun to play with, girls or boys?

Boy: Both.

Dr.: Are boys too rough sometimes?

Boy: Yes.

Dr.: How about girls? Are they rough too?

Boy: No, they're more calm. . . . I play airplanes sometimes.

Dr.: Do you ever make believe you're someone else when you play airplane?

Boy: A passenger, or I am [in affected voice] the beautiful stewardess.

Dr.: You make believe you're the stewardess?
Boy: Yeah.
Dr.: Which is more fun to make believe, a pilot or a stewardess?
Boy: Stewardess.
Dr.: Why is that more fun?
Boy: Well, because they're so pretty.
Dr.: Uh huh. How about being a boy versus being a girl? Do you wish, do you ever wish you'd been born a girl?
Boy: Yeah.
Dr.: What makes you think it would have been nicer being a girl?
Boy: I don't know, but you know I just feel like being a girl.

Logical, articulate replies are not always readily obtainable. Thus, the advantages of doll play, drawing pictures, and other devices of the child therapist-researcher.

Dr.: Do you always feel that way or sometimes?
Boy: Well, sometimes. I'm quitting more and more.
Dr.: Why?
Boy: Now that I'm really doing it, I really feel that it's not nice. Playing girl I think is not nice.
Dr.: Why don't you think it's nice to play girl?
Boy: Because girls are girls and boys are boys, *that's* why.
Dr.: Do you think that boys can ever become girls?
Boy: No.
Dr.: Was there a time when you were younger when you thought that boys could become girls?
Boy: Yeah.
Dr.: How long ago was that? When did you think that?
Boy: They think they're gonna change when they're three.
Dr.: Oh, at three boys think they can change into a girl?
Boy: Yeah.
Dr.: Did you used to think that you would change?
Boy: Yeah.

(A five-year-old looks back at the immaturity of his youth.)

Dr.: How did you think that was going to happen?
Boy: Well, I thought about it, and then I thought, well, if I ate a certain *plant* it might happen.

Not a new theory. Recall here the American Indian myth, referred to in Chapter 1, of sex change resulting from eating the arrowseed.

Dr.: If you ate a certain plant you might change into a girl?
Boy: Yeah.
Dr.: Did you know what kind of plant?
Boy: The ivy leaf.

Dr:. What gave you that idea, I wonder?
Boy: Because I know that you could eat plants, and I was just trying to taste, but when I tasted the ivy leaf, "phh."
Dr.: Did you try eating the ivy leaf thinking it would turn you into a girl?
Boy: Yeah, but I spit it out, and I forgot about being a girl.
Dr.: Did you try eating it again?
Boy: No! Because when I knew what it taste like, "yuk."
Di.. How long ago was that? How old were you then?
Boy: Three.
Dr.: What gave you the idea that it would be nicer to be a girl?
Boy: Because I'm pretty.

It was noted earlier that feminine boys are often exceptionally attractive and pretty. They are typically aware of this and that prettiness is culturally feminine.

Boy: And they can do more stuff than boys.
Dr.: What kind of stuff can they do?
Boy: Clean the house for their children.

An example of identification with the mother's role.

Boy: Men can really just make money and go to work.

The father's role for young boys is frequently poorly defined and painted in unattractive tones.

Dr.: That doesn't sound like as much fun to you?
Boy: No. I felt it was being nicer being a girl. Now I've stopped feeling like being a girl because I know that—I know that I'm not going to be a girl.
Dr.: Do you know any other little boys that wished they'd been born little girls?
Boy: Yeah.
Dr.: Who?
Boy: Most of my boyfriends. In fact, all of them.

Is this "projection," unconsciously ascribing unwanted personal attributes to others? There is a familiar echo here of the adult homosexual who in self-support attributes "homosexuality" to public figure after public figure.

Dr.: They wished they'd been born girls?
Boy: Yeah.
Dr.: What do they say?
Boy: They say, "I'd rather be a girl."
Dr.: Why do they say that?

Boy: Well, they're trying to copy me, and they think I'm still pretending I'm a girl. I'm not.

Dr.: What makes them think that?

Boy: I don't know. Oh, I think it's because sometimes I stay near my mother.

Dr.: Uh huh.

Boy: Like a girl.

Here this boy equates mother-son physical closeness with girlishness, an "insight" into psychologic theories.

Dr.: When you were younger was there a time when you used to want to be a girl and that you used to dress up like a girl? Did you ever like to wear girls' clothing?

Boy: Yeah.

Dr.: What kind of clothing did you like to wear?

Boy: Dresses. High heels.

Dr.: Dresses and high heels? What's it like to wear high heels?

Boy: Oh, *hard* to walk in.

Dr.: I'll bet it is. Are you able to walk in them, or do you fall?

Boy: I'm able to walk in them a little, but one time I tried to go outside with them and they got stuck in the doormat.

Feminine boys who like wearing women's high-heeled shoes persevere in their effort to master the art.

Dr.: What's fun about high heels?

Boy: I think I just wore them. That's really all. Usually I dress up for about an hour, changing clothes 'till I find one that perfectly fits me, and then I go walking around with a purse.

Dr.: What does your mommy say when you do that?

Boy: She says, "Get it off."

Dr.: Did you ever think that maybe your mommy wants you to be a girl?

Boy: Yeah.

Dr.: What made you think that?

Boy: I don't know. Usually it's hard to understand when you're so young.

Dr.: Did your mommy ever say anything to you that made you wish you had been born a girl?

Boy: Yeah.

Dr.: What?

Boy: She said, "Would you like to have a girlfriend over?" And then when she was over we dressed up like girls.

Dr.: Does she know that you're going to dress up when your girlfriend comes over?

Boy: Yes.

Dr.: She knows that?

Boy: Yes, because I've done this often now.
Dr.: So, she sort of knows that, and lets you do it?
Boy: Yeah.

Could this boy here be "reading" the unconscious of his mother in apparent contradiction with her statement that she discourages cross-dressing, or could this be "wishful thinking" that mother "secretly" does approve?

Dr.: I see. How about your daddy? How does he feel about it?
Boy: Well, he's not around usually, so he doesn't know.

Quite true. Fathers have much less awareness of their sons' femininity due to a lack of opportunity and willingness "to see."

Dr.: Do you think your daddy ever wanted you to be born a girl?
Boy: No.
Dr.: Just your mommy?
Boy: Yeah.
Dr.:. How about now? Do you think your mommy still wants you to be a girl?
Boy: No.
Dr.: What makes you think she's changed her mind?
Boy: Because she really just likes me to be a boy. So, it can be very hard to keep concentrating. I stopped being a girl, but, like, once you do something, you feel like doing it. I keep on doing it.

If behavior is positively reinforced and adopted, then considerable difficulty may ensue when parental cues change. This would be even more difficult if cues are inconsistent, that is, not uniformly negative, or are ambiguous.

Dr.: Is it hard to stop dressing up once you've already started it?
Boy: Yeah.
Dr.: How does it make you feel when you dress up?
Boy: Nice, sometimes, and boring others.
Dr.: When you dress up, like a girl, does it ever make your penis stand up stiff and straight?
Boy: Yeah.
Dr.: It does?
Boy: Yeah.
Dr.: When you dress up?
Boy: Yeah.
Dr.: Does that always happen when you dress up?
Boy: Yeah.
Dr.: It always does? What other times does your penis get stiff and stand up?

Here attempts were made to secure internal validation of the statement that erections accompany cross-dressing. Other circumstances were sought in which erection might occur, and the original question was rephrased.

Boy: Right after I've gone to the bathroom sometimes.
Dr.: Any other times?
Boy: No.
Dr.: But always when you put on girls' clothing?
Boy: Yeah.
Dr.: How does it feel when it stands up like that?
Boy: It really hurts.

Again, the significance of erections to young boys may vary; the feeling of erection against clothing can be experienced as painful.

Dr.: It hurts?
Boy: Yeah.
Dr.: What do you do?
Boy: Take off the clothing.
Dr.: And then what happens?
Boy: And then it goes down again.
Dr.: Then it goes down again?
Boy: Yeah.
Dr.: Does it make your penis feel like you want to play with it when it stands up like that?
Boy: Yeah.
Dr.: Do you play with it?
Boy: Yeah.
Dr.: And how does that feel?
Boy: That's—that feels funny.
Dr.: Is it a nice feeling? You're smiling. Is it a nice feeling?
Boy: Yeah.
Dr.: When you do play with it, when you put on girls' clothing and it stands up, does that feel good?
Boy: Yeah.

This boy reports pleasurable penile feelings from cross-dressing. If one can extrapolate to adult behavior, one would predict later fetishistic cross-dressing. Follow-up research will decide the validity of that prediction.

Dr.: Do you play with your penis any other time?
Boy: No.
Dr.: Just when you dress up like a girl?
Boy: Yeah. That's about all really that I have to say about being a girl.

During a subsequent interview, the same boy relates a sexual fantasy of infantile seduction. There was no evidence from parental reports that these events occurred, and the story likely represents a little boy's idea of what goes on between father and mother, perhaps based on his own sex play with little girls. If such be the case, it might be a rehearsal for later heterosexuality.

Dr.: Who's your closest friend now?
Boy: A boy who lives six houses away.
Dr.: A boy. How old is he?
Boy: Six, and I'm five.
Dr.: And what sort of things do you and he do together?
Boy: Well, we play, oh, let's see, what do we play? Well, he has a sister, so mostly it's hospital.
Dr.: You play hospital with his sister?
Boy: Yeah.
Dr.: How do you play hospital?
Boy: Me and him are the doctors, and his sister who is four years old is the nurse.
Dr.: And what do you do as the doctor?
Boy: Sometimes we do the operations on the nurse 'cause we want to see her feelings.
Dr.: Uh huh.
Boy: So we know how she feels about the baby.
Dr.: Do you examine her?
Boy: Yeah.
Dr.: Do you take all her clothes off to examine her?
Boy: Yeah.
Dr.: How does she feel about having her clothes taken off to examine her?
Boy: She feels, "Oh, goody, I can run around the house like this." And then my friend's mother comes in and sees her like this and says, "Who took off her clothes?" And he says, "I don't know." Ha!
Dr.: Um hum. Do you take off your clothes too? Does you friend take off his clothes too?
Boy: We all take off our clothes. As soon as the mother finds the game interesting, she takes off her clothes too.
Dr.: Does she really?
Boy: Yeah.

Here the story sounds fanciful.

Dr.: Um hum.
Boy: And we're all patients. First, there's a bare doctor, and then there's a bare nurse, and then there's a bare doctor again, and then there's a bare nurse again.

Dr.: What is it like to examine a little girl with the way her body's different from a little boy's? What does it make you feel like?

Boy: Like, uh—oh, dear.

Dr.: Oh, dear?

Boy: Yeah, I can't figure it out.

Dr.: Well, what do you make of that difference? Little girls have different bodies, don't they?

Boy: Yeah.

Dr.: What is the difference?

Boy: The penis is different.

Dr.: Do you think little girls have a penis?

Boy: No.

Dr.: Right.

Boy: They have a vagina.

Dr.: They have a vagina, right. What about when they're born?

Boy: They have a very little vagina.

Dr.: A very little vagina. They don't have a penis.

Boy: No.

Dr.: That's right. Why is that?

Boy: Because they don't get a penis.

Classic psychoanalytic theory holds that young boys believe both males and females to have a penis at birth. This boy's statements, though not supportive of that theory, do not rule out, of course, that he may have held such a view earlier.

Dr.: Where is the vagina?

Boy: Here.

Dr.: Right. How about inside? Is there something inside the girl?

Boy: Uh, well, there's a—there's an egg that's inside the mother, and there's a sperm inside the boy.

Dr.: Uh huh, that's right. . . . What does this little girl say when she sees your penis or sees her brother's penis?

Boy: Euu. Does *she* scream.

Dr.: Does she?

Boy: She runs up to the top of the bunk bed and screams like a screech owl.

Dr.: Why does she do that?

Boy: Because she's scared.

Dr.: She's scared of the penis?

Boy: Yeah, because she knows it's going to go to the bathroom and when she knows that she screams.

Dr.: I'm not sure I understand what you're saying.

Boy: Well, because when the boy goes to the bathroom, she's afraid it'll come and get her wet.

Dr.: And how about when you see her vagina, how do you feel?

Boy: Boy, do I—boy, do me and my friend scream too.
Dr.: Why?
Boy: We're afraid of her going to the bathroom, so we scream at the top of the bunkbed, and hop under the covers.
Dr.: I see. Is there anything about seeing her vagina that makes you feel anything else?
Boy: No. Sometimes we both feel like girls. Sometimes we both don't feel like girls. Sometimes she feels like a boy.

Again, one wonders about "projection."

Dr.: What do you mean that sometimes you both feel like girls?
Boy: I can't explain.
Dr.: Well, what does she feel like when she feels like a boy? Can you tell me that?
Boy: She does boys' games. She dresses up in police clothes.
Dr.: Uh huh.
Boy: She dresses up in her cowboy clothes.
Dr.: I see.
Boy: She reads boy books and when we feel like girls, we read girl books, and we dress up in girls' clothes.
Dr.: Does your boyfriend get dressed up like a girl?
Boy: Yeah.
Dr.: What clothing does he put on?
Boy: The same clothing I do.
Dr.: The same you do?
Boy: Dresses, high heels, stuff like that, but I don't do that at home.
Dr.: What happens if you do that at home? Do you get scolded?
Boy: No.
Dr.: Does anybody get angry with you at home if you dress up?
Boy: No.

An absence of parental discouragement. This was supported by his parents' statements that, in their view, feminine role-taking would broaden his development.

Dr.: Remember what you told me last time about putting on girls' clothes? How it makes your penis get big and stiff?
Boy: Yeah.
Dr.: Remember that?
Boy: Yeah.
Dr.: Does that happen to your friend too?
Boy: Yeah. He tells me it does.
Dr.: What does he say?
Boy: He says, "Euu, my penis is standing up straight. It feels like a giant."
Dr.: When does he say that?

Boy: When he gets dressed up like a girl.
Dr.: When he gets dressed up like a girl? The same thing that happens to you then?
Boy: Yeah.

If so, this is quite extraordinary. Or is it? Perhaps (though it is unlikely) all boys when they put on girls' clothes get an erection. There is a paucity of data on this. In all likelihood the friend does not experience erection with cross-dressing.

Dr.: How do you like that feeling? What's it like when it stands up big and stiff?
Boy: It feels like a giant again.
Dr.: And what do you do then?
Boy: I take those clothes off fast.
Dr.: Do you?
Boy: I get into my boy clothes and say, "Bye-bye. I'm going home."
Dr.: Do you ever play with your penis so it feels different?
Boy: Yeah.
Dr.: When do you do that?
Boy: When I like to. Ha, ha.

(A pretty straightforward reply.)

Dr.: How about when you look at this little girl and she's undressed? Does that make your penis big and stiff?
Boy: Yeah.
Dr.: It does? Has she ever seen your penis get big and stiff?
Boy: Sometimes.
Dr.: So, if you look at this little girl when she's undressed, sometimes your penis gets big and stiff?
Boy: Sometimes.

If so, perhaps a harbinger of later heterosexuality. Again, data are lacking on penile responses of young males to nude persons of the same and opposite sex.

During still a later session, the boy related his reactions to nudity to feelings of gender identity.

Boy: When I see my *daddy* undressed, I feel like a *boy*. If I see my *mommy* undressed, I feel like a *girl*.
Dr.: When you see your mommy undressed, you feel like a girl?
Boy: Um hum.
Dr.: How is that? What do you mean?
Boy: I really can't tell you.
Dr.: What do you mean you feel like a girl?
Boy: Well, you know, what I mean.

Dr.: Hum?

Boy: I just act like a girl.

Dr.: I wonder why that is? I wonder what it is about seeing your mommy undressed that makes you want to act like a girl.

Boy: That one I can't tell.

A theory of female identity or lack of masculine identity in males is castration fear. At this point, in describing his feeling about being female when he sees his mother, he took notice of a stick figure on the desk before him, which to the therapist was unremarkable in the context to which it struck the boy's attention. It is cylindrical with crudely painted clothing details.

Boy: How come that wooden figure, he has only one arm?

Dr.: That's the way it was painted.

Boy: Maybe one arm *fell off*.

Here the need was felt to "interpret" the boy's statement. *Interpret* is used here in the traditional psychoanalytic manner, that is, to render conscious or apparent to a patient what was previously unconscious or unapparent.

Dr.: Do you think anything could happen to a little boy's penis? Sometimes little boys worry that something could happen to it.

Boy: I think that someone will step on it probably.

Dr.: Do you think little boys ever worry that something could happen and they might lose their penis?

Boy: No.

So here there is initially some expression of fear of penile injury, then denial. This was followed later by the therapist's search for the "advantages" of having a penis.

Dr.: What do you think? Do you think it's better to have a penis or to have a vagina?

Boy: Penis.

Dr.: Why do you think that's better?

Boy: I don't know.

Dr.: One of the things you can do is you can stand up and you can pee against the wall or a tree.

Boy: Little girls can't do that.

The therapist then returned to "Parental Nudity: Fact or Fantasy."

Dr.: What part of your mommy's body do you like the very best?

Boy: The, ah, the vagina.

Dr.: The vagina?

Boy: If she isn't undressed, I always take, you know, her pants down to look at her vagina.

Dr.: You take her pants down?

Boy: Um hum.

Dr.: What does she say when you do that?

Boy: She says, "You naughty boy, put those up again." And, I don't know, I just play with her vagina.

Dr.: You play with your mommy's vagina?

Boy: Tickle, tickle, tickle. Yes.

Dr.: What does she say when you tickle her vagina?

Boy: She laughs.

Dr.: Does she really let you do that?

Boy: When I feel like it.

Dr.: Is your daddy there when you do that?

Boy: He likes me to tickle his penis.

Dr.: He does?

Boy: But he doesn't like me to sometimes tickle his butt. But sometimes they like me to tickle their butt.

Dr.: Uh huh. How do you do that?

Boy: I go behind them and tickle my father, and I go "Bang, bang" to my mother.

Dr.: OK. When you play with your daddy's penis, does that make your penis be big and stiff?

Boy: No. Only when I play with a girl.

Another internal check on the earlier sign of emerging heterosexuality.

Dr.: Only when you play with a girl? How does a boy feel when he tickles his mother's vagina?

Boy: Like a girl.

Dr.: You do?

Boy: Yeah.

Dr.: When you tickle your mommy's vagina, does your penis get big and stiff?

Boy: Yes, it gets *very* big and stiff.

Whether this be fact or fantasy, fantasy may well be the more important issue, as has been known since Freud's historic discovery. Here then is a hint at disassociation in this male of sexual identity (female) and sexual-object choice (heterosexual). There are, in fact, adult males with a strong cross-gender wish, to the point of requesting sex change, who are erotically responsive to females. Interestingly, these males are frequently fetishistic cross-dressers, as this boy may also be, if his previous statements are valid.

Dr.: Does your mommy know that?
Boy: She sees it get stiff.
Dr.: And what does she say?
Boy: She says, "Oh, dear, you better get undressed too."
Dr.: And what happens?
Boy: And then I say, "OK, Mommy, bare bottom time."
Dr.: And is your penis still big and stiff?
Boy: Um hum.
Dr.: And then what happens?
Boy: And I say, "Oh, it's bedtime. I better get away. I don't want to go to bed."
Dr.: Why is that?
Boy: Because I like playing *girl.*

One may speculate here that the boy utilizes a "transsexual defense": playing girl to defend against fantasies of incest.

Dr.: How about her breasts? Do you play with her breasts?
Boy: Yeah.
Dr.: How do you do that?
Boy: By tickling them.
Dr.: When you tickle your mommy's breasts, does your penis get big and stiff then?
Boy: Yeah.
Dr.: Which do you like to tickle more, her breasts or her vagina?
Boy: Her breasts.
Dr.: What do you like about that more?
Boy: Because they remind me of when I was a *baby.*
Dr.: Do you remember getting milk from your mommy when you were a baby?
Boy: Yeah.
Dr.: What do you remember about that?
Boy: Because now I drink milk out of a glass, and I remember I used to couldn't.
Dr.: And how would you get your milk before you could drink out of a glass?
Boy: I'd suck my mommy's breast as hard as I could.

(Memory? Watching younger sibling? Confabulation?)

Dr.: Do you remember that or do you sort of think that probably happened, but you don't remember it?
Boy: I can remember it, but, then more and more I become a boy.
Dr.: How do you do that?
Boy: I say, "Oh, dear. I'm a boy. H-e-l-p!"
Dr.: Um hum.
Boy: I say, "Bye-bye, you girlie firley burley," and the girl says, "OK, you dumdum boy. You have more stuff than I do." Whee!

Example 12-4

This boy, aged four and a half, tells a story that broadens somewhat the perspective described by the first three boys. His interview is included here because near the end it includes a therapy tactic that may be used with troubled feminine boys. Chapter 16 will focus on treatment.

Boy: I play house with my friends.
Dr.: Who are your best friends?
Boy: Lisa is my best friend. . . .
Dr.: Do you get a chance to play the mommy part?
Boy: Um hum.
Dr.: When you're mommy, what part does she take?
Boy: She's the big sister.
Dr.: When you're playing the mommy part, what do you do? How do you make believe you're the mommy?
Boy: I make cakes and cook things.
Dr.: Is it fun sometimes to make believe you're the mommy? [Boy nods.] Can you tell me what's fun?
Boy: Making a cake.
Dr.: Is it more fun to play the mommy part?
Boy: Yes.
Dr.: When you grow up would you rather be a mommy or a daddy?
Boy: A mommy.
Dr.: A mommy? Why would you rather be a mommy?
Boy: Just because.

Direct questioning here leads to a roadblock.

Dr.: Do you think there are little boys that are sorry they're little boys and wished they'd been born girls?
Boy: Um hum.
Dr.: Why do you think some boys are like that?
Boy: I don't know.
Dr.: Could you make up a story for me about a little boy who wants to be a girl, and what reasons he had for that?

A more subtle approach, and easier for the child.

Boy: Once there lived a little boy, and he wanted to be a little girl.
Dr.: Um hum.
Boy: But he wasn't a girl, and wished he was born a girl, but his mother didn't want him to be born a girl. There were too many girls in their home.
Dr.: Go on.
Boy: He gets lost.

Dr.: Lost?

Boy: Because they went to the grocery store. The mommy leaves without him.

Dr.: But, what about his wish to become a girl, what's going to happen with that?

Boy: Well, he turned into a girl.

Dr.: How did he do that?

Boy: A magic man comes and turns him into a girl.

Dr.: Who would the magic man be?

Boy: That magic man would be his daddy.

Psychoanalytic theory sees the father as the potentially castrating agent along the Oedipal route to male psychosexual maturity.

Dr.: And how does the magic man make the boy into a girl?

Boy: He would have to look for a wand, and take it, and he would come home and turn the little boy into a little girl.

Dr.: For the boy to be magically changed into a girl, what would have to change about the boy?

Boy: Dress.

Dr.: He'd have a dress? Okay, that's one thing. Go on.

Boy: And he would have long hair. He'd have girl's shoes. Three things.

Dr.: Three things, right. What else?

Boy: Umm. 'Cause he would have girl's shoes.

His conception of a magical sex change pointedly ignores anatomic facts.

Dr.: How about—let's say the child's all undressed. There's no clothing at all. What would have to change with the little boy's body in order to become a girl?

Boy: Because—umm—his knee—umm—

Dr.: His knee? How about where a little boy goes pee out of? OK. Is that going to have to change too? [The boy makes no answer.] What is that called in a little boy? Do you know? Where do you go pee out of?

Boy: Tweener.

Dr.: Tweener? That's what a little boy goes pee out of? How about little girls? Do they have a tweener to go pee out of? Or do they have something different?

Boy: They don't have a tweener.

Dr.: Right. What do they have?

Boy: They have bottom.

Dr.: Yes, but what else do they have?

Boy: Girl's socks.

Dr.: Yeah, but how about where they pee out of?

Boy: They don't have nothing there.

Dr.: You think it's good to have a tweener?

Boy: I wish I didn't.

Dr.: Why do you wish you didn't?
Boy: I would never like to go pee.
Dr.: Why?
Boy: 'Cause I wouldn't have to go pee in a hurry so much.
Dr.: What about girls? Don't they have to pee?
Boy: No, they don't have to go pee.
Dr.: No, girls go pee. Girls have two holes, and one of them is for peeing. You just can't see it very easily, but it's there.
Boy: Girls have a hole to go pooh.

So, he is confused about male and female anatomy. An attempt is made to dispell his confusion, explaining the facts in simple terms.

Dr.: Girls have two holes. They go pooh like you do when they sit down, but they also have another little hole to make pee out of. Instead of a tweener they have something else there, but they have to go pee also.
Boy: Only one of the holes is for go pooh?
Dr.: That's right. That's the same on a boy and a girl. The hole they go pooh is the same on boys and girls. The one they go pee out of, that's different. But even if you didn't have a tweener, you'd still have to go pee.
Boy: Uh huh.
Dr.: So, now, knowing that girls have to go pee also, do you think it's good to have a tweener, or do you still wish you didn't have one?
Boy: I wish I didn't have one.
Dr.: So, what you're saying is you really wish you were a girl? Are you nodding your head? [Boy nods.] You want your tweener to go away?
Boy: Yes.

Strict adherents to the castration-fear theory of feminine identification in young males are being hard pressed by this boy.

Dr.: Does your tweener ever get kind of big and stiff and stand up by itself? You know what I mean? Sometimes it's kind of soft and down, and sometimes it gets stiff and stands up. Does that ever happen?
Boy: Um hum.
Dr.: What makes it stand up stiff like that?
Boy: Play with it with my hand.
Dr.: Is there anything else you can do to make it stand up?
Boy: Uh huh.
Dr.: How about when you make believe you're a girl? Does that make it stand up stiff?
Boy: Umm. Sort of.

It is difficult to assess here whether his response was due to the interviewer's suggestion or was based on his own experience. Perhaps the idea of sexual metamorphosis *is* arousing. The possibility is not so farfetched. An adult male was recently interviewed who claimed that his primary source of sexual arousal was *the thought* of sex change.

Dr.: Sort of? How about when you put on girls' clothing? Does that make it stand up stiff?
Boy: No, that makes it go back down.

At this point, a therapy tactic was considered more beneficial than further direct questioning.

Dr.: Well, I'll tell you something. You know that sometimes little boys do wish that they had been born girls, and that's a little bit sad. One reason is that it's not possible for little boys to become girls, and it's sad because there are so many fun things that boys can do. They can go places and do things more on their own.
Boy: Umm.
Dr.: They can go to work, and do the kind of things that daddy does, and that's fun. That's exciting stuff. And it's kind of sad that little boys think that maybe somebody with a magic wand would come along and turn them into a girl. That's kind of sad because there aren't any magic wands like that, see? Little boys, once they're little boys, stay little boys, and little girls when they're born as girls stay as little girls. They can't change back and forth even though they sometimes might like to, but it doesn't happen. There is no magic wand, no magic wand that will do that.
Boy: Sometimes you can turn a girl into a boy.
Dr.: That's not possible either. Once girls are born girls, they stay girls, and boys stay boys. So, I guess it's going to be a little bit easier if you can learn to like some of the boy-type things.
Boy: Um hum.
Dr.: Maybe do some things with your daddy. He does fun things.
Boy: I know.

Although these interview excerpts were not selected to illustrate tactics of therapy, a few have nevertheless been included, particularly those stressing the irreversibility of anatomic maleness and femaleness and those citing pleasurable aspects of being a boy.

Integration of themes verbalized by feminine boys during interviews, with what they reveal in psychologic testing, and what is described by their parents, demonstrates the broad base from which their "femininity" springs. They not only like doing the things girls do, but may also wish to be fully in that role to the point of wishing their bodies were anatomically female. They know the insignia of maleness, but, contrary to theories that posit the universal desire to have male genitalia (penis envy), these boys wish theirs to be gone. At an earlier age they may have been unaware of anatomic sex differences, or, if dimly aware, were still believing in some magical body metamorphosis. However, Freud's famous remark, "Anatomy is destiny," has begun to impinge on them when they first appear for study. Here is the glaring obstacle, unavoidably attended to many times a day, running counter to the themes of their identity. Unchanged with the passage of time, it may later emerge in the statements of adult male-to-female transsexuals that they sit to urinate, never or rarely masturbate, and do not use their penis in sexual relations. Anatomical sex change is then sought; penis removal is begged for; and, occasionally, in the face of medical intransigence, self-mutilation is resorted to. After surgery, such persons generally experience increased psychologic comfort.

13

FEMININE BOYS:
PSYCHOLOGIC
TESTING

Data collected through psychological tests complement that derived from clinical interviews. The data presented in this chapter were collected under standard testing situations that permit comparisons between groups of subjects. In this study the previously described feminine boys underwent extensive psychologic testing and were compared with masculine boys and typical girls. The groups of children were comparable for age, I.Q., ethnic background, and extent of their fathers' formal education.

As reported by their parents, the masculine boys showed no interest in cross-dressing or doll play, preferred boys as playmates, and did not play female roles. They enjoyed rough-and-tumble play and sports. The girls enjoyed wearing dresses, playing with dolls, participating in girls' games, and preferred girls as playmates. None was considered a tomboy, and none had expressed the desire to be a boy.

Testing procedures included standard tests previously proved to discriminate between boys and girls as well as original procedures developed specifically for this research. The standard tests given the children were the It-Scale for Children and the Draw-a-Person Test. Original tests were the Family-Doll Preference Test, and the Parent and Activity Preference Test. Additionally, observations were made in an experimental playroom. Finally, when both biological parents of a feminine boy were available for study, parents and child were tested together by the Family Communication Task.

STANDARD TESTS

It-Scale for Children. The child is presented with a faceless, unclothed figure of a child drawn without distinct clues as to gender (an "it"). The child then makes a series of selections for "it" from groups of cards depicting masculine and feminine toys, boy or girl playmates, and masculine or feminine activities. Finally, "it" can be one of four people depicted on cards: a normal-appearing boy, a normal-appearing girl, and two intermediate, partly cross-dressed figures. Normal boys and girls, within the age range of the boys studied here, show significant differences in their card selections (Brown, 1956).

Draw-a-Person Test. The child is given a blank sheet of paper and a pencil and told to draw a person. After the picture is completed, he is asked to identify the person, then to turn the page over and draw someone of the opposite sex. Published reports indicate that boys are more likely than girls to draw a male first (e.g., Jolles, 1952). The sex of the first drawn person is presumed to be a reflection of the drawer's sexual identity.

FIGURE 13-1.

A two-card set used in the Parent and Activity Preference Test, depicting activities that are gender-typical: father sawing wood paired with mother sewing.

FIGURE 13-2.

A *two-card set used in the Parent and Activity Preference Test, depicting activities that are gender-atypical: mother repairing a car paired with father dusting.*

ORIGINAL TESTS

Family-Doll Preference Test. A set of dolls representing a family (grandparents, parents, boy, girl, and infant) is given to the child, who is instructed to make up a story utilizing the dolls. The duration of time the child utilizes each doll figure within a ten-minute test period is recorded.

Parent and Activity Preference Test. A series of twenty-eight two-card sets of pictures, one depicting a mother and the other a father in an activity, is presented to the child. The activities pictured on the two cards may be gender-typical, e.g., father sawing wood paired with mother sewing (eight such sets); gender-atypical, e.g., mother fixing a car paired with father dusting (eight such sets); gender-typical for one parent, e.g., both sewing (eight such sets); or gender-neutral, e.g., both reading (four such sets). Representative sets are illustrated in Figures 13-1-13-4.

The child is told that the two picture cards constitute the beginning of a three-card story and is then given two more cards, one showing a child having joined the mother in her activity and one showing a child having joined the father in his. The child selects one of the two cards. The pictured child is a boy when the child tested is male and a girl when the child tested is female. The activities and the sequence in which they are presented are the same for boys and girls. Figures 13-5-

FIGURE 13–3.

A two-card set used in the Parent and Activity Preference Test, depicting an activity that is gender-typical for one parent: both mother and father sewing.

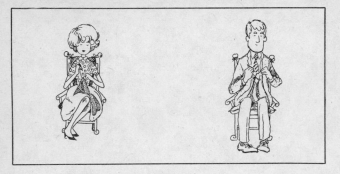

13–8 show the options a child may select to complete a three-card story.

Experimental Playroom Observation. Children are placed alone, for fifteen minutes, in a playroom stocked with typically masculine and typically feminine toys (e.g., truck, gun, doll, tea set). They are observed through a one-way mirror observation window, and the time spent playing with each toy is recorded.

FIGURE 13–4.

A two-card set used in the Parent and Activity Preference Test, depicting an activity that is gender-neutral: both mother and father reading.

FIGURE 13–5.

A two-card set used in the Parent and Activity Preference Test, depicting the options of a boy joining one parent in an activity that is gender-typical: father sawing wood or mother sewing.

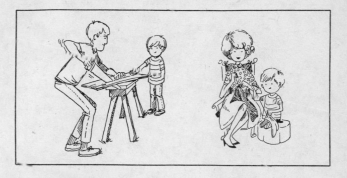

Family Communication Task.* This procedure is designed to delineate social power and dominance within families. The task is to describe a novel graphic design to another family member so that he is able to identify the design from an array of possibilities before him. Each

FIGURE 13–6.

A two-card set used in the Parent and Activity Preference Test, depicting the options of a girl joining one parent in an activity that is gender-atypical: mother repairing a car or father dusting.

* This aspect of the research was conducted by Katharine Smith, M.A., doctoral candidate, Department of Psychology, University of California, Los Angeles.

FIGURE 13–7.

A two-card set used in the Parent and Activity Preference Test, depicting the options of a boy joining one parent in an activity that is gender-typical for one parent: father sewing or mother sewing.

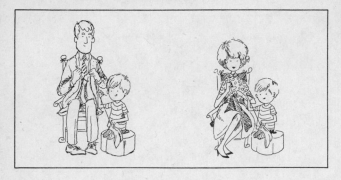

family member (mother, father, and boy) is visually separated from the others by an opaque barrier, but they may verbally communicate via a microphone and earphone connection. Each family member takes turns at being the *sender* of communication, that is, the one who describes to the other family members (the *receivers*) which design has been selected from the array of possibilities. Verbal communication is struc-

FIGURE 13–8.

A two-card set used in the Parent and Activity Preference Test, depicting the options of a boy joining one parent in an activity that is gender neutral: father reading or mother reading.

tured so that the first description is sent to both receiving family members simultaneously, but the flow of subsequent questions about the design from receivers to sender is controlled by the sender. This is accomplished by a switch, under the control of the sender, that allows communication with only one receiver at a time. Thus, communication flows at any given moment between only two family members (the sender and one receiver).

After the child has functioned as sender, he leaves the room, and the parents are instructed to tell him when he returns that he must try harder and to insist, as is their prerogative as his parents, that he do better (role-playing by the parents). When the child reenters the room, he is told by the tester that both his parents have something to say to him, one at a time. He then operates the microphone-earphone mechanism so that first he receives a directive to do better from one parent and then a similar directive from the other. The family members then take turns again describing and guessing at the graphic designs (Figure 13–9). This procedure was adapted from work by Alkire (1969).

FIGURE 13–9.

The array of graphic designs used in the Family Communication Task.

TEST RESULTS

It-Scale for Children. Fifty-five boys were administered the It-Scale. Thirty boys constituting the feminine boy group scored very similarly to typical girls. By contrast, the twenty-five boys in the masculine boy group scored similarly to other typical boys. The difference between masculine and feminine boys, as can be seen in Table 13–1, is statistically significant. Thus it was shown that the boys described as feminine by their parents, when making selections for a child (presumably themselves), chose culturally typical feminine toys and activities, preferred female playmates, and depicted themselves as women or feminine men.

Draw-a-Person Test. The same fifty-five boys were asked to draw a person. The sex of the first-drawn person by the group of thirty feminine boys was female 57 percent of the time. Similar-aged girls draw a female 82 percent of the time (Jolles, 1952). By contrast, the sex of the first drawn person by the masculine boys was female only 24 percent of the time. Other similar-aged typical boys draw a female 20 percent of the time (Jolles, 1952). The difference between feminine and masculine boys, shown in Table 13–2, is statistically significant. Thus, if the thesis is valid that the sex of the first-drawn person is reflective of the drawer's self-concept, the majority of the feminine boys showed evidence of having a female identity.

Family-Doll Preference Test. Thirty-five feminine boys, twenty-five masculine boys, and thirty-four girls were tested. Feminine boys scored similarly to girls and differently from masculine boys. Data and levels of statistical significance are shown in Table 13–3.

Thus, feminine boys, like girls, utilized female family-doll figures more often in their storytelling (presumably as a reflection of their

TABLE 13–1
It-Scale for Children

	MEAN SCORE
Feminine boys (N = 30)	41.2*
Masculine boys (N = 25)	72.6*
Typical boys (Brown, 1956)	66.4
Typical girls (Brown, 1956)	38.4

* $P < 0.05$, U — Test.

TABLE 13-2
Draw-a-Person Test

	SEX OF FIRST-DRAWN PERSON	
	MALE (PERCENT)	FEMALE (PERCENT)
Feminine boys (N = 30)	43*	57*
Masculine boys (N = 25)	76*	24*
Typical boys (Jolles, 1952)	80	20
Typical girls (Jolles, 1952)	18	82

* P < 0.02, chi square.

identity and role preference) than did masculine boys and additionally, in such fantasy, were involved to a greater extent in infant care, a role more typically taken by females.

Parent and Activity Preference Test. Thirty-five feminine boys, thirty-six girls, and twenty-six masculine boys were tested. In terms of parent preference, feminine boys selected the card depicting the child having joined his mother more often than did masculine boys. There was no difference between feminine boys and girls as to selecting the mother card. In terms of activity preference, feminine boys selected the card depicting the child having joined a parent in a feminine activity more often than did masculine boys. Girls selected the card depicting the

TABLE 13-3
Family-Doll Preference Test

DOLL	TIME SEGMENTS (MEANS AND STANDARD DEVIATIONS)		
	FEMININE BOYS (N = 35)	MASCULINE BOYS (N = 25)	GIRLS (N = 34)
Mother	12.1 ± 8.6*	6.4 ± 5.9* [x]	12.5 ± 5.9 [x]
Father	8.0 ± 5.5	11.0 ± 9.0 [o]	6.9 ± 4.6 [o]
Grandmother	9.3 ± 4.9* [†]	5.0 ± 3.5*	6.0 ± 2.8 [†]
Grandfather	5.7 ± 4.9	7.8 ± 9.8	4.6 ± 2.9
Boy	7.9 ± 6.0	9.5 ± 9.8	5.8 ± 4.5
Girl	10.1 ± 7.0	8.0 ± 8.9	8.5 ± 6.1
Infant	12.2 ± 9.3*	5.9 ± 6.5* [x]	12.5 ± 6.9 [x]
Masculine dolls (all)	21.7 ± 12.7	28.3 ± 20.8 [x]	17.3 ± 9.2 [x]
Feminine dolls (all)	31.5 ± 13.9*	19.4 ± 13.9* [o]	27.1 ± 10.1 [o]

Significance levels (T-tests):
  * P < 0.01 feminine boys vs. masculine boys.
  [†] P < 0.01 feminine boys vs. girls.
  [x] P < 0.01 masculine boys vs. girls.
  [o] P < 0.05 masculine boys vs. girls.

TABLE 13-4

Parent Card Selection: Mother (Feminine Boys vs. Masculine Boys)

	0-6 CARDS	7-13 CARDS	14-20 CARDS	21-28 CARDS
Feminine boys making selection (N = 35)	1	5	23	6
Masculine boys making selection (N = 26)	7	13	5	1

$\chi^2 = 20.7$, df = 3, P < .001

child having joined a parent in a feminine activity even more often than did the feminine boys. Card-selection differences are shown in Tables 13-4–13-7.

Thus, on parent preference, feminine boys proved to be considerably more like girls than like masculine boys, and on activity preference to be intermediate between masculine boys and girls. The data corroborate parental reports that a feminine boy strongly prefers being with his mother to being with his father and that he shows some preference for her activities to those of his father.

The parent and activity selections that best discriminated masculine boys, feminine boys, and girls were:

Child Joins: mother cooking or father flying kite.
    Result: masculine boys joined father; feminine boys and girls were divided between joining mother or father.
Child Joins: mother sewing or father sawing wood.
    Result: masculine boys joined father; feminine boys were divided between joining mother or father; girls joined mother.

TABLE 13-5

Parent Card Selection: Mother (Feminine Boys vs. Girls)

	0-6 CARDS	7-13 CARDS	14-20 CARDS	21-28 CARDS
Feminine boys making selection (N = 35)	1	5	23	6
Girls making selection (N = 35)	0	5	28	2

$\chi^2 = 3.4$, df = 3, P < .5

TABLE 13–6

Activity Card Selection: Feminine (Feminine Boys vs. Masculine Boys)

	0–5 CARDS	6–11 CARDS	12–17 CARDS	18–24 CARDS
Feminine boys making selection (N = 35)	1	22	12	0
Masculine boys making selection (N = 26)	4	22	0	0

$\chi^2 = 13.2$, df $= 3$, P $< .01$

Child Joins: mother cooking or father building a model plane.
     Result: masculine boys joined father; feminine boys were divided between joining mother or father; girls joined mother.
Child Joins: mother or father sleeping in bed.
     Result: masculine boys chose father; feminine boys and girls chose mother.
Child Joins: mother or father driving car.
     Result: masculine boys chose father; feminine boys and girls chose mother.

Experimental Playroom Observation. Fifteen feminine boys were compared to fifteen masculine boys and fifteen girls. Feminine boys and girls spent more time playing with culturally typical feminine toys and less time with masculine toys than did masculine boys. Toys that best separated the masculine and feminine boys were the doll (the feminine boys' and the girls' favorite) and the truck (the masculine boys' favorite). Thus, in an experimental setting, parental reports of feminine boys' preference for doll play was corroborated, as was their aversion to toys considered typical of boyhood. These differences in

TABLE 13–7

Activity Card Selection: Feminine (Feminine Boys vs. Girls)

	0–5 CARDS	6–11 CARDS	12–17 CARDS	18–24 CARDS
Feminine boys making selection (N = 35)	1	22	12	0
Girls making selection (N = 35)	0	5	28	2

$\chi^2 = 20$, df $= 3$, P $< .001$

toy preference and levels of statistical significance are shown in Table 13–8 and Figure 13–10.

Family Communication Task. Data analyzed to date indicate that communication is more efficient in intact families of masculine boys than in matched, intact families of feminine boys. This difference is consistent with that found by Alkire (1969) whose patient or "emotionally disturbed child" families communicated less effectively than normal families.

In our study, mothers and fathers of masculine boys understood their sons' communication more accurately than mothers of feminine boys. (Accuracy of communication is based on the receiver's correctly identifying the graphic design based on the sender's descriptions.)

In both groups fathers asked more questions of mothers in attempting to identify the design when mothers were the sender than mothers asked of fathers when fathers were the sender. Feminine boys asked more questions of their mothers than did masculine boys (49 vs. 16). There was also a trend for feminine boys to ask more questions of their fathers than control boys, but the difference was not significant.

With respect to the effects of role-playing by the parents, again differences appeared between the two groups. When the boys were told that both parents had something to say to them privately, but that they had to listen to only one at a time, feminine boys more often

FIGURE 13–10.

Average time spent playing with masculine and feminine toys during Experimental Playroom Observation, based on groups of fifteen members.

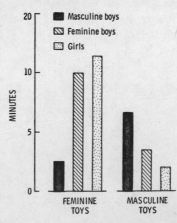

TABLE 13-8
Experimental Playroom Observation

	MINUTES SPENT IN SPECIFIC TOY PLAY PER FIFTEEN-MINUTE PLAY PERIOD		
TOY	FEMININE BOYS (N = 15)	MASCULINE BOYS (N = 15)	GIRLS (N = 15)
Doll	6.8 ± 1.4**	1.6 ± 1.0** †	5.7 ± 1.3†
Embroidery	1.9 ± 1.2	0.8 ± 0.6	3.6 ± 0.9
Carriage	0.2 ± 0.1	0.0	0.2 ± 0.1
Handbag	0.1 ± 0.1	0.0	0.3 ± 0.2
Tea set	1.1 ± 0.6	0.1 ± 0.1††	1.7 ± 0.5††
Truck	1.3 ± 0.4*	4.0 ± 1.0* ††	0.8 ± 0.5††
Gun	0.9 ± 0.4	1.4 ± 0.4††	0.1 ± 0.0††
Rocket	0.2 ± 0.1	0.4 ± 0.1	0.4 ± 0.2
Wagon	0.2 ± 0.2	0.2 ± 0.2	0.0 ± 0.0
Ball	0.3 ± 0.2	0.3 ± 0.2	0.6 ± 0.5
Punching dummy	0.5 ± 0.3	0.6 ± 0.2	0.1 ± 0.0

Significance levels (analysis of variance):
* $P < 0.02$ } feminine boys vs. masculine boys.
** $P < 0.01$
† $P < 0.02$ } masculine boys vs. girls.
†† $P < 0.01$

chose their mothers first. Ten of twelve feminine boys chose their mothers first, compared to only two of eight masculine boys.

Communication theory holds that information is asked of people who are seen as having social power. In other words, communication within a social hierarchy is directed *upward* (Back et al., 1950; Kelley, 1951; Hurwitz et al., 1960). Thus, our findings are consistent with the thesis that mothers in feminine-boy families hold relatively greater social power than do mothers in masculine-boy families, as perceived by the *child*.

Parents of feminine boys were rated as more effective in role-playing. Eleven of sixteen control parents did not engage in role-playing, whereas all the parents of feminine boys played their roles as directed. This is of interest in that feminine boys also appear unusually adept at role-playing (see Chapter 10). It could be that feminine boys learn role-playing by observing it in their parents, or one could further speculate that the capacity for role-playing is in some way an inherited personality trait.

After the role-playing intervention, there was a marked shift in the capacity for the fathers of feminine boys to understand their sons' communication. Their capacity improved to the level previously shown by the fathers of masculine boys and their sons. Thus it may be that a feminine boy is responsive to his father's directives once the latter assumes a position of authority. If such is the case, it bears an implication for one strategy in family therapy.

The psychological test results summarized here offer more objective data to support the subjective impressions obtained from clinical interviews. Particularly striking is the degree of concordance between feminine boys and girls. In these test situations, feminine boys did not emerge as "a third sex." Instead, they exhibited preferences for roles and activities similar to those of typical girls and distinct from the average male of the same age.

14

"IDENTICAL" TWIN BOYS: ONE MASCULINE, ONE FEMININE

Twin studies hold a venerable place in the history of research into psychosexual anomalies. Investigation has generally focused on twin pairs concordant for behavior in an effort to assess the extent of genetic loading behind these various patterns. Kallman, for example, found that among forty pairs of twins judged to be monozygotic (though not proven "identical" by more sophisticated means) when one was homosexual, so was the other (Kallman, 1952). This study with its startling finding has been criticized by several investigators, including Kallman (1960), on methodologic grounds, but it is nevertheless provocative. Since that classic paper of 1952, a number of cases have appeared in the literature of monozygotic (identical) twins discordant for homosexuality (e.g., Klintworth, 1962; Davison, Brierley and Smith, 1971). Studies of such twin pairs can be a useful model for isolating critical experiential variables when genetic contributions are held relatively constant.

The following case material describes two eight-year-old boys demonstrated to be monozygotic (identical) twins,* one of whom is feminine and the other masculine.

Example 14-1

The twins are monozygotic with more than 99 percent probability.† One twin was referred at age eight for evaluation of feminine behavior that included cross-dressing, doll play, taking the role of a female in games, and an avoidance of rough-and-tumble boyhood play.

GENERAL BEHAVIOR

Doctor: How different are the two boys in regard to masculinity?
Mother: Very. First of all with actions. Frank Jr. [masculine] walks like a clodhopper. Paul [feminine], on the other hand, walks femininely. He is on the prissy side. He has a feminine ring to his voice. He is like a female when he gets upset. . . . He thoroughly enjoys playing with dolls. He and his sister can play day upon day upon day. His brother will deliberately go out and get into a football game or anything with the older boys in the neighborhood. . . . Paul will still dress in women's clothes, but he's getting out of the habit because he knows it really aggravates us. He will put hair clips in his hair. . . . When they play house, Frank is always the father and Paul is always the mother or the sister.

EARLY DIFFERENCES

Dr.: Did they look different at birth?
Father: Paul [feminine] looked a great deal heavier and rounder, a good-looking baby. The other like a spider monkey.
Mother: Frank [masculine] was very badly mutilated. Oh, he looked like a drowned baby bird. He was a very ugly infant. Paul had big eyes and was a pound heavier, so his face was fuller.
Father: He was the best looking of the two.

The prefeminine infant appeared to the parents to be more attractive and to others as feminine.

---

* Dr. Robert S. Sparkes, Associate Professor of Medicine and Pediatrics, Division of Medical Genetics, School of Medicine, University of California, Los Angeles, kindly performed the tests required to rule out dizygosity in this twin pair.
† The total ridge count on ten digits for both boys is 192. The probability of finding this in dizygotic twins is 0.25 percent. Both boys have identical findings for the following red cell antigens: ABO, Le, Rh, Go, MNSs, Fy, Lu, Kk, Jk, P, Vel. Phosphoglucomutase, haptoglobin, 6-phosphogluconate dehydrogenase, and adenylate kinase electrophoretic types are also identical in both boys. Karyotyping of each twin reveals 44 + XY chromosomal configuration.

Mother: We always got comments in the double stroller, "Oh, how nice! A boy and a girl." You can guess *who* they thought was the *girl* and *who* they thought was the *boy.*

Dr.: Paul was the girl?

Mother: It was Paul they thought was the girl! It used to infuriate me. The two of them dressed identical. Never did I put lace or frills on.

Dr.: What were they responding to? Why did they think Paul was the girl?

Mother: Because Frank just took off like a little old man. He never looked like a baby. Never. Paul did. He looked the picture, with the rosy cheeks, round face, blue eyes, blond hair. . . . Paul was always the cuddlier of the two boys. You could hold him. You tried to hold Frank, and he would do everything but bite you.

The prefeminine twin was also more cuddly.

Dr.: Was one twin more active?

Mother: Up to four months there was nothing you could identify. After that I would say Frank [masculine] over Paul [feminine]. When they were still in the playpen, which puts them a little under a year, Frank reached over and bit Paul on the ear something fierce, and Paul didn't do anything. He just curled up.

Dr.: Were there as many times that Paul was dominant?

Mother: I would say it was almost equal.

Dr.: Did you have a preference when you were pregnant for a boy or a girl?

Father: A boy.

Mother: Personally, if I were given the choice, I would have rather had a girl. However, he wanted a boy. He's the last Frank Riley. And therefore because he wanted a boy I wanted a boy. I had to have a girl too.

The mother indicates wanting a girl as well as a boy.

Dr. (to father): You're the last Frank? You named one of the boys after you?

Mother and Father: Yeah.

Dr.: How did you decide which twin to name Frank Jr.?

Mother and Father: First born.

Father: We found out before they were born they'd be twins, and we decided the first born would be Frank Jr.

The first born, named for his father, was the premasculine twin.

Mother: Now I wish we could go back and change their names.

Dr.: Why?

Mother: Even though we haven't gone into detail in front of the children as to why Frank was named after his father, it almost looks—I can see, looking through Paul's eyes—that he got Daddy's name because he's *the one that Daddy liked.*

ONSET OF BEHAVIORAL DIFFERENCES

Dr.: When did you start noticing a difference?

Mother: Four, four and a half. Paul preferred the friendship of the little girls in the neighborhood and enjoyed playing with dolls and took more of an interest in his sister than his brother. His brother was becoming very masculine at the time. Paul didn't want to participate in sports. He'd much rather clean house. I don't know whether it was a preference for me or for what I did, the fun of getting all dressed up or putting on makeup or doing dishes or grocery shopping. These seemed to be the things he preferred to do. I was the one who did them.

At age three, the prefeminine boy had contracted an infectious disease involving lymph nodes of the axilla and neck. His illness radically modified the roles that each parent played with each twin. For two and a half years, the mother repeatedly drove the prefeminine boy to a hospital (an hour each way) for extended evaluation and treatment. Meanwhile, the father was at home with the premasculine boy.

Father: I think the reason I kind of laid off a lot of sports with Paul was because he was down here in the hospital, and I had a chance to be with Frank more and tried to keep him occupied with sports during these periods of time. The reason I didn't push Paul that much was because his little arm was bad at the time, and it was hard to make him do it. I gave up on him until the last couple of years. I was upset because he didn't want to do it.

Mother: Paul was always invited to be included with his brother, to participate, whether it was kite flying or basketball or baseball, but he didn't. . . . All the females in the family said, "You can't do that to him. That isn't his cup of tea."

Father: The operation [surgery on the right axilla] affected his arm, and he wasn't quite as active. Everything has been toward the fact that maybe you can't push him like that because he's that way.

Mother: It gave him an excuse for not competing with his brother. This is where his aunt came into the picture. . . . "Well, he can't throw a ball like Frank, because he has a hurt shoulder."

The illness differentially affected the expectations others had of the two boys.

Mother: Frank didn't necessarily want or need the affection. When I say "need," I mean he didn't *crave* it like Paul did. Because Paul found that, being in a hospital, he got waited on. Things happened his way. When he got home, things happened his way. He could play on this, the fact that he had been sick.

The mother was aware of the difference in her relationship with the two boys and conscious of displaying more affection to the sick child.

Psychologic Testing

On the Draw-a-Person Test, the sex of the first person drawn by Paul was female; that drawn by Frank was male. Evidence exists that the sex of the first-drawn person is reflective of the child's gender identity (see Chapter 13). On the It-Scale for Children (Brown, 1956), Paul scored 38 and Frank 72. Published norms for boys and girls indicate that Paul's score is in the normal range for girls; Frank's is in the normal range for boys.

On the Bene-Anthony Test of Family Relations (Bene and Anthony, 1957), more positive outgoing and incoming feelings between father and son were described by Frank (masculine), and more positive outgoing and incoming feelings between mother and son were described by Paul (feminine). With respect to negative feelings, more were described between father and son by Paul than by Frank. These data are shown in Table 14–1.

The twins were also administered the Parent and Activity Preference Test described in Chapter 13. Paul chose the "boy and his mother" card seventeen times; Frank chose it only three times.

Comment

This case report does not rule out a neuroendocrine or other constitutional basis of cross-gender behavior. Monozygotic twins need not have an identical prenatal hormonal milieu, any more than an identical nutritional one; witness the long-recognized differences in twins' birth weights. Intricacies of somatic development do not proceed identically in two persons derived from the same fertilized ovum. Otherwise, par-

TABLE 14–1

Bene-Anthony Test of Family Relations

	PAUL (FEMININE)		FRANK (MASCULINE)	
	MOTHER	FATHER	MOTHER	FATHER
Outgoing positive	7	5	3	8
Incoming positive	8	2	5	8
Outgoing negative	1	1	1	0
Incoming negative	1	4	4	2

ents of monozygotic twins would be unable to distinguish them on the basis of physical appearance.

This report does, however, point to the value of exploring postnatal experiences in detail and of guarding against oversimplification that ignores that myriad of experiences. To do so would be to ascribe gender behavior purely to a prenatally written neural program.

In this twin pair, some behavioral differences were apparent soon after birth. The prefeminine twin was a more attractive infant. Additionally, the prefeminine twin was more cuddly, which may have facilitated more mother-infant contact. This seems to have been a significant influence in eliciting different reactions from adults to him and his brother. Stoller (1968) has found such variables to be critical in the development of femininity in boys. The activity level of the premasculine twin may have been greater, and there is some evidence that he was the more aggressive.

Coupled with these differences between the infant boys were possible differences in parental attitudes toward the twins. The premasculine infant was named for the father. This may have influenced the father's behavior toward the two boys, causing him to favor the son who bore his name. Further, it may have facilitated the premasculine boy's identification with his father while retarding a similar identification by his prefeminine brother.

The critical event, however, appears to have been the illness of the prefeminine boy, starting at three, which greatly altered the role each parent played with each twin. During the years in which gender identity consolidates, one twin was spending considerably more time with his father, engaging in sports and rough-and-tumble play, while the other twin was spending more time with his mother, drawing solicitous attention because of his label as "the sick child."

Thus, two male children with a similar, if not identical, genetic makeup, can diverge in the development of masculinity and femininity, in accordance with a differential chain of events beginning at birth and continuing through childhood.

15

FEMININE BOYS: HOW THEY GET THAT WAY

An obvious question for the behavioral scientist is "What causes femininity in a young boy?" (We need also ask, "What causes masculinity?") The question of what causes femininity is most easily answered by those who have never studied a single case history. Unfettered by facts, they adapt with ease their theoretic bias and provide essentially logic-tight explanations, some of which are: a dominant mother, defense against castration fear, early conditioning, a neuroendocrine disorder, and so on. Those who have studied a very few cases, and are favored by chance, will find a few variables constant from one to the next. From these will be synthesized: the etiology. Those who are driven to study larger and larger numbers of cases jeopardize the comfort of such security. It is the disquieting reward of the "expert" that the more data he collects, the more research knowledge he collates, the less he is *sure* he knows.

This chapter's cat will now be let out of its bag: I do not have a simple explanation of what causes boyhood femininity. To those for whom this disappointment has not dissuaded further reading, that remark will be expanded.

All feminine boys are not the same. Nor did they arrive at their femininity via the same route. It is possible to cite for many feminine boys variables that appear to bear some plausibility as being influential in *that* case. The variables vary from boy to boy, the numbers growing as the number of boys grows. Furthermore, their concurrence with feminine behavior, and perhaps the word *coincidence* would be more suitable, does not prove *causality*.

A necessary condition for further clarification of the causes of boyhood femininity may be delineation of subgroups of feminine boys. Feminine adult males may be subdivided according to varying degrees of feminine identification: masculine heterosexuals who cross-dress with sexual excitement, effeminate homosexuals who sometimes cross-dress, feminine males requesting sex change who have been partially successful in male roles, and males requesting sex change who have never functioned as males and "pass" as acceptable women (Stoller, 1968).

With a graded system of classification, both for children and adults, a theory may be constructed (and tested) in which several ingredients, in combination, are postulated as essential for yielding the most extreme degree of femininity, with lesser degrees resulting when fewer ingredients are present. For the moment, however, theoretical reductionists will have to settle here for a list of possible contributing factors, based on the cases so far evaluated that have been globally assessed "feminine."

THE VARIABLES

The following factors have been found in association with the emergence of boyhood femininity. It may eventually be learned which, if any, are *necessary* or *sufficient* causative factors and which, if any, must appear together *in constellation* to be effective.

A Listing

1. Parental indifference to feminine behavior in a boy during his first years.
2. Parental encouragement of feminine behavior in a boy during his first years.
3. Repeated cross-dressing of a young boy by a female.

4. Maternal overprotection of a son and inhibition of boyish or rough-and-tumble play during his first years.
5. Excessive maternal attention and physical contact resulting in lack of separation and individuation of a boy from his mother.
6. Absence of an older male as an identity model during a boy's first years or paternal rejection of a young boy.
7. Physical beauty of a boy that influences adults to treat him in a feminine manner.
8. Lack of male playmates during a boy's first years of socialization.
9. Maternal dominance of a family in which the father is relatively powerless.
10. Castration fear.

Examples

Each of the following examples is focused on one of the variables listed above. However, because these variables are frequently and variously intertwined, several may appear in one picture.

PARENTAL INDIFFERENCE TO FEMININE BEHAVIOR

Parents may seek counseling and evaluation only because of pressure generated outside the family. (This has been true in about 50 percent of the families in this study.)

Doctor: What are the things that you've been most concerned about?
Father: The reason we came here is because we were recommended to come here by Doctor—I can't remember his name. He says my son has a problem. Other than that, I'm not sure.
Dr.: Do either of you feel that your son has a problem?
Father: The way this doctor puts it, yeah. He definitely has a problem. The fact that he wants to be a girl all the time. I mean, we lived with it five years. Six years, I guess.
Dr.: What's your feeling about that?
Mother: Well, I don't know. I have mixed emotions really. I don't know. It's never occurred to me to bring him anywhere. I used to get real disgusted with him the way he would act and everything, but all the time I'd just ignore it. I never thought there was anything really to worry about.

Mothers may have a neutral attitude toward a variety of feminine behaviors in their son. (Neutrality was the initial attitude in about 80 percent of the cases.) First, this mother describes her attitude toward her son's doll play.

Dr.: Does he play with dolls?
Mother: Yes.
Dr.: Exactly what does he do with them?

Mother: He dresses them up, and he undresses them, and he puts the clothes right back on again.

Dr.: Are these boy dolls or girl dolls?

Mother: Girl dolls.

Dr.: And how often does he do this?

Mother: Every chance he gets to get hold of a doll.

Dr.: And how do you feel about the doll playing?

Mother: I don't mind it. I don't see anything wrong with it.

Dr.: When did you first notice his interest in doll playing?

Mother: Since he was very little, very little. About three.

Dr.: Is your son aware of how you feel about the doll playing?

Mother: I think he knows *there's nothing wrong with it* [emphasis added].

Then, she describes her attitude toward his use of cosmetics.

Dr.: Has he shown any interest in makeup or cosmetics?

Mother: Yes, he has. He likes to put on my lipstick, and he watches me closely to see how I put mine on, and then he tries it.

Dr.: And how do you feel about that?

Mother: I don't like him to get into my cosmetics, so I tell him to keep away from them.

Dr.: Why don't you like him to do that?

Mother: Well, it's *my* stuff, and things that are *mine* I don't like my children to get into.

Finally, the mother reveals her attitude toward her son's playing the role of mother.

Dr.: Does he play house or mother-father games?

Mother: He plays house a lot.

Dr.: Do you know what role he takes?

Mother: He takes the mother. He gets like a doll, or a stuffed animal, and pretends he's the mother. He spanks it if it's mean, or if it's bad, or he says, "You know Mommy doesn't like for you to do that" or "Mommy doesn't like that."

Dr.: And what's your feeling about this?

Mother: I don't see nothing wrong with it.

A mother's attitude may be ambivalent thereby communicating a mixed message.

Mother: His younger sister got one of these artificial sets of cosmetics. About four days ago he came out painted up like he was going to a circus from the eye shadow, and I said, "Get in there and get that off your face." (*He really looked good.*) And I made him wash it off, and he got mad and said, "Well, it was there to play with. You really *don't* mind do you?" And he said, "Well, if my *hair* were *longer,* I'd look better."

When parental concern does develop over a son's feminine behavior, mothers are characteristically more concerned than fathers. (True in about 80 percent of the cases.) This family demonstrates how two parents differentially interpret the same behavior.

Mother: I feel that he is not what I would consider all-boy, and I'm very concerned about him. I have noticed it, and I'm sure my husband has noticed it, but he has chosen to ignore it. I spoke to him several years ago about it, and he didn't react in any way except to say that he'll outgrow it; there's nothing wrong I've been aware of it; for some reason he seemed to want to ignore it. I don't know why.

Father: Well, I would say it was lately when I first noticed, but I just thought it was something natural.

Mother: I don't see how my husband can say that when we have a son that's older than this boy. Why he would feel that this is just something natural? That's what I tried to point out to him. If there isn't something wrong, why doesn't the older boy act this way?

Mother (to her husband): Do you think it's just a natural thing when you have eight brothers and a son?

The next dialogue strikingly illustrates a father's unconcern over his son's femininity.

Dr.: What have you been concerned about?

Mother: Why don't you tell Dr. Green what you're concerned about?

Father: I'm concerned about him as a child. He's—I don't know—the other two kids, you—he's always got an answer and even though he knows he's wrong, the answer is right. For instance—

Mother: But you're not really concerned about *that*. I mean—

Father: But this is all part of it.

Mother: Yes, but you're concerned really about him being *feminine*, aren't you?

Father: That seems to be—

Mother: Is it going away, or is it—

Father: I don't know. But you can't *talk* to him. The two kids can play, and they can play good for hours on end. They fight, yes, but as soon— he's not got to be in there two minutes, and then they're fighting, the whole three of them. He causes the trouble, and then away he goes, and then that's it. It seems he lives to make trouble. This is the whole thing.

Dr. (to mother): What have you been concerned about?

Mother: Well, wishing to be a girl.

Father: This feminine thing hasn't bothered me as much as the trouble, you know. You can tell him something, and he'll completely contradict you. It's like you tell him to clean up his bedroom, and you go in there, and it's exactly the same.

Mother: He would put scarves on and play house and be the woman and never be the man, and he's always played with girls instead of boys.

Dr. (to father): Were you aware of his taking the role of the female in games?

Father: Yeah, three or four years ago, or maybe four or five years ago, but I figured that was just a *fad*, you know, a kid goes through. But [continuing undaunted] the thing that's got me is, the other two you can tell them to do something and they'll do it. The boy's not as good, but the girl, every time you tell her to do something, she does it.

Mother: I was doing the dishes one day, and he came out and stood by the sink and said, "I'm going to be Miss America."

PARENTAL ENCOURAGEMENT OF FEMININE BEHAVIOR

A mother's reaction to her son's doll playing may be positive.

Mother: About two years ago I got his sister a complete Barbie set for Christmas. The doll house and the carrying case and everything, and this is the *only* time I had a real problem with him doing anything I considered socially unacceptable. He actually *swiped Barbie clothes from the dime store for that doll.* Boy, I really went into such a fit over *that.* I marched him into the store, and I embarrassed him in front of the manager and made him replace all of the items, and *that was the only time that I have ever forbidden him from playing with dolls* [emphasis added]. It irked me so bad to think he would go to the extent of stealing. I said he would have to save his money and *then* he could buy clothes for the dolls!

A mother may want a daughter so badly that she sees her baby son as a girl. (True in about 10 percent of the cases.)

Dr.: What was he like as an infant?
Mother: Real tiny. Real delicate. He was a beautiful child. He had the body and the face—everything—of a little girl, very dainty.
Dr.: What would you say about his face that was like a girl's?
Mother: His eyes, his eyebrows, and his hair.
Dr.: What about his eyes?
Mother: His eyes were just like a little girl's. Just beautiful, just beautiful. Eyelashes real long just like a little girl should have.
Dr.: What sort of personality did he seem to have?
Mother: A little girl's.
Dr.: In what way?
Mother: Well, to myself, I see him like a little girl. I see him like a little girl. I wanted a girl so bad, to me he was a little girl.

An occasional mother's reaction to her son's feminine behavior has been negative.

Dr.: To what extent do you think he thinks you disapprove of the feminine behavior?
Mother: Well, he sees my reaction. I don't scream or shout, but he could see my facial expressions that I don't like it. And when he put on the

powder before going to school, I told him, "Now, when you go to school you won't see any other boys wearing powder." And he said no, and I said, "I don't even wear that much powder myself. Makeup is for ladies. Not for little boys." So I said, "Do you realize what you are doing?" He said no, and I said, "Can you help yourself?" He said no.

CROSS-DRESSING OF A YOUNG BOY BY A FEMALE

The onset of this boy's feminine preferences occurred when, at one and a half, two girls dressed him in girls' clothes. Everyone thought he was cute.

Mother: It seemed to me when it first started he was a year and a half and these two little girls took him and they dressed him up completely, from a wig all the way down to shoes. And he started to play with dolls then. Now I noticed him then. We never had any dolls for him before then, and he played with his toys, but from then on he started wanting the [high-heeled] shoes, and he wanted a doll, and a little at a time he would want something else.

Dr.: He was a year and a half old?

Mother: Yes. And that was the first time. Well, now he would play with little dolls before, but no big deal. He really was just a year old, just a toddler.

Father: Everybody thought it was cute and everything. Everybody laughed.

Mother: Then when he'd try and get the high heels, everybody thought it was cute, you know, because he was wanting to wear them and everything.

Father: I'd say that's what started it all. And maybe the fact that I didn't stop it soon enough.

Mothers may dress their sons in girls' clothes. (True in about 15 percent of the cases.)

Mother: As a matter of fact, when he was little I used to dress him. Maybe it was my fault. I don't know.

Dr.: Tell me about that.

Mother: He was very, very tiny at the time. I used to dress him like a little girl. I wanted a girl so bad.

Dr.: How would you dress him?

Mother: I would put little girls' clothing on him. (I would never take him out anywhere like that.) At the time I didn't think it would hurt him, because he was very tiny, only a couple of months old.

Dr.: What sort of clothing would you put on him?

Mother: Little dresses, little hats, little slippers, a girl's blanket.

Dr.: How old was he when you first dressed him like that?

Mother: Oh, he was about three or four months old.

Dr.: And over how long a time did you do that?

Mother: I guess till he was about nine months old.

Dr.: What made you stop dressing him as a girl?

Mother: I realized to myself that he wasn't a girl, that he was a boy, and I was supposed to dress him like a boy. So I stopped. I said to myself, "Why kid yourself? He isn't a girl. He's a boy."

Others in the family also dressed him as a girl.

Dr.: As far as you know, has anyone else ever dressed your son in girl's clothing?

Mother: Yes, my sisters. They used to dress him quite often, too, in little girl's clothes because they used to love to see him the way he looked. He was about two or three months.

Dr.: Did this continue over some period of time?

Mother: Oh, until he was about one.

Dr.: Why would they do that?

Mother: Because they thought the way I did: that he was just adorable as a little girl.

Dr.: How often would they do that?

Mother: Quite often. Every time they had the chance. His eyelashes were so long they used to say, "Give me your eyelashes."

Dr.: After his first year, has anyone dressed him in girl's clothing?

Mother: Yes, my mother-in-law did, one time. I found out about it. She dressed him up to see how he would look like a little girl, and everybody just laughed about it.

Boys have been dressed in girls' clothes by a sister. (True in about 8 percent of the cases.)

Here are two examples.

Father: Our daughter, who is now sixteen, ever since she heard about this, she has been blaming herself. She has a guilt complex. She thinks because when he was younger she used to like to—she wanted a sister—and she used to treat him like a sister, and she thinks because of that this is why he has gone this way.

Dr.: How would she treat him as a sister?

Father: She would do his hair, and she would play dolls with him, and she'd dress him up as a girl.

Mother: She was telling me she dressed him up, you know, with a bonnet and so on. And he was like two years old maybe.

Dr. (to second mother): What was your daughter's feeling about his using her clothing at that time?

Mother: At that time, she thought it was cute. She dressed him up.

Dr.: She did?

Mother: Yeah. Yeah. We all thought it was cute because he was just a little guy playing around. My daughter she'd dress him up and play like he was a little girl. She wanted a little sister.

Dr.: Did your daughter ever dress up the youngest boy?

Mother: No. By the time he was at that age we realized this must have been going on too long with this boy, so we never encouraged it again. (I mean, *allowed* it again.)

A mother or sister need not be the apparent feminizing influence. About 10 percent of the boys evaluated may have been so influenced by their grandmothers.

Dr.: How do you think this preference developed?

Stepmother: He was dressed up and his hair curled and stuff like this when he lived at his grandmother's. And fingernail polish put on him. He lived with his grandmother since he was a baby, and she raised him until about a year ago. He was there until he was five.

Father: Around three or so it was something cute to her—painting him up with fingernail polish.

Dr.: Besides nail polish, what other feminine things, if any, did she do?

Father: He was allowed to clomp around in high heels if he wanted.

Stepmother: Your brother and sister-in-law have both said they've seen him dressed. After he came back and was with the other children, he didn't know how to play with them most of the time. And he evidently had not been moved to do anything that most kids that age would do because he would get dirty. In fact, one day I did want to take him to the beach, and he told me he couldn't because his clothes might get dirty and his grandmother would be upset. And I said if his hands got dirty he could wash them with soap and water. "It comes off!"

Dr. (to father): During those three years were you aware that your mother was doing some of these things?

Father: When I spotted them, I put my foot down. Of course, it did me no good to put my foot down, because when my back was turned or I was out of the house, she was back to it.

MATERNAL OVERPROTECTION

A mother describes differential treatment of a prefeminine boy compared to his siblings.

Mother: He was a very delicate baby. He didn't belong out there with the other boys! He belonged inside with *me*. I didn't want him to get dirty. I wanted him to be clean all the time, and I used to make him little shirts with little panties. Of course I made my other sons that, but with him it was *special*. Because I wanted a *girl* so bad, and he had the features of a girl.

Dr.: What was his reaction to being held?

Mother: Oh, he loved it. He was always smiling.

Dr.: Do you think he seemed to enjoy being held more, less, or about the same as your other children?

Mother: More.

Dr.: To what extent would you hold him when he was an infant?

Mother: Oh, a long, long time. Gee, most of the time I would spend holding him, because my other two—they were big already and they didn't need my attention that much. Or they would go outside and play with my little sisters or something.

Dr.: How would you rate the amount of time you had available for him the first year compared to your other boys?

Mother: More. He was a very delicate baby. I watched over him con- stantly, whatever he did, [to see] if he'd fall. My kids never had a scratch on them when they were little. I was always right after them, but him it was *more.*

Others describe inhibiting early boyish behavior.

Dr.: How did you feel about his participating in rough-and-tumble play?

Mother: I didn't want it to be too rough. If I saw that he was going to be hurt—now this was before he was five years old—he went out once and the other boys, his own age, were going to push him down the concrete steps—and I stopped them, stopped him from getting pushed. And I think I did more of that than I needed to.

Dr.: Can you give me other examples?

Mother: Well, there *is* another thing that sticks in my mind. When he was about two years old, my husband wanted to take him to the *men's* bathroom, and I said *no,* and I think this is all wrong, I know now.

Dr.: You didn't want your husband to take him to the men's public bathroom?

Mother: Yes, I didn't think it was clean enough.

Dr.: So you took him to the girls' bathroom, the women's bathroom?

Mother: Yes, I protected him—

Father: Anything that would hurt him. Any physical way that would hurt him.

Dr.: Can you say how?

Mother: Running too hard. Riding a bicycle pell-mell like boys normally do. I would take him to the bus stop instead of letting him go by himself when he started kindergarten.

EXCESSIVE MATERNAL ATTENTION AND PHYSICAL CONTACT

A father offers his theory of why his son is feminine.

Father: The trouble started when he was born a boy, because a boy had never been born in my wife's family and he was spoiled rotten.

Dr.: How's that?

Father: Oh, picked up everytime he opened his mouth to cry or do something. Every time I saw him he was being held by my wife's sister or mother. He was just spoiled rotten, that's all there is to it.

Dr. (to mother): What's your opinion about that?

Mother: I think he was made a lot over.

Father: Well, he *was*. He was picked up every five minutes.

Mother: Well, he used to cry a lot.

Father: And that's probably why he cried a lot, because he knew as soon as he opened his mouth he'd get picked up again.

Mother: My sister used to visit quite a bit, and, of course, we lived with my mother, so she used to give him some attention.

Father: Twenty-three hours a day!

Dr.: How would you compare the amount of holding he had in his first year compared to your other two children?

Mother: Well—

Father: I'd say they got about 75 percent of what he had. When he was a baby, there was your mother, and invariably a sister or two, in the same house so as soon as he cried, he was picked up. But when we had the other two over here, there was just us two, and if she were busy and they cried, they cried.

A mother describes having more time for cuddling her feminine son than her other children.

Mother: My husband was working all those hours. And oh, probably he didn't cry too much, but when he cried I was Johnny-on-the-spot to pick him up and soothe him, especially since he had this asthmatic cough. I couldn't stand to hear the wheezing.

Dr.: What would stop his crying?

Mother: When I'd pick him up.

Dr.: What was his reaction to being held?

Mother: Oh, he loved it.

Dr.: Was he cuddly?

Mother: Oh very, very much. Very affectionate.

Dr.: Did he seem to enjoy being held more, or less, or about the same as your other two children?

Mother: I think he preferred being held more. I held him more. My husband was working and the other boy was four, four and a half, and I was there every minute twenty-four hours a day. I had this little toy [*sic*]. And I lavished all my emotion I guess on him by cuddling him. It would be something to do. Well, I had more time for him. With her and the other boy I just didn't have time. With him, that's just about all I had was time.

She also describes making him a uniquely important person in her life.

Mother: Now this brings something to mind. I think I put him before my husband, but not with the other two. I would feed him first—it didn't matter what else was going on—I would feed him, but not with the other two.

Feminine boys may frequently sleep alongside their mothers. (True in about 20 percent of these cases.) This increased contact may impede formation of a separate identity. It may also require inhibition of sexual arousal to female bodies, a protective mechanism against the intimacy resulting from such contact.

Dr.: Do you recall instances in which he would sleep in the bed with you at night?
Mother: The second year, yes, because his daddy was gone. And many nights he slept with me. I was pregnant. I was very, very tired. If I went to bed early, I'd go to bed with him. He slept with me as many nights as he didn't.
Dr.: What about your two older children? Did they sleep with you at night?
Mother: No.
Dr.: It was only him?
Mother: Yes.

ABSENCE OF OR REJECTION BY FATHER

About 20 percent of the boys were abandoned by their fathers before their fourth birthday and had no substitute father. Additionally, *physically present* fathers may be *psychologically absent*.

Mother: My husband wasn't any good. He never worked. I was always the one that was working. He was always loaded on something. That's why he is where he is today, in prison.
Dr.: Loaded on what sort of things?
Mother: Well, he was going overboard with bennies. He was dropping a hundred a day, which is enough to kill anybody. He'd stay up four or five days in a row, then come back and shake for a couple of hours after taking a handful of reds, to go to sleep for a couple of days, while I was getting up, going to work, and taking care of the baby, cleaning, cooking, and everything else. So his father was asleep or gone. Then he started with acid and methedrine and was just going hog wild on everything he could find, and there were many times that he would get mad at me, and he'd take it out on me. He hit me many times.
Dr.: During the boy's first years of life, how much time was your husband home?
Mother: Quite a bit of it. I went back to work when he was five months old, and he was home, supposedly baby sitting for me. I would come home and he would be asleep and the baby would be soaking wet in his crib where he'd been all day, because he would be home but he just wouldn't watch him. After staying up four or five days, when you finally fall asleep you're in a dead sleep, so he supposedly didn't hear anything. He was gone so much of the time—*mentally*—that his presence wasn't really felt that much.

Another pattern of psychological absence.

Mother: He doesn't have the male companionship that he should have. There is absolutely no outside sports that a mother can put her son into, and if the father doesn't do it, then I imagine the majority would tend to stay with their sisters and mothers.

Dr.: Is there anything in his relationship with your husband that you feel is influencing his feminine behavior?

Mother: Yes, like when Daddy is home he doesn't take him anywhere. If the TV is on, he'll sit and watch ball games, and if I'm baby sitting or something, no matter where I am, my boy will come to me and seek me out for companionship. I'll say, "Go to your father now. This is the time to be with your father. Talk about the game that he's watching," and because it's interrupting my husband's visual end of it, and he can't concentrate on the game, my son recognizes it, and he'll soon leave. He won't have the companionship that he needs. He'll come back to me.

The next boy's experience with adult males during his first three years was extraordinary. These men *did* change into women by putting on women's clothing. They were "drag queens."

Mother: When I was living back East I was staying with my sister. I came home from work, and I noticed she had these fellows impersonating themselves as females, and I was very shocked when I walked in the door, and I asked her what was going on. She said they were dressing, and I said, "You have children here" and "That's not normal." She said, "There's nothing wrong with it." He was three years old at the time.

Dr.: I'm a little bit confused. Could you fill in a few more details? Who were these people, and what were they doing?

Mother: My sister had some fellows in the house impersonating themselves as females. They would get dressed and go out at night to make money.

Dr.: At what period of his life was he exposed to these men?

Mother: He was three years old. I only stayed there for six months at my sister's house, and then I moved.

Dr.: And are you saying that it was on a daily basis that he was seeing this?

Mother: Yes, and I didn't know anything about it. But he would ask me questions, you know. He would say, "Mommy, didn't you tell me boys don't wear earrings and makeup?" I said yes. He said, "Well, my aunt had some men over there and they had earrings."

Dr.: Were they drag queens? Do you know what that term is? They are homosexual men who dress as women.

Mother: Yes, they were.

Dr.: How did your sister come by knowing these people?

Mother: Well, my sister is a lesbian.

Dr.: What about his father? Was he aware of any of this?

Mother: He has no interest in him. His real father didn't want him. I moved out when my son was two months old.

Dr.: Did his father see him after those two months?

Mother: Oh, no.

Dr.: Was there another man living with you as a sort of substitute father?

Mother: No.

Dr.: No uncles or anything? No men that he could have looked at and said, "That is a man."

Mother: No.

Dr.: Except the drag queens.

Mother: That's right.

Paternal rejection of the feminine boy may stand in contrast to the father's relationship with the boy's masculine brother.

Dr.: How would you compare the kind of relationship he had with his father to the relationship between his father and your other son?

Mother: He wasn't as close to his father as the other brother. None of the children were very close to him, but his father was more proud of the oldest boy and his interest in sports. He would stop and listen to him because they talked on the same level. His father would make comments like "That's going to be my *All American*. This will be my *drum majorette*."

However, the time spent in father-son activity may be described as similar for both masculine and feminine brothers (reported by about 25 percent of these families). In some of these cases this degree of participation is considered average and in others less than average.

Dr. (to first father): Compared to most fathers and their sons, how would you rate the amount of time you had for him during his first year or two?

Father: As far as a dad from day to day, I had less time, but having, as far as time off goes, like a whole day with the children, I had more time than most normal fathers do.

Dr.: What about time available for him compared to his brother during the years three, four, and five?

Father: Whenever I play with one, I always play with the other one.

Mother: They're both right there.

Father: We're either out wrestling or playing catch or running around in the grass or something. It's pretty much the same.

Mother: Because if he'd start playing with one, he'd always call for the other one to come.

Father: They get pretty much the same attention.

Dr. (to second father): Compared to your other children, how would you rate the amount of time you had for him during his first couple of years?

Father: About the same. I've never been one to come home and pick him up and play with him.
Father (to his wife): Wouldn't you say about the same?
Mother: About the same? I don't think you played with him at all, really.
Father: That's what I *mean,* about the *same.*

PHYSICAL BEAUTY IN A BOY

Some little boys are so beautiful that they are mistaken for girls. (About one-third of the feminine boys in this series have been "pretty" children.)

Dr.: How would you describe his face as an infant?
Mother: When he was younger, people would mistake him for a girl. He had curly blond hair, and he was a beautiful baby. Up until the time when he was about three, people kept mistaking him for a girl, and I was kind of *pleased* by it. I was pleased that he was such a beautiful child, but I would always say, "He's not a girl. He's a boy." I would tell them so that he knew he was a boy and they were wrong.

A second boy is still mistaken for a girl at age seven.

Mother: I look back on things that I have said not thinking it might make an impression on him. His eyes are beautiful. They are definitely *girl's* eyes with the long lashes. I have stated that, when he was a baby. I didn't think he might have noticed. He could have. Even the other day, my aunt stated that she gets him and the oldest daughter mixed up. She said she was having trouble and was calling him Nancy. And I said, "Oh, dear me, that's a no no." But everyone has always commented like that, even I have at times.

Comments by adults such as; "He's so pretty, he should have been a girl," or adults mistaking boys for girls so far appear to be more frequently reported by mothers of feminine boys than mothers of masculine boys. Thus these boys' appearances may influence others to treat them in a manner that reinforces a feminine identity.

LACK OF MALE PLAYMATES DURING EARLY YEARS OF SOCIALIZATION

About one-third of the families interviewed described an absence of boys with whom their sons could play during their preschool years.

Mother: There were no boys on the street.
Dr.: Only girls?
Father: Only girls.
Dr.: We are talking now when he's how old?
Father: Two, from two and a half to four, he only had girl companions.
Mother: Right, there wasn't a boy on the street, and we decided—

Father: So, we moved. So we moved into an apartment where there were eight million kids—boys and girls—and he still played mostly with his sister's friends.

Dr. (to a different mother): You mentioned his interest in playing with girls. How far back does that go?

Mother: Well, actually it goes all the way back to the time he was born. A lot of this could be environmental. Unfortunately, everywhere we moved there was no one but girls to play with. Now where we are there are a lot of boys. He's even given the freedom to take off on his bike and go seek out boys, but he won't do it.

Boys, though available, may be considered too rough.

Dr.: When he first had other friends available to play with were they boys or girls?

Mother: Boys.

Dr.: In the very beginning they were boys?

Mother: Yes, but *he wouldn't play with them.* He would always—if they hit him he would cry and run upstairs.

Dr.: At what age?

Mother: He was two. He would come to me crying and hanging on— my legs.

Dr.: And were there girls there for him as substitutes for these boys?

Mother: Yes, he always found a girlfriend to play with.

Unusual circumstances may make it easier for a boy to relate to female rather than male peers. This boy and his mother both think that a disfiguring scalp infection, at age four, initiated his feminine behavior. Boys teased him; girls did not.

Dr.: And are you in your new school?

Boy: Yes.

Dr.: And what's that like?

Boy: It's been better than my other school. The children don't make fun of my head, and they're more friendly with me. See, I cut my head when I was four years old, and it got infected, and I had to go to all these doctors and everything, to see what they could do. And I had to start kindergarten late, so I'm not as good as the other children are. I missed a lot of kindergarten because of my head.

Dr.: It was at around that time that you used to make believe you were a girl?

Boy: Yes.

Dr.: Why did you do that? Can you tell me?

Boy: I don't know. I guess I lived in a neighborhood that really wasn't too much filled with boys, and I knew more girls than I knew boys. Mommy didn't like me to play with the girls because I would dress up.

Dr.: When you would play with the girls and dress up like a girl, did you think you were a girl?

Boy: No, I remembered what I was, but I acted like a girl. I didn't change my thought or anything. I just remembered I was a boy really. I acted like a girl.

Dr.: Were there times when you were playing with the girls when you wished you had been born a girl?

Boy: Sometimes. Sometimes when I was dressing up I wished I was born a girl.

Dr.: I'm wondering whether, because you felt uncomfortable about your hair, that that was one of the things that made it more difficult for you to play with boys.

Boy: I guess that's probably why.

Dr.: Or was it that there weren't any boys?

Boy: No, that's not it. There were lots of them.

Dr.: It was easier for you to play with girls?

Boy: Yeah. Because the girls wouldn't tease me or anything. They'd understand what happened, and they wouldn't keep on asking me what happened to my head.

The mother confirms her son's story and agrees with his reasoning.

Dr.: Were you aware of the preference for feminine things and female companions before all this business with the hair, or did it all seem to follow after?

Mother: It seemed more afterwards. I noticed a change in him.

Dr.: Did you feel there was a relation between the hair business and the preference for girls as playmates?

Mother: I didn't at first. Maybe I was looking for an excuse, I don't know, but I began to think so because girls were nicer to him. They didn't as a rule tease him about his hair or ask questions or anything like that, and the boys would, and the play was rougher.

Dr.: That's the same story that he tells me.

Mother: Oh, it is?

Dr.: The way he describes it the boys gave him a much harder time than the girls did. The girls didn't tease him as much.

Mother: No, the pressure was off him, I'm sure. And I didn't worry so much about him playing with girls. It was when he started dressing like the girls that I got concerned.

DOMINANT MOTHERS AND SUBMISSIVE FATHERS

Family decisions may be made mostly by the mother. Recall here the theories of learning that point to the importance of power attributes of "models" with whom children identity. In this family, mother is boss by default.

Mother: I've always tried to make my husband make the decisions, but I feel he is a little weak in this line. Like I'll say, "Gee, honey, it's your weekend. You've got a long weekend. Where shall we go?" And he'll say,

"I don't know. Why don't you choose?" So I may take three choices, and I'll say, "Which one of these three do you want to do?" And he'll say, "Oh, I don't know, whichever you want to do." And this is the way it's always been.

Dr.: How about finances?

Mother: Finances. We've shared finances back and forth, and, right now, I am the one who is paying the bills.

Dr.: Who signs all his report cards?

Mother: I do.

Dr.: Who do you think your son considers to be the boss in the family?

Mother: If you just out-and-out asked him, he'd probably say me.

Dr.: Who do you think the boss is?

Mother: I would like my husband to be. I've always been one that—I feel the husband should be the strong one.

Dr.: And who do you feel is the boss in your family?

Mother: I feel he is pushing me into it.

Fathers' decisions may not be those which are evident to their sons.

Mother: You see, my husband makes a lot of decisions, but they are not decisions the boy sees. I wouldn't say I run the whole show. I run the show that my boy sees. I don't think I overrule. I really think this is the way we have mapped out our lives, and, you know, this is my area.

Dr.: What if you are in a car going somewhere, and he wants to stop and get a hamburger or get an ice cream, who will he ask? And how will the decision be made?

Mother: I am the one who grants permission and discipline. I think pretty much my husband doesn't care about these things. I really feel that I would like to become less important in my son's life, and I would like my husband to become more important.

Dr.: In terms of seeing decisions made about his life, how does he see things?

Mother: It is all me. My husband doesn't wish, he doesn't choose, to make decisions in this whole area.

This next family, dominated by the mother, includes a feminine boy. One must, however, guard against oversimplifying explanations of the etiology of feminine behavior in such boys. This same family produced four other boys, all masculine.

Mother: Well, I'm not afraid to speak up or tell anybody anything. I didn't used to be like this. I used to be afraid of everybody. But now if I disagree with someone, I don't care who they are, I usually tell them, and I guess I am aggressive that way.

Dr.: How about in terms of your relationship with your husband?

Mother: I'm probably more domineering than he is.

Dr.: You think you are more domineering?

Mother: I think he wants me that way. I don't know.

Dr.: In what sort of things would you be domineering?

Mother: I think I make most of the decisions. This is from years of experience. My mother was a widow, and we just made decisions from the time we were children.

Dr.: What are the decisions in the family that you make?

Mother: Well, I do all the shopping, and I balance the checking account and pay the bills. I discipline the children more because I'm home more. If we go anywhere or do something, I seem to be the one that does it.

Father: I don't speak up. It's the way I was raised, I guess. Lots of times I know I should speak up more, but I just can't do it. I haven't grown up with men, and if I'm in a group of fellows I'm limited as to what I can talk about.

Additionally, in other families with a feminine boy, decision-making may rest with father.

Dr.: What sort of things do you disagree on?

Mother: Oh, petty little old things. Well, now, we disagree about the boys. I think he should go ahead and let them do this, and he won't, and so we usually end up working it out somehow or another. There's no major things that we really disagree on. I usually let him do—have things his way unless there's just something I absolutely want to do. He is the head of the house. I mean we all pretty much do exactly what he says.

(Marital roles are discussed further in the next section of this chapter.)

CASTRATION FEAR

Traditional psychoanalytic theory sees the height of the male's fear of loss of his penis during the Oedipal period from ages four to six (Fenichel, 1945). This adolescent describes a real trauma to his penis at age five that may have induced concerns over its preservation.

Patient: I was circumcised when I was five years old. And my brother told me according to the Freudian psychology this is a very dangerous age to be circumcised, because it can lead to the castration complex. That's what he told me. He's an M.D.

Dr.: Do you remember when you were circumcised?

Patient: Yes. I remember that I didn't like it. Three days after the circumcision there was a lot of suffering because I couldn't urinate. I have a pretty good idea that must have something to do with it.

Traditional psychoanalytic theory also sees the fetish, an inanimate object that becomes associated with sexual arousal, as a psychologic device to defend against fears of penile loss. Women's shoes and feet are classic examples. This person describes such a fetish as an accompaniment of his penile surgery.

Patient: Approximately around that age is when I began to have a type of complex about shoes, you know, women's shoes. Before that it was women's feet, just the foot. I don't understand why. The first thing that I remember of any type of sexual thing is that my sister and I used to play around. I was very little, so we used to play cards, and she was always barefooted and I was usually naked because I was a very little boy. There was a great difference of age, and it didn't matter, but I remember that sometimes her foot would just rove through my genitals, just as a mistake as we were sitting there. I don't know why I remember that, but it must have had an influence on me later on.

An argument for conditioning may also be made here to explain his sexual arousal in conjunction with women's feet.

Dr.: How old were you then?
Patient: Oh, I was about four or five.
Dr.: And how old was your sister?
Patient: About twenty. In the early stages of my childhood I just enjoyed very much the presence of women's feet, especially when they would take their shoes off. I remember all my life I have always had an obsession about women's feet.
Dr.: Did you have an erection while thinking about feet?
Patient: Yes, that's right.

Foot fetishism progressed to shoe fetishism, then to women's clothes in general, and on to fantasies of sex change.

Patient: I just began to enjoy high heels. And this thing about women's shoes, especially high heels, began about a year before I began to look through the wardrobe of some girl, and I don't know why. I assume it had a relation with the feet, but why I all of a sudden began to enjoy girls' clothes, I didn't stop to think. A year after that I began to wear girls' clothes.
Dr.: Was it sexually exciting?
Patient: Wearing girls' clothes? Yes, very much.
Dr.: Was any particular piece of clothing most appealing to you?
Patient: In the beginning it was the shoes, and then after that it was other parts, especially skirts. But now I feel different. You see, now it's specially the underwear, and still something about the shoes.
Dr.: What do you think about when you masturbate?
Patient: It always involves being dominated or dominating the person who is with you. Sometimes it is a woman, sometimes a man.
Dr.: Do you think of yourself as a woman—with a female body—when you masturbate?
Patient: Sometimes.
Dr.: Is that an attractive thought to you?
Patient: Sometimes, yes. Why I don't understand.

INTRAFAMILY RELATIONSHIPS

Specific areas of a family relationship are so frequently cited as crucial for the emergence of atypical (and typical) sexuality that they demand special attention. Among them are father-son separation, marital-role division or the relative power within a family of mother and father, parent-child emotional closeness, and sibling sequence. The following sections summarize these features for the families in this study.

Father-Son Separation

Before their fourth birthday, seventeen of the thirty-eight boys experienced a separation of at least three consecutive months from their natural fathers. In only four of these cases were the separations temporary, due to the father's business or military duty. Thus, thirteen of thirty-eight boys (34 percent), before they reached age four, were separated from their biological fathers by divorce, abandonment, or death. This percentage of father-son separation is higher than the norm. In the typical white American family (thirty-five of the thirty-eight families studied are white), 92 percent of children under five live with both biological parents (1970 census). A more important finding, however, may be that in twenty-five of the thirty-eight families, the father *was* living in the home, for this statistic poses an obstacle to ascribing boyhood femininity merely to absence of a father.

TABLE 15-1

Age of Feminine Boys (N = 38) Separated from Biological Father and Incidence of an Adult Male Living in Household.

SEPARATED FROM BIOLOGICAL FATHER		ADULT MALE LIVING IN HOUSEHOLD		
BOY'S AGE AT SEPARATION (YEARS)	NUMBER OF BOYS	BOY'S AGE (YEARS)	YES	NO
0–0.5	5	0–0.5	36	2
0.5–1	2	0.5–1	36	2
1–2	4	1–2	35	3
2–3	3	2–3	35	3
3–4	3	3–4	30	8
4–5	0	4–5	28	7

Furthermore, although one of three boys was separated from his father, about four of five boys (thirty of thirty-eight) did live in a household which included an adult male (see Table 15–1). The father-substitute was usually a stepfather or grandfather. Thus, only about 20 percent lived in households with no adult male figure. However, this percentage is also higher than the norm. In typical white American families, only 7 percent of children under five live with only one parent (their mother) and no father substitute (1970 census). Still, it should be kept in mind that older males, potentially capable of serving as models for identification, *were* living in the homes of the majority of the feminine boys studied.

An additional, technologically introduced, "father-substitute" further complicates the issue. The likelihood of a total lack of opportunity to witness models of masculine roles is becoming increasingly remote. Male images are beamed into nearly every household through the "miracle of modern television," rendering isolation from a male *image* practically impossible. However, the capacity for a gray-toned, two-

FIGURE 15–1.

Mothers' view of marital-role division: Families of feminine boys.

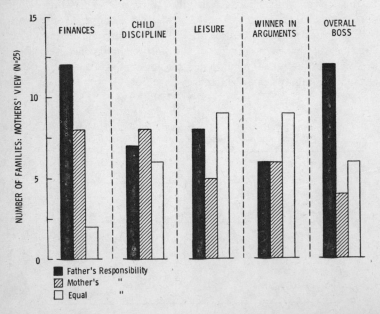

dimensional, nonrelating image to promote identification is questionable, although there is evidence that the behavior of children can be modified by showing them filmed representations of adults (Bandura, 1965).

Marital-Role Division

Role division was assessed in the twenty-five families of feminine boys in which the boy's biological parents were still married and living together. Five major categories of marital-role division appeared to be similar in these families of feminine boys and a comparison group of twenty-five families of masculine boys. Few differences were found, either in gross role division or in the way each member of the couple saw that division. (See Figures 15–1–15–4.)

No significant differences between the two sets of families were found in areas of handling finances, child discipline, and the typical winner in disagreements. In both groups of families finances were

FIGURE 15–2.

Fathers' view of marital-role division: Families of feminine boys.

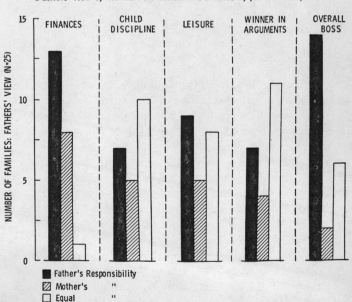

FIGURE 15–3.

Mothers' view of marital-role division: Families of masculine boys.

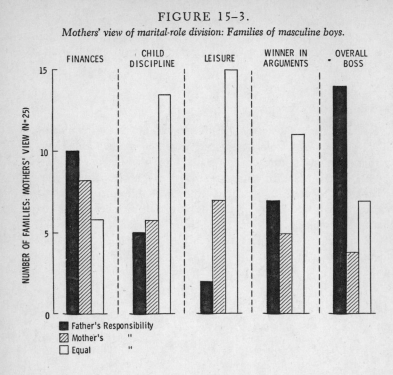

handled more often by the fathers, child discipline was handled by both parents, and either parent was likely to win out in a disagreement.

Two differences that were found involved planning leisure-time activities and determining who was the "overall boss." In families of masculine boys, both parents generally agreed that leisure-time planning was equally shared. In families of feminine boys, the father seemed to be the parent more often primarily responsible for planning leisure-time activities. Most of the fathers of feminine boys saw themselves as the "overall boss." Most of the fathers of masculine boys, on the other hand, saw both marital partners as co-holders of the title.

Thus, at the gross level, examination of marital-role division does not produce a consistent pattern of association of mother-dominated homes with boyhood femininity. The finding that little difference exists in *gross* family-role division is not surprising. Consider that none of the families with *a* feminine boy has *two* feminine boys. All male siblings

FIGURE 15-4.

Fathers' view of marital-role division: Families of masculine boys.

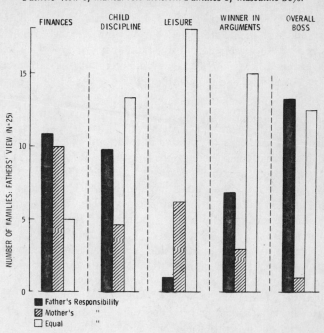

Father's Responsibility
Mother's   "
Equal   "

of the feminine boys studied are masculine. To implicate the single variable of a mother-dominated home as leading to boyhood femininity would require that *all* boys from such homes be feminine. This is not to contradict the impression from previous interview excerpts that in some families fathers of feminine boys maintain a low profile of visibility and influence. Disparate mother-father influence *may* be important in *some* families, but it cannot be simplistically implied to be operative in *all*, or to be the *sole* etiologic variable.

It becomes necessary, therefore, to look closely at individualized relationships within families with two or more boys, *one* of whom is feminine. We hear from the narrative reports of parents that relationships with each sibling are frequently different, subtleties lost in the gross categories of "marital-role division." One example was illustrated in the preceding chapter. Our research interviews attempt to examine intrafamily alliances and relationships and to discover extenuating circumstances affecting the time parents have available for each child. Our research is also exploring, in greater depth, processes of family decision-making and parameters of family-member influence. Varieties of situations are presented to families of children suffering conflicts of sexual identity, and assessments are made of styles of interaction. These assessments may reveal more subtle distinctions than the gross role-division parameters cited here. The Family Communication Task described in Chapter 13 is a model of one such strategy.

Parent-Child Emotional Closeness

Thirty-eight mothers and twenty-five fathers of feminine boys were asked to describe their feelings toward their sons. Twice as many mothers indicated "very close" rather than "moderately close." Conversely, more of the fathers said "moderately close" rather than "very close." About 75 percent of the feminine boys were described as preferring their mother, and only about 7 percent as favoring their father. (See Figure 15–5.)

In contrast, parents of the masculine boys so far assessed do not show a similar discrepancy in appraising the extent of their emotional closeness to their sons. More than half of *both* mothers and fathers have described their feelings as "very close," and only about one of three as "moderately close." About half the masculine boys are said not to favor either parent, and when one parent is preferred there is a lesser tendency among the boys to prefer their mothers.

Emotional closeness and distance are complex phenomena, not only with respect to the ways in which they are manifested from family to family but also with respect to their origins. The answer to the question "To what extent are such feelings activated by parents or children?" varies from family to family.

Consider, for example, a family with two boys, one ten, who is interested in sports, and one four. Assume that the father enjoys playing ball. When he is not working, he may well spend more time with his older, sports-minded son than with his four-year-old, who is too little to participate and is relatively ignored. Denied access to his father, the younger boy may find the only available companion for activity to be his mother. Thus, primarily as a consequence of his younger age, the boy may experience rejection by his father. The creation of emotional distance between father and younger son would seem here to have been activated more by the parent than by the child.

FIGURE 15–5.

Preferred parent of feminine boys and degree of emotional closeness between each parent and child.

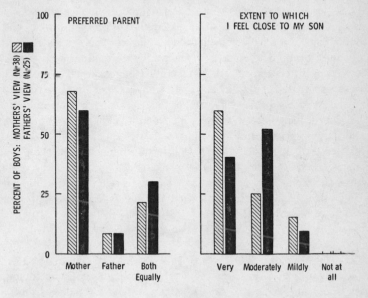

On the other hand, consider another family in which the father initially takes a genuine interest in his son and, although tired at the end of each workday, tries to engage him in rough-and-tumble play or sports. The boy may, however, have little interest or ability in sports, perhaps being "temperamentally unsuited" for such vigorous activity. The father, gaining no or only a reluctant response to his endeavors, may soon withdraw them. This boy, too, may experience rejection. Here, however, the emotional distance seems to have been activated more by the child than by the parent.

Regrettably, such distinctions are frequently lost in the study of adults who recall an alienated relationship with their fathers and an intimate one with their mothers. Too often the conclusion is drawn that the active participant in determining the relationship was the parent, with the child the passive partner or victim. Such is not always the case. Not only may parents train children, but children may also train parents.

Sibling Sequence

A variety of predictions could be made about sibling sequence and how it affects the development of masculinity in a boy. An older sister could provide a female model for identification as well as feminine toys and clothes. The birth of a younger sister could evoke jealousy; a boy seeing his central role with his mother eroded could come to the conclusion that to be a girl is to be favored. Older brothers may provide male models for identification, or they may cause a younger brother to feel inadequate in relation to his more mature siblings.

So far in this research, no significant pattern of sibling order has emerged. Five of the feminine boys have no siblings, and of those with siblings, twelve boys are the oldest in the family, and eleven the youngest. A trend exists for feminine boys to have a younger rather than an older sister (eighteen versus eleven), but the difference is not statistically significant. (See Table 15–2.)

The Necessary Variable

Finally, whatever the circumstances that promote boyhood femininity, what comes closest so far to being a *necessary* variable is that, as any feminine behavior begins to emerge, there is *no* discouragement of that behavior by the child's principal caretaker. This has been true, so far, in nearly every family. For some extended period of time, at least months, and usually a year or more, parents do not consider the behavior distasteful, unusual, or in any way significant in terms of the boy's future. These parents, and parents generally, are unaware of the significance in young children of sex-typed behavior and the early

TABLE 15–2

Incidence of Feminine Boys (N = 38)
with Younger or Older Male
or Female Siblings

SIBLING	YES	NO
Older sister	11	27
Younger sister	18	20
Older brother	18	20
Younger brother	15	23
No siblings	5	33

timetable for fixing gender identity. The age at which most parents
consider male and female gender identity to be *emerging* is essentially
when it has already established *rigid footing*. The male child beginning
school with a strong identity and role-preference as a girl is well into a
stabilized personality trait, and the "passing stage," seen at two and a
half, was when gender building blocks were rapidly being set in place.
Recall, for example, that although half the boys when first seen for
evaluation were between eight and ten, none had commenced cross-
dressing after the sixth birthday, and three-quarters had commenced by
the fourth.

AN ETIOLOGIC PATTERN

The disparate descriptions presented in this chapter make it clear that
no consistent etiologic pattern exists for extensive boyhood femininity.
From details frequently reported in these cases, however, something of
an etiologic pattern can be sketched. The sketch is not an exact likeness
of the history of any one boy or his family. It is composed primarily for
those who experience a compelling need for law and order in their
theoretic universe.

This composite approximates Stoller's theory of the etiology of
extreme femininity in boys (Stoller, 1968; 1969). Here, however, less
emphasis is put on certain psychodynamic concepts, such as the symbolic meaning of the boy to his mother and her own bisexuality, and
more weight is given to certain socialization factors, particularly peer-
group interaction for the young boy. It also postulates the manner in
which a neuroendocrine factor may influence early socialization.

1. A mother considers her infant male child to be unusually attractive. She finds him extremely responsive to being held. Whether her perceptions are objective judgments, reflecting innate features of the infant,
or whether they are subjective distortions, reflecting her own psychological needs, is not known. However, that distinction may not be a
critical factor. Her perceptions of her child—whatever their origin—will
affect her behavior toward him.

2. The mother's time commitments are such that she is able to devote
considerable attention to this boy. Her other children are separated
enough in years so as not to detract from the child's early mothering
experience. Her affective or emotional commitments are such that she
has few other avenues for channeling her feelings of caring and love.

3. As the child begins exploring his environment for objects for play, the many colorful accessories belonging to his mother are available to him. He begins to play with these objects, which may be shoes, cosmetics, and jewelry. To a degree, he imitates the person with whom he is primarily in contact, his mother.

4. These early behaviors are considered to be cute. The responses obtained by the child are supportive—additional attention, benign laughter, being shown off.

5. The father, if present, is a much less significant person in the boy's life than his mother. He is much less often in the presence of the child and interacts minimally with him when present. His possessions and accessories are not so attractive as objects for early play and role-taking.

6. The father, too, when witnessing his son's early play with feminine objects, experiences it as funny, cute, or neutral, and does not object.

7. As the child begins peer relationships, girls are primarily available. The few boys available, if any, are more aggressive than he, intimidate him, and meet with parental disapproval. The boy asserts that he likes to play with girls because boys are "too rough." Possibly here too an innate feature is operating to influence early socialization. A lower level of aggressivity, influenced perhaps by an intrauterine endocrine factor such as lowered androgen levels, may facilitate his companionship with girls because he is more comfortable in their play activities. Hence, his earliest learned social skills are those more typical of girls.

8. The father having anticipated a developmental time when the boy would be able to take part in father-son, rough-and-tumble play instead finds that his son has little interest in such vigorous activity. The boy is more in tune with the calmer domestic activities of his mother. The father experiences rejection from his son and deems him a "mama's boy." A degree of father-son alienation ensues. The frustration of the father is transmitted to the son, who, becoming aware of his father's demands and annoyance, retreats further toward the accepting reactions of his mother.

9. Earlier socialization to feminine skills and companionship now poses an obstacle to same-sex peer integration during the first years of school. Accustomed to female playmates, the boy does not relate well to his male schoolmates. Because of his feminine interests and greater comfort with female companions, he is teased, resulting in further alienation from his male peer group.

10. The mother continues to respond positively to the boy's interest in cross-dressing or improvising feminine costumes and to his attentiveness to her clothing and grooming. During the most positive moments, her response is approving; she regards his behavior as funny or cute. During the least positive moments, her response is neutral. She asserts that boyish or girlish behavior during these years is inconsequential with respect to later masculinity or femininity. She may be encouraged by his play with girls as a sign of his later being "a lady's man."

11. The emotional distance between father and son continues to increase because of the boy's low interest in his father's activities around the home and his reaction to his sense of paternal rejection. The father begins to feel that he has failed in his responsibility for providing a male image for his son. Rendered anxious by this, he tends to deny the existence and/or meaning of his son's femininity. Statements such as "All boys go through that" and "It's only a passing phase" become his outward attitude, even when other sons in the family have not manifested similar behavior.

12. During the next few years the boy's increasing identification with females is revealed by a degree of feminine affectation. He displays feminine hand gestures, a feminine style of walking, and feminine vocal intonations. His manifest femininity increases social stigmatization and causes the child to be labeled a sissy or "a girl."

Finally, an adult outside the family, typically a school teacher or neighbor, repeatedly brings the boy's behavior to the attention of his mother. The boy reports being continually teased at school. The parents develop some concern. The child, now about seven years old, may be referred to a clinic for consultation.

THE RESEARCH DESIGN

Clinical data, currently being gathered on these boys and their parents, may lead to a better understanding of etiology(ies). The research design includes extensive interviewing of the parents of both feminine and masculine boys with the same series of open-ended questions. Interview questions are directed toward many areas that include initial parental reactions to feminine and masculine behavior, extent of mother-son and father-son contact, family decision-making, and psychosexual development of the parents.

All interviews are tape recorded and transcribed. Ratings are made on a variety of attributes, such as the relative degree of attention a prefeminine boy received from his father during his first three years compared to (a) his masculine sibling, if one exists, and (b) a masculine boy from a different family.

When this is fully accomplished, it may then be possible to correlate several variables with not only gross manifestations of the boys' behavior (whether they are "masculine" or "feminine") but also with more microscopic analyses, such as in *what ways* are they masculine or feminine? Not all the boys who have been evaluated are feminine to the same degree, or in the same way. The extent of cross-dressing differs; the extent of female role-taking differs; the extent to which they state their wish to be girls differs; the extent to which they display feminine mannerisms differs; and their responses to psychological testing differs.

Progress is being made. First, we had theories in search of a population. Then we obtained a population in search of a methodology. Now we have a first approximation of a methodology in search of findings. Perhaps, in turn, these findings will yield new theories.

16

FEMININE BOYS: TREATMENT

To treat or not to treat is a complex question engaging both ethical and research considerations.

The foregoing chapters have stressed the conflicts of adult male-to-female transsexuals and their parallels in the lives of feminine boys. However, not all feminine boys are on the road to transsexualism. This is evident from four studies. Bieber and his colleagues (1962) reported that one-third of 106 adult male homosexual patients recalled having played predominantly with girls and four-fifths recalled not having participated in competitive group games. John Money and I recently conducted assessments of five young adult males we initially studied (but did not treat) twelve to fifteen years ago. As young boys they had been very feminine. Three are now clearly homosexual. A fourth, who refuses to return for an interview, is reported by his family to collect photographs of nude males. A fifth has had a heterosexual affair but about one-third of his masturbatory fantasies are occupied by memories of male-male oral-genital experiences during early adolescence. Additionally, within a month of this writing, two noteworthy events have occurred. First, he purchased a bikini-cut, rayon pair of men's underpants. To his surprise, trying them on and viewing himself in a mirror produced an erection. He had not cross-dressed since age six. Second, he was invited to the apartment of a male neighbor who asked, "Would you like a blow-job?" He found the sexual experience exhilarating and reports a compelling, but conflicted, drive to continue the relationship. Zuger (1966) has evaluated six adolescent and young adult males seen previously during childhood for feminine behavior. He found that three were homosexually oriented and a fourth possibly transsexual. Finally, Lebovitz (1972) has found that of sixteen previously feminine boys, three are now transsexual, two are homosexual, and one a transvestite.

Thus not all feminine boys are pretranssexual. Some are prehomosexual, others preheterosexual. Considering both their current behavior and their future sexuality, should any treatment be instituted now? An argument can be made for intervention for two reasons: one concerns the adult, the other the child.

Adult male-to-female transsexuals experience extraordinary social hardship as they grapple with an identity in conflict with their anatomy and the expectations of society. As children they were called "sissies." As adolescents they were labeled "fags" and "queers." During adulthood these troubled people frantically seek sympathetic physicians who will grant their wish to bring their body into conformity with their sexual identity. Those successful in their quest (within the limits of technical feasibility) must still face the challenge of time. The degree to which they will achieve their long-sought security remains uncertain.

Adult male homosexuals experience hardship in consequence of societal censure. In most of the United States their sexual conduct is illegal, subjecting them to legal harassment. They experience job discrimination, most people disapprove of their activities, and most church groups consider their orientation sinful. Should they wish to marry their loved one or adopt a child, they are legally prohibited. While these societal biases are hopefully becoming attenuated, and some may vanish, the rate of change may not be rapid enough for today's atypical boy.

Many homosexual adults contend they are proud to be "gay." Their pride is not challenged here. However, some homosexuals do suffer because of their sexual orientation. Some long for a family. Those who undergo expensive psychoanalysis or painful aversion treatment do so not only out of feelings of guilt or fear of discovery; some genuinely seek the features of a life-style currently available only in a heterosexual union.

Feminine boys experience considerable social hardship. They are teased, ostracized, and bullied. It would be well if the difficulties experienced by those with atypical gender-role behavior could be avoided. Their extraordinary conflict might be prevented if society were to radically modify its standards so that any degree of feminine behavior in males and masculine behavior in females was fully accepted. In the early 1970s we read and hear much about a "unisex" movement— the blurring of sex roles. This ethic may be taking hold in some segments of the population, but it has not filtered into the day-to-day lives of these children. Furthermore, unless the whole of society changes dramatically during the next few years, the distress already experienced by these children will augment and their alienation will increase as society continues to stigmatize them. While one might prefer that society immediately change its often irrational values of what constitutes desirable gender-role behavior, realistically, there is more basis for optimism in helping a single person to change.

Opponents of treatment aver that intervention will stamp out esthetic, sensitive qualities in the child and crudely press him into the stereotyped mold demanded by a sexist society. Proponents of treatment disagree. When consulted by the family of a boy whose atypical behavior causes him current hardship and portends increased distress, our goal is to reduce that social hardship. The aim is not to suppress sensitivity and compassion, nor to promote a thirst for aggression and violence. Rather, it is to impart greater balance where a radically skewed development has precluded a comfortable range of social integration. We believe that by so doing, the child may suffer less immediate distress and may subsequently have available to him a wider range of social and sexual options.

Thus, the ethical basis of treatment intervention considers both the child and the adult. Whether the very feminine boy is pretranssexual, prehomosexual, or preheterosexual, he currently experiences the *same* social hardship. Should his adult sexuality be atypical, the problems facing him will in all likelihood be greater than those of the heterosexual.

Finally, there are advantages for the behavioral scientist in attempting to modify atypical sexual identity during childhood. The opportunity is presented for testing hypotheses about the development of atypical behavior by directing intervention toward its suspected developmental causes. Also, if attempts to change behavior utilize a variety of strategies, a comparison of their relative effectiveness further adds to our knowledge. Moreover, the possibility of contrasting the adulthoods of treated and untreated children will tell whether behavioral change effected during childhood remains meaningful in the long run or whether it is merely a temporary masking of an already fixed personality attribute.

Various approaches to treatment of feminine boys have been instituted in our program. In spite of their seemingly disparate vantage points, each is based on the same underlying tenets: (1) developing a relationship of trust and affection between a male therapist and the feminine boy; (2) educating the child as to the impossibility of his changing sex; (3) stressing to the child the advantages of participating in some of the activities enjoyed by other boys, and promoting greater comfort in such activity; (4) educating the parents as to how they may be fostering sexual identity conflict in their child; (5) advising the parents of the need for them to consistently disapprove of very feminine behavior and to consistently encourage masculine behavior, if they desire change in their sons; and (6) enhancing the father's or father-substitute's involvement in the feminine boy's life.

These general procedures have been followed, using three specific strategies of intervention: (1) individual sessions with the boy and separate sessions with his parents; (2) group sessions with several boys plus group sessions with their mothers and group sessions with their fathers; and (3) teaching parents to act as therapists by instructing them on specific aspects of behavior which should be systematically encouraged or discouraged at home.

INDIVIDUAL SESSIONS

The parents are interviewed together during their initial evaluation session. The boy is seen separately and engaged in some pleasant procedures such as drawing pictures and playing with toys. Following extensive parent interviewing, individually and together, as well as extensive testing and interviewing of the child, treatment sessions may be instituted.

Example 16-1

This family was concerned about their seven-year-old son's extensive femininity and the considerable social hardship the boy was experiencing. They were seen for two hours a week over a period of three years. The case example illustrates several stages in evaluation and subsequent treatment.

PRESENTING PICTURE

Mother: As far as my first noticing it, perhaps one day at a friend's house—she has four little girls. He likes to go over there, and he likes to go back in their room and play with their dolls. He went back there and grabbed a doll and wanted to make a dress. He took Kleenex and paper towels and tore them and folded them and poked holes in them and really made a very attractive dress with these dolls. And my friend commented on it and said, "Gee, I think he's going to be a dress designer."

Doctor: How old was he?

Mother: He was four, four and a half. You know, I don't know what I'm afraid of—if it's homosexuality. I even hate the *word*.

Dr.: What else?

Mother: I think a lot of it is that he likes the sight of feminine things. He would tie aprons around himself. I got so that I never kept aprons in the house anymore, because he'd get my aprons and tie them around him—here up at his shoulder or under his arms—to make a nice long skirt, and would go around the house in aprons. He'd have to have an apron tied around up here with a nice full skirt and then one tied around his head to make a nice flowing hood. He would go around the house in two aprons like this. Like an old lady. I got so that if there was nobody in the house, I would *let* him do it. It got so that we were taking aprons and just sticking them places and hiding them, and even today I go around and find aprons wadded clear back on closet shelves where we had tried to hide them, just in a fit of panic.

Dr.: How would others react?

Mother: His grandmother lived here, and we used to come and visit, and he'd get to her house and go right to the kitchen and get an apron and start tying it around him as a long skirt with the long hood. She would always bring out the apron in him. Always. At first she encouraged it. She thought it was kind of *cute*, you know.

Dr.: Are there other things which concern you?

Mother: He won't play with boys. They tease him. He has said he wants to be a girl. I don't know if it should worry me or not. That's why I am here. Maybe it's something that he can grow out of. Maybe it's something that he's going to need some *help* to grow out of.

As a small child the boy had been seriously ill, finally requiring genital surgery. Greatly concerned, his mother became overprotective.

Mother: He had a lot of illnesses. He has had a lot of history of ear infections.
Dr.: When was that?
Mother: Oh, it started when he was less than a year. Finally, with the backache, they sent me to a urologist. He did kidney surgery on him about a year ago. He was there three different times. He came up once for a couple of pieces of surgery through the penis with the cystoscope.
Dr.: During those early illnesses did he require special care in any way?
Mother: Yes, I guess. The fevers scared me. I would have done anything to get rid of the fever, and then a lot of times, many visits to the doctor, you know, that other children don't have, and then, of course, the kidney surgery. He's had the cystoscope and catheters and everything else up his penis, and the blood—and he had a little narrow place at the tip of the penis, all up and down that tube, and they had to cut that and widen it in some way. So there's been enough to terrify him, really.
Dr.: How did this affect the way you treated him?
Mother: He was sick so often that I would have done anything to keep him well. Other mothers would send their kids out in the water or out in the wet sand or out in the high wind, and here I would always have little caps tied around him. He'd go in swimming, and I'm there with a Q-Tip, you know, going around the ear. And all the other mothers—the kids running around with wet heads, you know, and I'm following him around with towels trying to wipe his ears out. I just couldn't see another earache. He was getting all this extra attention and concern. He's probably just geared to that. "Put your hat on. Zip up your jacket." Whereas my other boy can run around, and I hardly say anything. I figure if he's cold, he's going to come in and do something about it.

TREATMENT

The boy and his parents have been seen for more than three years. The excerpts that follow are representative of interviews and therapy sessions that spanned that time. During an early session with the child the irrevocability of being a boy or girl was stressed. An office fish tank stocked with guppies became a therapeutic ally.

Dr.: I guess you are a little bit scared about coming here. You've been to see doctors so many times. It must scare you a bit, huh?
Boy: Uh huh.
Dr.: We're different kinds of doctors than the other doctors you've been to. We're just *talking* doctors. We don't have any needles or anything to hurt you with. . . . I'd like you to draw a picture for me. OK? Tell me when you're finished. . . . Oh, that's nice, very nice. Who is that?
Boy: Mary Poppins.

Dr.: Mary Poppins? OK. Do you ever sometimes like to make believe you're Mary Poppins?

Boy: Sometimes.

Dr.: Can you tell me how?

Boy: Well, I take a sheet and put it around me, and then I hold it around me. Then I wrap a blue blanket around me, and I look like Mary Poppins.

Dr.: What do you do when you look like Mary Poppins?

Boy: I make an umbrella out of Tinker Toys.

Dr.: Do you act like Mary Poppins?

Boy: Well, yeah.

Dr.: Have you ever gone out dressed like Mary Poppins?

Boy: Uh uh. 'Cause every time, my mommy saw me.

Dr.: I see. You think people might not understand why you dress up that way?

Here his awareness of the social consequences of feminine behavior is discussed.

Boy: Because I'm a boy, and boys aren't supposed to dress—go out dressing like girls. My mommy has to make me stay in the house.

Dr.: But you like to dress up like a girl sometimes?

Boy: Not all the time. If I dress like a girl when a friend comes over, they won't want to play with me.

Dr.: Why is that?

Boy: Well, because a boy is a boy and a girl is a girl, so they want to go home.

Dr.: You know, sometimes little boys your age wonder whether it's possible for them to become little girls. I wonder if you ever think about that.

Boy: I think about that. I think that it's possible for them to become— sometimes I don't want to be a girl, and sometimes I want to be one.

Dr.: What's nice about being a girl?

Boy: Well, girls don't have to fight. Sometimes girls scream, and then I scream and then I get mixed up with them.

The dialogue then shifts to the irreversibility of being a boy.

Dr.: Do you think it's possible for little boys like you to become little girls?

Boy: Yeah, it's possible.

Dr.: Tell me how you think it can happen.

Boy: I mean, it isn't possible.

Dr.: Oh, it's not possible. Do you know why it's not possible?

Boy: Girls wear dresses and boys wear pants. That's all I can think of.

Dr.: Are little boys and girls built the same way, or are their bodies different in some way?

Boy: Their bodies are different.

Dr.: How are they different?

Boy: Uh. Well, girls don't have to fight and boys do. That's one good thing about it. That's all I can think of.

Dr.: Is your mommy's body the same as your daddy's body?

Boy: Uh uh.

Dr.: No? How are they different?

Boy: Mommy wears a dress all the time. Daddy wears pants all the time. And Mommy has long hair.

Dr.: Let's say you have a boy or a man, OK? And this boy or man has long hair and wears a dress. Does that make him a girl, or is he still a boy?

Boy: He's a girl.

Dr.: You mean, if a boy lets his hair grow and wears a dress—? Does that make him a girl, or is he still a boy?

Boy: He's a little girl.

Dr.: Not really.

Boy: I know. 'Cause he's still a little boy.

Dr.: He's a boy who's *dressing up* like a little girl.

Boy: That's just got long hair down to here.

Dr.: That doesn't make him a girl, does it? Do you know why it doesn't make him a girl?

Boy: No.

Dr.: Well, let's look at these guppies in the fish tank here.

Boy: Yeah.

Dr.: Do you know where the baby fish come from?

Boy: From under there. See, it's the mommy's fat place.

Dr.: Right. So the mother carries the little baby fish. OK. Now can a daddy fish carry the babies too?

Boy: No.

Dr.: That's right. So that's another difference between boys and girls. Isn't it?

Boy: See, here's the fat place. And then the mama has babies.

Dr.: Right. So then that's only in the mommy fish. Now, do you think if that daddy fish wanted to become a mommy fish, he could do it?

Boy: No.

Dr.: Why couldn't he?

Boy: Because he would not have the same thing that babies come out of.

Dr.: That's right. His body is different from the mommy fish. Just like the bodies of little boys are different from the bodies of little girls. Now what if that daddy fish were to dress up and look like a mommy fish?

Boy: He'd just have to paint hisself ugly.

(Fortunately, male guppies are more colorful than females.)

Dr.: And he wouldn't be a girl because his body would still be different.

Boy: Yes.

Dr.: Have you ever seen a little girl undressed?

Boy: No.

Dr.: Have you ever seen your mommy undressed?

Boy: Yes.

Dr.: OK. And have you seen your daddy undressed?
Boy: Uh huh.
Dr.: And can you tell me how your mommy's body is different from your daddy's body?

Here an effort is made to help the boy categorize himself as being more like his father.

Boy: Well, uh, they don't have the same kiki. A kiki is on the bottom.
Dr.: They have different bottoms. Can you tell me how it's different?
Boy: Well, the daddy has a long kiki and the mommy has a short kiki.
Dr.: Yes, that's right. And the inside's different 'cause the mommy has a place to hold little babies.
Boy: I know, and the daddy's breast is little and mommy's breast is big.
Dr.: That's right. Is your kiki more like your daddy's or like your mommy's?
Boy: Like my daddy's.
Dr.: That's right.
Boy: Only daddy's is bigger.
Dr.: Because he's a bigger person. He's a bigger man, and you're a little man. And how about when you grow up? What do you think is going to happen?
Boy: Like my daddy.
Dr.: You'll look like your daddy, that's right. So you do know a lot about the differences between a boy and a girl, don't you? So you know that it's more than just letting your hair grow long, or putting on different clothing.

During a session with the parents, both the mother and the father showed great reluctance to accepting any responsibility for their son's femininity. They preferred seeing the causes of his behavior in disordered chromosomes or a hormonal imbalance. Intervention here was directed not so much at discounting biological contributions as at focusing on influences over which the parents retained some control.

Mother: Is there such a thing as taking a hormone count to see whether anybody's femininity—
Father: Like chromosomes?
Mother: No, I don't mean chromosomes. I've asked him that before.
Dr.: This is a *new* approach to the nonexperiential genesis of feminine behavior. It doesn't have anything to do with one's *environment* or what happens in one's life or one's family.
Mother: No, I'm not ruling that out, but I can't really completely and honestly rule out this other thing also.
Father: You have a sexometer? I know a doctor who sells monkey glands.
Dr.: It could be astrology, but we can't do anything about that. In

today's play session your son has shown he's really afraid to do "boy things." He's terribly frightened of—

Mother: Like what?

Dr.: Playing anything with a ball. He is just terrified that somebody's going to hurt him. Like he's going to be terribly, terribly hurt. He's really physically frightened. I'm not sure I know why.

Father: He shows this a lot around the house.

Dr.: Why should he be so frightened?

Mother: I'm sure I've overly cautioned him. I don't know. I'm sure that I've not let them do things that I really should have them do because I was frightened that something might happen that they were not capable of handling in some way, or something.

Dr.: Has he ever really been hurt by playing ball?

Mother: Not that I know of.

Father: He never *played* ball!

Mother: My husband won't play ball with him. Damn it, I don't know what I have to do. He won't even fix the fishline for him. Last week they were coming in and wanting to fish. Well, I don't like bait or worms or fish or anything, and he doesn't either, but [to her husband] of the two of us I think it ought to be *you* that's going to bait a hook, and not *me*. That's one area where I get *off* the hook.

Father: Maybe we can get *artificial worms.*

Mother: The other boys in the neighborhood fish. This is an activity that the kids in our neighborhood happen to do, OK? Then our kids don't fish. I think it would be great to give them something that everybody else in the neighborhood does.

Father: If he would have said, "Dad, I want to play ball," I would have done it.

Mother: Yes, but he would never say that. I'd be *disappointed* if he were a ball player, but he should be adequate, you know, so that if he has to he could catch a ball.

A strategy here was to pose an alternate model, other than behaving as a girl, to a boy not adept at athletics.

Dr.: I guess my position with him tonight in play was that I can understand that everybody doesn't like to play ball, but I didn't think he would be hurt. I didn't understand really why he should be so afraid of being hurt. I can see where not every kid wants to play ball, but at the same time he doesn't have to do *girlish* things. That's something, doing sissy things, that people make fun of. He can do boyish things but not dangerous things; he's going to be very unhappy doing sissy things. He heard me. He just sat there. He was playing with a doll while I was saying it. He got a little upset and put the doll away.

Mother: Just this week he said to me, "Are there some men who grow up and when they get grown they want to be a woman?" I thought maybe this was something you had discussed with him.

Dr.: No, I told him that as he grows up, and if he continues to do sissy things, that he won't have many friends, and people will make fun of him, and that he'll be very unhappy. Now, he may infer from that that there are some people that don't outgrow it. He may have inferred that. My guess is that he's hoping that there are some people maybe who are like he is.

Mother: Yes, that's what I kind of sensed.

Dr.: You know, if he asks you again "Are there some men who grow up and still have the idea they would like to be a woman?" you might say, "Usually they are very unhappy, because they can't be women, and so why try to be something you can't be?" See, he doesn't have to do girlish things just because he avoids boy things. There are plenty of boys who aren't athletic and competitive, but they do *boyish* things. When I told him that tonight, he started building. He was building things

Instruction was given to the mother to reward specifically masculine behavior.

Mother: In Cub Scouts they were playing a game. It was real boyish and real good. It was fine. In a game he is rough and tough, and he is one of the last ones in there. It's a game where you eliminate people by trying to pull them over a circle, and boy, they yank them and crack them around a whip and make them fall.

Dr.: When you see him doing these things, do you tell him that you're pleased and reward him for it?

Mother: No, I don't.

Dr.: I think you should. Say, "Gee, that's really great. You really held your own. You really did beautifully."

Mother: Well, I didn't do it enough. I should do it more. I didn't really do it.

Dr.: That's the kind of nonathletic boyish behavior I think he should be encouraged in so that he doesn't have to retreat and back off into feminine things.

More father-son involvement was encouraged.

Dr.: Rather than his being in Cub Scouts, I would still rather see him go into Indian Guides, because that's father and son instead of mother and son. You've got to get these mothers *out of the way.* Feminine kids don't need their mothers around.

Mother: Just with daddys and boys.

Father: Well, I might look at their schedule. I hate to get *involved.*

(A response somewhat short of enthusiastic.)

Mother: See, he's just like my son. He doesn't like to do group-type things.

Dr.: You know, it doesn't matter what it is, as long as it is primarily involving boys and fathers. It should be the two of you.

Two and a half years later, some change was apparent in the boy's behavior but his mother was still not consistently discouraging his femininity.

Mother: How's he seem?
Dr.: I think he's doing great.
Mother: Yeah.
Dr.: Yeah, I think he's really much different. One of the things I had him do today was draw a picture. I haven't had him do that in a long time, just draw a person. . . . Do you remember who he drew the first time he ever did that?
Mother: Oh, probably some shape.
Dr.: No, he drew a person the first time. He drew Mary Poppins about three years ago.
Mother: Uh huh.
Dr.: And today he drew Frankenstein. [Both mother and doctor laugh.] Some shift in identity. I suppose, another three or four years, he'll be pretty well straightened out.
Mother: I can see little things just every day where he's making tremendous strides in the right direction. . . . But then I see little things also that just seem unnatural for him. Like when he gets out of the shower, you know, he'll go around wriggling his butt around with a towel. I usually leave him alone on that. That's just a mannerism.
Father: Yeah, but—
Dr.: If you feel it's very feminine, say something.
Father: Yeah. It's more like something a girl would be seen doing.
Dr.: I think he can become more conscious of that and control it.
Mother: You just can't move in on *everything*.
Dr.: The thing is that it's done *gradually*, and in *stages*, you know.
Mother: Yeah.
Dr.: At the beginning you move in on the most *gross* manifestations, and as the time goes by and he shows change, start moving in on the finer issues. You're not ruining his life; you're not saying he can't walk or talk; you're saying just don't do that one little thing when you walk or talk that causes you to be teased. You have to be consistent with it.

Attempts continued toward improving the father-son relationship.

Father: I got mad at him a couple of days ago, and I called him a little *shit*.
Dr.: OK.
Father: And she chewed me out.
Dr.: What's the matter with that? He probably *was* a little shit.
Mother: Well, I'd rather see my husband go off and *hit* him and not call him names.
Father: I'd rather get my frustrations out rather than hitting them all the time.

Dr.: Why would you rather see him whomped than called something?

Mother: I just don't like to see a father calling his son a name like that.

Dr.: Why would you rather see a father hit his son?

Mother: Because it seems more like a father-son relationship to haul off and whomp him than to call him a little shit.

Dr.: What do you think the effect is on a relationship in which a kid gets whomped a lot of times when the father gets mad? What do you think it does to the father-son relationship? What do you think it does to the son's perception of what the father is like?

Mother: I don't know, Dr. Green, you, you've got to think—

Dr.: What do you think it does?

Mother: Well, I'm not sure you might think that it might make the son think that his father was mean. And on the other hand the kid's not stupid, and he thinks that if my daddy doesn't hit me my daddy's *weak*.

Dr.: But he is responding. He's letting the kid know that he doesn't want him to do something in a way that's not including hitting him. He's not doing nothing.

Father: Verbally chewing him out.

Dr.: Uh huh. I think that if a father is someone who whenever he gets angry hits the child that the son gets to fear him, and it's doubtful that this builds a very positive bond between the two. If anything, I think the child will move back and retreat, withdraw from the father. You want to build up a more *positive* thing.

The mother had continued to restrict her son's free movement into a circle of male companions. *Considerable* effort was expended here to persuade her to allow him further out on his tether, by pointing out the possible benefits of giving him more freedom *and* the possible consequences of *not* permitting him autonomy.

Mother: When I watch him come home from school, there'll be a group of boys and a group of girls getting off the bus, and then finally, all at once, he comes through all by himself. And it looks kind of pathetic, and it breaks my heart to see all these youngsters off the bus together and he's alone.

Dr.: I thought he was more integrated now into groups of boys?

Mother: Well he is, but the neighborhood always shifts and changes, and then they all stop at the malt shop on the way home and I don't think it's—my husband agrees with me—it's a real crummy place, and we're all trying to close it down.

Dr.: Do the kids stop in there? Do the other boys stop?

Mother: Oh, yeah.

Dr.: Don't you feel, though, that if you're concerned that he's not integrating with a group of boys, you're making it much more difficult for him by saying he can't stop here, that he is an exception?

Mother: I—I know it, but you know—

Dr.: What's going to happen to him in the malt shop?

Mother: It's not—there's a bunch of hippies in there.

Dr.: What does *that* mean?

Mother: Well, I know that they use dope openly in there. You know, they smoke marijuana. At least they seem to do it.

Dr.: He's not going to start taking heroin if he goes into that malt shop. But if he's isolated from other boys, then you're going to perpetuate the kind of problem you have with him. He's not going to feel comfortable in a group, in a peer group of boys. And what's left to him? Either being completely by himself, or retreating into the security of a group of girls. That's what we're trying to *undo*. It seems to me the dangers, the long-term dangers, of his being a social isolate are a lot more than sitting around in a malt shop.

Mother: The malt shop is not so innocent. You have to be familiar with what it is.

Dr.: No matter what it is, you're not going to be able to isolate him from the culture in which he's living. It's impossible. What you can do, which I think is harmful, is make him a social isolate. He's living in a culture, he's a part of that culture. Maybe 50 percent of his friends in his class, no matter what you think or do, are going to be smoking marijuana. And if you really try to isolate him from everybody else, he'll grow up as an isolate with all the problems he was having some years ago and maybe even worse.

Mother: Then you'd let him associate with people who smoke marijuana in a place with card playing and a pool table? There are dirty hippies in there.

Dr.: Considering the problems that he has had, I would lean over in the direction of allowing him to do the things that other kids are doing. I think in the long run that's going to have a more helpful payoff for him than protecting him from that kind of environment. He's an exceptional kid, and he needs that kind of exposure.

Mother: All right. But you still don't know the whole story of that crummy place.

Dr.: I don't care *what* they're doing. I don't care if they're performing *abortions* underneath the *malted milk counter.* The issue is that he has to become integrated into a group of kids his age. *Boys.*

Mother: You know, I don't think it's very fair. You don't really understand the situation.

Dr.: We began this story by saying how pathetic it was to see him off by himself. I agree that it is pathetic and that it is important that he feel that he can integrate into a group of his peers, which has always been an issue with him. If he can't be with boys, he's going to want to be either completely alone, away from everybody, or else be with girls. And that's exactly where he was three years ago. You may feel more comfortable in that, and more secure, but in the long run he's the kid that loses out. These are the years he needs to form his masculine identity. If you want that, you've got to take some risks.

Three years after his first session, the boy gave his reasons for having had a "big, fat girly problem."

Dr.: Do you remember back three years ago, when you were seven, why your mommy and daddy brought you here?
Boy: I think 'cause my eyes weren't trained to do anything.
Dr.: What do you mean by that?
Boy: I saw things backwards.
Dr.: You had problems reading?
Boy: Mm hm, and I saw letters backwards, and then, you, they brought me to you.
Dr.: Am I the kind of doctor that examines your eyes or how you read?
Boy: No. All kinds of problems I had.
Dr.: What kind of problems did you have?
Boy: A big, fat *girly* problem.
Dr.: What do you mean by a "big, fat girly problem"?
Boy: I put big, fat girly dresses on.
Dr.: Do you remember why you used to do that?
Boy: 'Cause I wanted to look funny. 'Cause I wanted to look like a big, fat weirdo with a girly dress on. All funny.
Dr.: What else about that big, fat girly problem can you remember? Besides dressing like a girl.
Boy: Sometimes I'd act like one.
Dr.: How?
Boy: I'd go, "Yippee," or scream.
Dr.: Do you remember any other ways you acted as a girl?
Boy: I'd play house, and I'd have a little dolly. I threw it away.
Dr.: Did you? When was this?
Boy: I think it was a couple of weeks ago. A little dolly. It was real ugly. I just got so mad I threw it away, 'cause I ripped all the hair off it. I threw the whole thing away.
Dr.: Do you remember any time when you actually wished you had been born a girl?
Boy: Yes.
Dr.: What do you remember?
Boy: I think a long time ago when I was four or five.
Dr.: Do you remember why?
Boy: Only girl neighbors lived right next door to me, and they'd always come out to play with me and babysit me. Then when I was about four or five, I got all this stuff about girlies.
Dr.: What did you like about being a girl?
Boy: Well, I could babysit people and get lots of money.
Dr.: Were there any other reasons?
Boy: Yeah. When I got older I thought they looked so pretty and stuff. Then, you know, nobody is mean to girls. Nobody pushes them all over the place.

Dr.: Who pushes little boys around?

Boy: Big people. Most of the times, boys.

Dr.: What about your mommy and daddy? Do you think they would have treated you differently if you were a girl rather than a boy?

Boy: Yes.

Dr.: How?

Boy: I would get dolls and dresses. I'd probably have hair ruggings all over the floor, and dolls all over the bed and things. Maybe I would have a cat. That's why I was always probably wishing to be a girl, because if you're a girl you get a pet, a cat.

(He later got a *dog*, a gift from the therapist.)

Dr.: And would your daddy treat you differently if you'd been a girl?

Boy: Mm hm.

Dr.: How?

Boy: He would probably have paid me attention.

Possibly, a telling etiologic note.

Dr.: How would that be?

Boy: Usually when I asked him things, he wouldn't do it.

An earlier lesson was reviewed to reinforce the irrevocability of his being a boy.

Dr.: When you used to think you wanted to be born a girl, did you ever think you *were* a girl?

Boy: No, girls have long hair, and they have dresses.

Dr.: But what about if you'd put on dresses and had long hair? Would you have been a girl?

Boy: No.

Dr.: Why not?

Boy: 'Cause I wouldn't speak like one. I got a real hoarse voice and everything. Then when I was a girl, my legs would get all hairy, and I'd grow a beard and moustache. One time I saw a lady with a moustache, and it was so *weird*.

Dr.: Are there any other reasons why you couldn't grow up to become a lady?

Boy: No.

Dr.: Is there anything different about your body and a little girl's?

Boy: My body grows hair.

Dr.: Anything else? ·

Boy: Uh uh. Nothing else.

Dr.: What about your bottom? Is your bottom the same as a girl's?

Boy: Yes. A bottom—a bottom is a bottom. A girl's bottom is the same as a boy's bottom.

Dr.: Is it really?

Boy: They look different.

Dr.: How are they different?
Boy: A girl's vagina is inside and a boy's penis is outside.
Dr.: That's right. So that's another reason why a little boy couldn't become a little girl. . . . Do you think some of those girl things might come back again?
Boy: No.
Dr.: Why don't you think they might?
Boy: 'Cause I won't be asking for girls' hats.
Dr.: Do you feel now that you prefer being a boy?
Boy: Mm hm.

Thus, after more than three years of individual sessions with the boy and his parents, treatment had yielded some results. Despite the resistance of the parents to some of the therapist's suggestions, they had seen the merit of others, and had acted on them. The boy seemed to have accepted his anatomical destiny and was getting along considerably better with his schoolmates. Teasing had stopped and he had a wider circle of friends, both boys and girls.

GROUP SESSIONS

Group therapy offers some potential advantages over individual treatment sessions. It is more economical in that several patients may be seen concurrently. For the boy it can afford an initial socializing experience with other boys. For the parent it affords an opportunity for sharing with others similar experiences and conflicts over the sex-role development of their children. A potential disadvantage is dilution of any one patient's experience with the therapist.

The Boys

A group was formed of six boys experiencing conflict due to their atypical sex-role development. For one year, the boys, aged four to eight, met for weekly play sessions in a recreational area furnished with toys and equipment chosen to facilitate boyish play: a tether ball, a slide, a Frisby, a basketball and hoop, a kickball, monkey bars, and a running area.

The aim of these play sessions was twofold: to promote male peer-group identification and to provide additional exposure to an adult male identity model. For two of the boys, others in the group have constituted their first male playmates. For another two, the therapist constituted their first adult male "authority" figure.

Each boy was aware of the reason for his being in the group, although the degree of explicitness with which the parents presented this reason to each boy varied. Generally, all the boys saw their common problem in terms of liking things usually preferred by girls and of having difficulty getting along with other boys.

Early sessions were devoted to establishing friendships within the group. The therapist's participation was aimed at creating an informal atmosphere in which the boys would be at ease and in which they might develop a friendly trust in the therapist. If a boy experienced difficulty in integrating into the group, he received support from the therapist.

During the sessions, boyish play, usually unstructured, was encouraged. The boys were praised for such feats as scaling the heights of the monkey bars or plunging head-first down the slide, and for displays of agility, such as running or kicking a ball. Even inept attempts at handling a ball or at climbing were complimented, and repeated attempts were strongly encouraged. In all verbal reinforcements of behavior, masculine nouns were prominently used: "That's a good *boy*. Come on, *guys*! You're getting taller; you're going to be a big *man* when you grow up;" and so on.

Further, displays of feminine gestures were casually but firmly censured. When a dramatically feminine mannerism of the type that typically evokes teasing by nonfeminine boys was shown, it was met by the therapist's disapproval in some such comment as "Hey, don't run like that." The boys generally knew what the admonition referred to. Playing female roles was also criticized. In an "airplane" game, for instance, a boy who suggested that he play a stewardess was redirected to a masculine role by "You don't *look* much like a stewardess. You look more like a pilot. I think you'd make a better pilot."

One of the distinct advantages of exposure to a group context has been the use of "projection" by group members. When one feminine boy criticized another feminine boy for some feature of femininity, his criticism frequently focused on an aspect of his own behavior. For example, a boy with an effeminate lisp once took severe exception to another boy's speech, citing a lisping quality. The second boy's speech seemed unremarkable to the therapist, and when the latter wondered aloud whether the criticizing boy had ever *also* had difficulty in his manner of speaking, this was initially denied.

"Identifying with the aggressor" also occasionally occurred. A potentially feminine toy, such as a stuffed animal, has been, with great show, rejected as a "sissy" object, thus revealing that a feminine boy was identifying with masculine boys who usually teased him.

Discouragement of female role-playing, in particular, has produced noticeable results. During early sessions the boys would permit such role-playing, but they eventually began identifying with the therapist, criticizing such feminine play in others in the group, and offering negative reflections on it.

In these ways, through support of a masculine identity, projected criticism of common feminine traits, discouragement of grossly feminine mannerisms which typically yield social conflict, and encouragement of boyish play, masculine behavior of these boys has been augmented. The boys have enjoyed the group experience. Comments by their parents which follow indicate the degree to which the boys' social interactions outside the group have changed.

The Mothers

At least as important in promoting behavioral change in the boys have been the separate group sessions with mothers and those with fathers. Mothers met once a week with male and female* co-therapists. The mothers, prior to the group's inception, had never shared concerns over the management of a feminine boy's behavior with someone in a similar situation. Because of the age differential of boys in the group, some mothers found themselves in positions comparable to those held by other group members several years previously. A mother of a five-year-old might say, "My son in kindergarten won't play with boys. Should I say something to the teacher?" A mother of a seven-year-old would then describe what happened when she did. A mother of a five-year-old might deny the significance of her son's repeatedly making believe he is a mommy. The presence of a mother of an eight-year-old whose behavior at five was identical would then be speedily mobilized to help dispel her head-in-the-sand self-reassurance.

Again, as for the boys, it was frequently easier for a mother to find fault in another's approach to her son's behavior than to see that she herself behaved similarly. Once she found the fault in another, she was better able to find it in herself. Parents would thus discover and rehearse

* Marielle Fuller.

ways to modify feminine behavior in their own sons by instructing other parents.

The Fathers

Fathers met every two weeks with the male therapist. For them, perhaps the most important feature of their group experience was the revelation that there are other fathers also less than enthusiastic with the prospect before them. Not all fathers relish playing games with their sons after a grueling workday or surrendering the Sunday TV football classic to take them fishing. Nor does every father welcome the idea of joining Indian Guides for a glorious camping weekend with other father-son pairs, eating dirt- and cinder-laced eggs for breakfast and trying to remember clean clothes. However, the presence within the group of a father who reluctantly joined Indian Guides with his son and, to his amazement, found it to be highly enjoyable helped others over the same hurdle. Recognition that other fathers may also be reluctant to devote much time to father-son activities, coupled with the awareness of the specialized needs of *their* sons, may assuage guilt and lend group support to the undertaking.

The following examples, excerpts from group sessions with mothers and fathers, illustrate these points. The relative merit of this approach toward modifying the behavior of the feminine boys, as with the other approaches cited, must await the test of follow-up assessment.

Example 16-2 (Mother Group)

Mother A: I am so glad to meet you because you are the first women I have ever met with the same problem.

Mother B: Well, everybody thinks they are unique, but then they find out there are other people with the same problem, and you are happy to meet them.

Doctor: Tell us what you've been concerned about.

Mother C: Ronny wants to wear my stockings all the time, and I tell him no.

Dr.: What do you do?

Mother C: He says, "Can't I wear them?" and I say, "No, you can't." I think he has begun to realize, because now when I say no, he gets a funny look on his face like he knows why. Sometimes, though, I feel that the die is cast, and it's almost too late. I can't get over feeling that way. Which way is he going to go? And can I push him one way or the other? I feel like he is going to slowly meander into it.

Mother A: But he is only five, and my boy is nine. I felt the same way when Danny was about five. I felt it was hopeless. That's when it was at its worst, between five and six, that's when it was so obvious. I don't know exactly why, but the older he got, the more he was able to control it. I don't know about inside, but outside he was more able to control it.

Thus, a mother's pessimism about the irreversibility of her son's femininity was countered by another group member.

Mother B: You know what I think? I think it's a combination of heredity and environment. I really do. If kids have these things when they are born, then environment plays into their hands.
Mother A: Where do you think they have a heredity for homosexuality?
Mother E: I think if one has a tendency to be swishy, it can be directed.
Mother D: Well, aren't we all that way? Don't we all have—what's the word I'm looking for—don't we all have latent homosexual tendencies? On some people it shows more than on others.
Mother C: I think it's a biochemical thing.
Mother B: I'm not going to blame it on heredity, I'm just going to say that part . . .

A typical attempt to look away from parent-child experiences and toward heredity as the cause of an atypical sexual identity.

Mother D: Two weeks ago when we were driving home, Bobby asked me why he was coming here, and I told him because—well, first of all because I wanted it. He kind of accepted it, and then he said, "Why?" And I said, "Doctor Green is interested in your behavior, the way you do and act like a girl sometimes." And he said, "Well, Danny doesn't act that way." And I said, "What about Ronny?" And he said, "Yeah, Ronny does. Ronny is always playing with the girls, whatever they're playing. They were playing airplane, and Danny and Bobby were the pilot and co-pilot, and Ronny was the stewardess. [Considerable laughter in the group.]
Dr.: Tell me something. When you describe how they are playing and you say Ronny is a stewardess, everybody laughs?
Mother D: It's funny.
Dr.: Why?
Mother B: If it was your own kid, would you laugh or cry?
Mother D: If Bobby was the stewardess, I would have laughed very hard.
Mother B: I think what Doctor Green is trying to say is our laughing accepted it in a way. Does it get the message across?

A classic example of how mothers can, without conscious awareness, show approval of their sons' feminine behavior.

Mother E: I think Ronny, perhaps, according to my son, is the one they make the most fun of.
Mother C: The boys at school and the boys after school have picked on

him, and then he either plays by himself or with girls. And the kids in the neighborhood are rougher than he is and won't have anything to do with him. We thought by moving we would get him away from the kids that already know him as he is, and maybe it will be a change for him.

Dr.: I have heard so many times that boys play too rough and that's why these boys play with girls.

Mother D: Why don't the other girls [sic] in the neighborhood want to play with him if he plays calmly and quietly? There is that one little girl in the neighborhood. She's always at the door. "Can Bobby come out and play?" But she's a tomboy. She looks like she will outgrow it, but I don't know about Bob.

Mother B: There is an inconsistency in that too, though, because as much as Alan doesn't like roughhousing, I have seen him, much to my absolute surprise, on an occasion he will come on with a real tackle from across the room. And I will just gawk, because I have never seen him do things like that, you know. He has aggressive sides. They just don't seem to come out very often.

Dr.: Do you make remarks when you see him do this? Like "Gee, that was a great tackle" or something like that? To encourage him to do this again?

Mother B: Usually not. I usually stay out of the whole thing.

Dr.: If once in a while you see him doing something out of character, if you give him some confidence, you might increase that kind of behavior.

A mother laments that her son is picked on by rougher boys. However, she also does not encourage his rough-and-tumble play.

Mother B: Alan made a remark the other day which I thought was good. I took him down with the bike, and I had a girlfriend with me, and she said, "Oh, Alan, you have such a nice mommie to go through all this trouble to take your bike somewhere." And he said "She's OK, but my dad's nicer." Really. I hadn't heard that before, and that was good.

Dr.: That was good. You don't feel insulted? Second best?

Mother B: I don't feel insulted at all. I really don't. I know he loves me. There's no doubt in my mind. But too long he loved me, and there was not enough with his dad.

Dr.: What do you think is responsible for this shift?

Mother B: Well, perhaps I have not spent as much time with him, and I have been trying to spend more time with his sister, and I've been involved with other things, and he wants me to do things with him and I don't want to, and my husband will come home and he will read to him. I almost purposely don't do it, because I don't want to get sucked into being the one he always comes to all the time. That's good.

Thus, one mother described to others her gradual disengagement from her son.

Dr.: What do you think about Ronny's gestures? Do you feel that they are still pretty feminine?

Mother C: Yes.

Dr.: His posture is very feminine?

Mother C: Yes.

Dr.: How do you feel about it?

Mother C: I don't like his posturing.

Dr.: Where do you think he gets that?

Mother C: I wonder if he gets it from me.

Dr.: Do you stand that way?

Mother C: Well, I used to stand like this when I would be thinking about something. Well, I quit doing it, because he was always copying me, so I tried to stop. I used to do that, but I don't know if I do it any more, but he still does it.

Dr.: I guess that is the most characteristic thing about Ronny, how feminine his posture is.

Mother: But I'm not going to follow him around saying, "Don't do this and don't do that. Keep your hands down. Don't put your hands on your hip." I'm just not going to reduce myself to doing that.

Dr.: "Reduce yourself"?

Mother C: I don't think it really helps to keep after somebody like that.

Mother A: It does. It helps to stop it.

Mother C: It may stop it, but I just don't want to stop the posture. I want more than that. And I feel that I want to go in and get to the heart of it before I do any superficial thing which might only make the heart of it worse, just by giving those superficial symptoms attention. I want to get down to the bottom of it.

Mother D: Is there really a bottom of it?

Mother B: Yeah, there is.

Mother C: What do you think it could be?

Mother B: It has to do with identity. The title "Gender Identity," that's the whole thing.

Co-therapist: I know, but you're talking about a years and years and years kind of a thing. If these boys grow out of this feminine thing, it's going to be a long-term endeavor. It's not something that's going to happen in six months or a year.

Mother B: If you don't get rid of the superficial things, when you get to the heart of the matter you are still going to have to deal with the superficial things anyway. And if you eliminate them as you're going along, then you're eliminating the problems.

Mother C: I don't think so.

Mother A: If you find the reason why he is the way he is and can get this out of his mind, do you think that everything else is just going to stop like that?

Mother C: I think the desire to be a girl could be wiped out, and he would stop standing like that.

Mother B: But how can you wipe out the desire? The habits have to be changed. The habit of his standing with his hand on his hip. You can get him out of that habit.

Dr.: What if there is only one way you ever learned how to walk, and there is only one way you ever learned how to stand and use your hands, you are going to continue to show those gestures no matter what you feel inside.

Mother C: Yes, I see what you mean. You have a point there. So what should I do? Start saying, "Stand up this way"?

Dr.: There's one more thing, too, that when you behave femininely, your environment responds back to you, as though you're a feminine boy. If he comes across like a swishy little boy, then his friends are going to treat him as such, and that's going to make it hard for him to change what he thinks of himself inside.

Mother C: Shall I just tell him to quit standing that way?

Mother B: It is hard. It is really hard. It's obnoxious to me, but I did it, and Alan has really changed in terms of the way he postures himself. The change was remarkable. But it was really crummy, and I really hated doing it all the time—"Do this. Don't do that"—but it's changed his external appearance.

Co-therapist: Do they respond differently to him?

Mother B: Sure they do. They respond like he is a *boy.*

Mother C: Yes, I will just concentrate on the posture for a while, and later when that improves then—

Dr.: He is probably not even conscious at this point of it. It has to be brought to his awareness. Until he becomes conscious of it, he's not going to be able to—he's going to have to get sensitized to his feminine behavior.

Mother D: Now, with Bobby, all I had to do was to look at him while he was doing it, and he would realize that that was what I meant and he stopped doing it.

The group has the force of numbers. Note in the foregoing exchange that other mothers joined the doctor in challenging Mother C's attitude toward her son's feminine behavior.

Mother D: Generally Bobby has been behaving beautifully. In fact I got a call from the principal of the school that he and another boy had gotten themselves into trouble at school, and, of course, I couldn't tell the principal, but I was happy to hear it. They had climbed up into the band room on top of the auditorium, and it's dangerous up there. I didn't want any danger for him, but I was happy to see him doing boyish, mischievous things with another boy too, and not with any other girls [*sic*]. Of course, I had to punish him a little bit for it, but nothing serious. In fact, he had to write a letter of apology to the school that I had to sign, and I made him do it twice, and that was all. I just told him, "Don't do it again."

Dr.: Why did you feel that you had to punish him *at all?*

Mother D: Well, it was something that the—well, I didn't want him doing it again because it was *dangerous*, but, in here, I was glad that he had done something like that. But he had to be punished in some way. I just made him write the note, which he had to do anyway, but I made him rewrite it the second time so that it would be presentable to the school. But it wasn't really a punishment. He thought it was, slightly. I just said, "Don't do anything that's going to hurt you. You're going to get hurt. I don't want you to get hurt, and neither does the school, and it's dangerous. Don't go there any more." But as far as telling him not to play with this other kid and anything like that—no, no, not a word about that.

Dr.: Well, I guess it's kind of hard to know what your message meant to him.

Admittedly, she faced a complex situation. However she might have shown less protectiveness by suggesting other kinds of boyish play that would be equally adventurous but less dangerous. As it was, she transmitted a mixed message to her son for one of his most boyish actions to date.

Mother A: My son insists now that he doesn't want anything to do with girls, and he has only boyfriends. There is one little girl who calls him up to play with him, and he says, "I don't want to play with her. She's a dumb broad." I don't know if he is doing it to please me or if this is typical of boys that age.

Dr.: It could be both.

Mother A: It really pleases me. He hasn't done anything in months and months and months that has even worried me a bit.

Mother E: It's kind of odd that you want them to stay away from them, and later you want to make sure that they *don't* stay away from them.

Dr.: The thing is that before adolescence your companions are sort of reflective of your self-image.

Mother E: You mean if the nine- or ten-year-olds only wanted to play with girls it would be—

Dr.: It means he feels more comfortable with girls and participating in girls' activities.

Thus, the significance of boy playmates versus girl playmates during preadolescence was clarified.

Mother F: It's interesting that Rick's best friend is—the boy he has chosen to become best friends with—because we don't allow him to play with any girls outside of school—is a boy who I would suspect has got some similar gender identity problems. I have never seen anything overt, but he is kind of a feminine-looking, sensitive type of boy, not real aggressive.

Dr.: But does he do girl things?

Mother F: I don't think so. This is the type of person Rick is attracted to, a nonaggressive boy.

Dr.: That might be the only type of boy he can feel comfortable with.

Mother F: Mm hm.

Mother C: You know, Ronny used to be attracted to a very aggressive boy, and that worried us. It was about two or three years ago when he was about four. He would come over to use the toys. He didn't care anything about Ronny, and Ronny used to follow him around like a dog, but I felt that he was thinking of himself as the feminine part of the group. I didn't feel that he was looking at him as a boyfriend who would be aggressive. Plus, I hated the boy. The boy was horrible, and I was glad when he moved away, too.

Mother E: Why did you hate that boy?

Mother C: Because he was nasty and destructive and sick. He'd come and break things. Just that he was sneaky, and he had a lot of bad traits, and I didn't like him. But I let him in anyway. I didn't like him, and I was very glad when he moved.

Dr.: Are there other boys for him to play with?

Mother C: No, not right now. There is no one his age, so he is alone.

Dr.: There are no boys from school?

Mother C: No. No one lives in this area.

Dr.: Could you import boys?

Mother C: There is one boy, and I know his mother. His mother took care of him when he was a baby. If I made an effort, I could probably have him see that boy, so I'll try and make an effort. I have her phone number.

Dr.: Yes, I think that would be important.

Mother E: I used to do that. I used to just call mothers and ask if so and so could come over today.

Dr.: A lot of it is a matter of chance. Sometimes the odds aren't very evenly distributed. You can be a boy with five or six same-age girls, and for some kids it's all right, but for these kids it's something special, and sometimes you have to import boys into your environment, or export your own kid into another environment.

Mother E: I take my boy over to my sister's house. She's got a boy who is a year older. I try to get him with the other boys if he can't find one in the neighborhood. If he can't find someone to play with that day, I take him over to my sister's to play with my nephew because I don't want him playing with the girls.

Here a mother lent strong support to the therapist's suggestion that another group member provide male playmates for her son.

Mother B: Have you ever had a conference with his teacher?

Mother D: No, and in a way I don't want to talk to her about it, because I'm afraid—well, in one nursery school, she just started forcing him into all kinds of roles. I don't have much confidence in the teachers. This lady is nice, but I mean—I don't know how she would act. I want them to treat him normally, [to] let him think that he is part of the group and not to think that he has some special problem.

Dr.: In a way, she may be overlooking certain things that she doesn't think are significant. She may observe him doing some feminine things and feel it's not worth worrying about.

Mother F: She may let him dress up too, which is one thing he shouldn't do. I didn't think they did either at the school my boy was going to, but they had one day a week where they let the kids play with this one great big trunk of all kinds of clothes, and my boy was always picking out girls' clothes to wear, and when I told them about it they made a special costume to wear, a sailor suit or a cowboy suit. They still let him dress up, but in a masculine way, because they were aware of it, and they knew, and they tried to keep him away from only playing with the girls. They cooperated beautifully with me, and they were more than happy to help.

Mother D: Then I will make an effort to talk to the teacher.

Dr.: You have a lot of homework to do.

Mother D: Yes, I'm so used to sitting back and doing nothing. That's the way I've been all my life.

Reassurred by Mother F's story, Mother D resolved to try to enlist her son's teacher as an ally in attempting to modify his behavior. Acceptance and reassurance by a group of one's peers—in this case, other mothers of feminine boys—can greatly aid in breaking a habit of passively "doing nothing" and lead to positive action.

In a later session, the mothers reflected on some behavioral changes toward masculinity in their sons, and speculated on whether therapy might be due some credit for bringing them about. They also received encouragement to continue the sessions.

Mother C: I can only say—all of us, I only hope it's worth all the effort we put into it—that they will not only turn out to be the way we would like them to be as boys and men, but that they make something of themselves somewhere along the line.

Dr.: You see changes in your boy?

Mother C: Yes, I do. I asked him today when we were coming down here. He knows why he is coming here. And I said to him, "Do you feel that coming here is doing you any good?" and he said, "I don't know," and I said, "Do you still feel that you are acting like a girl?" and he said, "Oh, no!" He was very emphatic. And I said, "Well, do you still want to be a girl?" and he said, "Uh uh," and I just dropped it and let it go at that.

Mother B: My boy is changing his mind about being a girl. I think he's found too many things that other boys are doing and enjoying them. He's having fun.

Mother D: I think this is helping them. This group meeting—my boy has changed a lot, because he was talking about how he—there was a ladybug in the back of the car and he said, "Oh, I'm a ladybug," and then he quickly stopped and said, "Oh, I'm not a ladybug." He said, "Julie, she can be a ladybug." He said, "I'm just a bug."

Mother E: He's catching on.

Dr.: Has he said, "I am a girl" or "I want to be a girl"?

Mother D: He used to say both, so now he doesn't say either one, and I think he is changing and that he doesn't want to be one like he used to.

Mother A: How can there be any improvement? How can you attribute this place—

Mother B: I'll tell you this—that I think it is that they are probably beginning to realize that they can do certain things to make them happy because they are boys, things that they enjoy doing are masculine. Maybe that's what they're learning here. I don't know, but I get that idea, and that's good, so that he can enjoy some sort of association with the masculine sort of thing.

Mother F: But you're not directing anything down there are you?

Dr.: What is happening there is that these are boys who aren't particularly threatening to each other, and sometimes they are being critical of feminine things in each other. That is, frequently it is easier for people to criticize things they see in themselves when someone else does it, so they become critical of each other and at the same time not being aggressive and competitive boys, they can play together as boys. They do not have to depend on boys who will frighten them away. They may be feminine boys, but they are not girls.

Mother E: How long do you think this will go on?

Mother B: It might take years.

Co-therapist: This isn't the kind of thing where you expect people to change overnight. It takes four or five years to develop this kind of behavior.

Mother C: Do you feel that there is an improvement? What is expected?

Dr.: I think kids like this can change. I've seen some change. Some kids do and some kids don't.

Mother B: I know there is nothing guaranteed. There never is when it comes to this, but you think there is a good chance that something could—

Dr.: I think there is more chance of something happening if you focus on the behavior than if you just ignore it or just say, "Well, we'll wait a few years and see what happens."

Example 16-3 (Father Group)

Father A: My son and I have been really getting into the Indian Guides at the "Y." I'm the chief now, so we do that a lot. We enter into all of their things—I understand we have one of the most active groups—and he enjoys that a lot, you know.

Doctor: What sort of things do you do in the Guides?

Father A: Well, we have been on three overnight things. We went up on a snow trip, and then we went on to *another* one because there was *no snow*. We went in on a backpack trip and slept on the ground, which was a good experience, and which led us into some other things with the family. We had tribal games the other day. All the tribes got together on a ball field and went through the "little Olympics."

Dr.: Your boy seems to be liking this?

Father A: Yeah.

Dr.: How about you?

Father A: I *love* it.

Dr.: You do?

Father A: It's really forced us into a situation where we are together a lot more. It's at least two weekends a month.

Dr.: Does it surprise you, the fact that you enjoyed it?

Father A: Prior to this time I never would have had the time for it, and now I just have more time. It really is great. He is playing ball more than ever before, and he is riding his bike more than ever before, and he is also making friends with boys more than girls. I could check back six months ago or even a year ago, little girls were all he was making friends with. Suddenly he is improving.

Thus, to other fathers, one enthusiastically described experiences, with his son, in an exclusively father-son group activity, the Indian Guides.

Dr. (to Father B): How is *your* relationship with *your* son?

Father B: Well, I'm very busy myself. I'm forming a complete new thing in my business, as a matter of fact. I've been very, very busy, and I *should* spend more time with him. I'll be honest about that. As a matter of fact, I had the same opportunity for Indian Guides as he had, through my brother-in-law who is in it, and I told him I would join and, of course, I never did yet, but my *intention* is good, and I think that maybe in another four or five weeks—

Dr.: It might be good for your own unwinding.

Father B: I think so too.

Dr.: It would be good for you to get away from your own business.

Father B: I have thought about that too, and I might make some time regardless, and just get around and do it.

Dr.: You need that.

Father B: I think he would really enjoy it. He's been bugging me about it.

Dr.: Everyone feels the same way. But it's been good for the kids in every case. Really, *nobody* has the time.

A second father, with "good intentions," had been putting off a similar undertaking.

Father A: (In Indian Guides) They handle the competition thing. It exists, but nobody ever feels any kind of inferiority about it. Like with these tribal games, if you won as a team for first place, everybody got a first-place ribbon. During the meeting we all do a project, and if a kid is very creative his thing comes out a little differently, but there again everybody comes out with a product that they are all proud of, so they can be as competitive as they want, yet they don't feel a fear of this.

Dr.: The competition that these kids can handle is not in contact sports, the kind of thing where they choose up sides, and they're the last one chosen, so they are teased and called sissy, because they can't throw the ball. That's not an issue here. They ought to be able to deal with boys and not feel threatened by them.

Father A: I think everyone won a place, won a first place in something.

Dr.: These kids don't choose girls as playmates because there is something tremendously attractive about girls. It's because they are not a threat to them. They don't tease them.

Father A clearly saw the need by these boys for physically noncompetitive, male peer-group experiences.

Dr. (to Father C): How about your son in this respect?

Father C: I think that, as you mentioned, as long as there is no competition and you get involved, but the minute you want him to get in with the rest of the boys, then he will rebel, you know, and run off and say, "No, I don't want to do it. I can't do it."

Father D: I can't put my finger on anything that happened to my son as far as, you know, getting hurt. I thought maybe he might have been hurt by a ball. I know when he was a little kid he was scared to death of a glove. Inadvertantly I threw it out to him. He was around two, and he just panicked this one time, and, like, he sees boxing gloves or a baseball glove, and he doesn't even want to put his hand in it. I don't know if he still remembers that experience but—

Dr.: Well, I think the key is to find something that he can adjust to. Nobody is trying to make these kids into great athletes. The issue is that if they are totally incompetent and really in fear and fearful of a ball, there will be a social repercussion. They are going to be ostracized. I think the issue is to find something that he can do, even if it's just rolling the ball across the room, and reward him. Maybe *bribe* him. You know, he has to play with you for fifteen minutes for a reward. Maybe he needs a material thing like a special treat. Like, if he plays with you a little on Saturday, then afterwards you go out and get an ice cream.

The therapist here pointed out the social advantages for these boys in developing some degree of masculine skills and proposed a strategy for engaging the boy in such a venture.

Father D: From me this sounds like a broken record, but the *same* thing—like, I'm not in the professional field, but I come home *tired*. I'm a construction worker, and there are a lot of evenings when I don't *feel* like doing anything but just—

Dr.: Nobody does. There isn't *anybody* who comes home who does.

Father D: Just sit around and wait for your dinner. You know, "Go on and play, or go to your room."

Dr.: The easiest thing to do is make yourself a drink and pick up the paper, and hope the kid disappears somewhere.

Father D: Last week he came up to me and said, "Let's go to the park," and so I said, "OK, let's go." Usually I say, "No, it's too late."

Dr.: That's important. Any overture that the kids make.

Father D: So it was around seven thirty or eight, and it was cold and miserable and my wife said, "Where are you going?" and I said, "I'm going to take him to the park," and she said, "He's going to catch cold," and I said, "I'm going to take him to the park. Don't say *nothing.* We're going to the *park.*" So we went to around nine o'clock, and then I told him, "Let's go get a tasty freeze," and he liked that. And now every night when I come home from work, it's "Can we go to the park tonight?" I've been taking him pretty regularly.

Here the therapist empathized with a father's reluctance to become involved with his son at the end of a hard work day following which the father recounted the effect of his extra effort on his son's behavior.

Dr. (to Father C): What about your relationship with your son?

Father C: It has improved quite a bit. I have made a more definite time to stay with him. We made it to the zoo one Saturday, and he is interested in animals and this type of thing, so we went up to the canyon.

Father D: I know that—right now I'm involved with a softball team, and all the fathers take the boys out. So I'm always looking over my shoulder to see what type of activities he is in. And I've noticed the last few nights that I have taken him there's a group of older boys, and—he would leave the bench where we were sitting and go off to the swings or stuff—now he will get mixed up with the older boys. They were doing the playing, but he was handing them the bat and going after the ball, where two months ago he wouldn't. He wouldn't even come close to that.

Dr.: In listening to what you are describing in what's happening, I'm hearing you all say, "I'm spending more time with my boy now in contrast to whatever happened before." I'm wondering if you all are feeling kind of leaned on by the problem, or by your wives, or by *me,* whether you feel it is a *burden* and a pressure on you. I'm wondering if you feel that it was *your fault,* and you have to get out there and make up for your past sins and such.

Father B: With me it's not like that at all. I think that perhaps I should spend more time with him. I'm spending more time with him now than I have in the past.

Dr. (to Father A): How do you feel?

Father A: I feel a little bit leaned on, but I don't resent it at all. But I'm very aware of my time now. I'm trying to remember back to what my childhood was, and I can remember never seeing any fathers around, ever, weekends, weekdays, or anything, and I find myself saying, "Well, goddamn it, I spend so much time, much more time than any other father I ever knew," but my final analysis is that "Well, my son *needs* it. I didn't need it. Somebody else didn't need it, but he needs it, so I do have to."

Dr. (to Father C): How about yourself?

Father C: I don't feel leaned on, but what he said I could agree with, because my father had a store and that was his life, and fathers weren't just around. I don't think I feel leaned on.

Dr.: I feel that what he said is very true, that kids are very different. There are some kids if you just throw them out into the world and don't do anything for them, somehow everything falls into place, but with these kids it's different, for some reason.

Here the therapist tapped into feelings of resentment by the fathers for having to perform as "superfathers."

Father A: My wife came home with a poster a couple of weeks ago, and I had all kinds of mixed reactions, and I had to think about what it meant for a while. It's a big poster of a kid sitting by himself on a rock overlooking the ocean, and there is a quotation and in essence what it said was that if you don't hear the music everybody else does, let him march to his own music. Right, he hears a different drummer. So I think initially what that meant to us, "OK, he's different. That's fine. Why should we get so hung up about it? We should just accept that," which isn't good either because we don't want to accept it entirely.

Dr.: It's a memorable quotation. The problem is that in the real world there are certain rhythms you can march to and get by with, and others happen to give you a lot of problems.

PARENTS AS THERAPISTS

A third strategy employs parents as the therapeutic agents, utilizing a systematic design of rewards and fines. Parents make a listing of the feminine activities shown by their son. Another list is made itemizing the boy's favorite privileges and most sought-after treats, and a relative rank ordering of their value is noted.

From this information an individualized treatment protocol is designed. The model here is that children accumulate or lose points as a function of various aspects of their behavior. Rewards and fines are graded relative to their value to the child.

Several approaches may be used, the choice to be determined by data derived from parental descriptions of the boy under study and from trial and error. To a boy who usually takes a female role in "house" games, points may be given for taking the role of father. These points may be applied to a necessary total to gain some special privilege. Playing a female role may result in, say, five points being subtracted from that total. Alternatively, points may be independently accumulated toward a negative total whereby some routine privilege is temporarily lost.

For example, a positive total of thirty points may be needed for a trip to Disneyland, ten points for staying up an extra hour for an entire week watching TV, and five points for an ice cream treat for dessert. A negative total of five points may result in loss of dessert and ten minus points in loss of a weekend's movie privilege. Privileges withdrawn must not be masculine related, for example, a camping trip with father or swimming lessons. Scores may be kept on a prominently displayed, attractive graph, much in the manner of public billboards that chart progress in a community fund-raising drive.

Another strategy that can be employed allows the child to engage in a less desirable behavior, such as playing with a neighbor girl, his favorite playmate, only after first engaging in an alternative behavior, such as playing with a neighbor boy. The time required playing with the boy in exchange for playing with the girl is progressively increased. Other therapists have endorsed this approach for use with adult male homosexuals, desirous of reorientation. The patient is required to spend progressively increasing durations of time in heterosexual dating prior to being permitted a homosexual experience (Money, 1972).

A similar reward system may be developed for modifying parental behavior. Parents may put money into a "kitty" to be withdrawn as a function of their interaction with the feminine boy. The father may draw out money for time spent in an activity with his son; the more time, the more money; and the mother may draw money for time that would have been previously spent with her son but that she has reassigned by promoting his activity with another boy.

The utilization of parents as therapists is based on principles described for the treatment of children with other behavior disorders (Bijou and Baer, 1966; Patterson and Gullion, 1968; Sherman and Baer, 1969). It has the potential advantage of providing a day-to-day, consistent effort toward modifying behavior in a naturalistic setting.

In the treatment of boyhood femininity, the straightforwardness of such home-based intervention is deceptively simple. It ignores the intricate dynamics existing in some families. While great success has been reported in modifying a variety of undesirable childhood behaviors such as temper tantrums, fighting, sloppiness, and poor personal hygiene, boyhood femininity appears to be more complex. Dr. Kathy Mayers and I attempted to establish this treatment program in three families. We encountered a variety of obstacles.

First, the principles of the treatment system were explained to the parents in each family. They were given explanatory reading material by Patterson and Gullion (1968), a programmed text written for parents. Dr. Mayers then traveled to the home and remained for intervals ranging from a half-day to three consecutive days and nights. During these home visits preliminary baseline observations of the boy's masculine and feminine behavior were recorded by Dr. Mayers, and an attempt was made to train the parents to also systematically make and record observations.

Parental resistance was considerable. Although they had professed concern over their boys' orientation, to a remarkable extent they sabotaged the program. Profound difficulties ensued when mothers were required to record the frequency of various feminine behaviors. The family would not be at home when a joint observation session had been scheduled by the mother and Dr. Mayers. A variety of reasons was offered by mothers as to why previously agreed upon observation periods had not been conducted: "That was the day I went bowling," "Too time-consuming," "Menstrual cramps forced me to bed." Observation data sheets were lost.

Yet another obstacle was the degree of "spontaneous change" in the boy. The process of office evaluation and particularly the presence within the home of an observer brought the boy's behavior under critical scrutiny. Thus, during these periods, visible femininity diminished. This change in turn was interpreted by parents as full disappearance of the feminine identity and was seen as rendering superfluous any additional time commitment to the program. In-home observation by Dr. Mayers tended to confirm a degree of behavioral change, but it was not so considerable as reported by the parents.

Additionally, certain behaviors that appeared to the investigators as indicating a feminine orientation were interpreted by the parents as unequivocally masculine. One four-year-old boy, for example, was fond of carrying a purse. Wherever he went, he would dangle a purse from his forearm and carry it with his arm flexed at the elbow and hand turned upward. The boy then substituted a small briefcase for the purse. The parents saw this solely as modeling after his father. However, the boy carried the briefcase in precisely the manner in which he had carried the purse. His appearance to other children remained decidedly feminine.

Clearly, the degree of discomfort within the family ensuing from these boys' femininity is not comparable to that in which the child throws temper tantrums, assaults a sibling, or refuses to dress and wash. In part, these parents are troubled by their son's very feminine behavior. Also, in part, they are not displeased. As a consequence, their motivation for carrying the major burden of effecting change is compromised

The pitfalls encountered so far with these mothers and fathers have revealed more about parental attitudes toward atypical sex-role development than whether such behavior is amenable to change by a schedule of positive and negative reinforcement. Furthermore, the changes seen in the child during the period of preliminary, baseline observation, point up the need for control groups for comparing the efficacy of "treatment" intervention. A number of nonspecific influences may contribute to behavioral change. It may ultimately be found that the decision to bring the child for an evaluation and a desire to enter a treatment program of *any* type is the most important single contributor to whether a boy significantly "outgrows" his early femininity.

Be that as it may, for this home-based approach to be effective, it is obvious that a very careful assessment must be made of parental motivation to effect change in the child. In the absence of such careful family screening, the treatment strategy becomes little more than an exercise in ambivalence.

AN OVERVIEW OF TREATMENT STRATEGIES

Principles for treating these boys developed as my collaborator, Robert Stoller, began seeing very feminine males and their families in a search for etiology. Based on his observations, and aided by both an early treatment approach of Ralph Greenson (1966) and later work of Lawrence Newman (Green, Newman, and Stoller, 1972), several treatment principles have been formulated.

The first concerns the sex of the therapist. We believe that the therapist should be male for two reasons. By the nature of his behavior, authority, and prestige he will be available to the boy as an object for identification. The companionship provided by an adult male in many cases fills a void in the boy's experience left by an absent or psychologically unavailable father. The male therapist substitutes as a role model. The boy and man may involve themselves in activities that are typically boyish and within reach of the boy's ability. These may involve kicking a ball, running, or just going for walks. In this context, these activities are not competitive or threatening to the boy, as they might be with the feminine boy's more aggressive male peers.

Generally, parental attitudes toward the boy's very feminine behavior have previously been positive, in the sense that it evoked laughter or brought increased parental attention of a not unpleasant nature. Children have been posed and photographed in girls' clothes and shown off to friends and relatives. Many parents think such behavior is cute. Fathers, even more than mothers, tend to dismiss the behavior as "nothing to worry about," perhaps because femininity in their sons is seen as a failure on their part to serve as adequate models for male identification. Approval, implicit or explicit, should be interrupted.

Cessation of reinforcement for behavior that may cause a boy social distress should be accompanied by enhancement of approval for alternative activity. The mothers of the feminine boys we have seen are frequently ill at ease with rough-and-tumble, boisterous, messy behavior, and have difficulty permitting its expression. They may be able to accommodate to such behavior if stress is laid to the importance of allowing such expression for *their* son in consequence of his already emerging female identity. The fathers we have seen are themselves frequently disinclined to participate in activities such as roughhousing, playing ball, or other outdoor activities. Again, they may be better able to generate motivation for such ventures if the special nature of *their* son's needs are emphasized. The boy's contact with his father and with his male peers may be augmented by participation in some local program such as the Indian Guides. Many of their activities are of a noncompetitive nature, including excursions, outdoor cooking, and handicrafts. These boys should not be hurtled into Little League.

Boys feeling unable to compete in rough-and-tumble, aggressive play, may, with the logic of early childhood, choose the "only" alternative: being with girls and adopting their behavior. But another choice is available: they may build, draw, read, play board games, and play with boys who are themselves not wholly sports and roughhouse-minded. Fathers may be overly demanding of their sons, expecting them to be athletic and aggressive. The boys' inability to meet these fathers' definition of "masculinity" may cause them to view father and his activities as negative and to draw closer to mother and her activities.

Such fathers can be encouraged to engage their sons in activities within their *mutual* interest and competence.

When investigation of the boy's behavior reveals the presence of companions who appear to promote feminine activities, this can also be brought under control. Some parents actively discourage play with boys who are characterized as too rough and dangerous. Some report that dressing up and girlish game preference is considerably enhanced when a feminine boy plays with neighbor girls. Nonaggressive male peers can be invited home after school, or on weekends, to provide a not-so-threatening peer relationship for the feminine boy that may not be available in the immediate neighborhood.

Parental-role division may be such that the boy sees his mother as prime provider of rewards, protection, and sustenance. The father's role may be undermined, overtly or covertly, in the boy's presence, so that he comes to view the male role in a negative manner. Again, the special nature of the boy's behavior may be used as leverage to effect some redistribution of influence. Some fathers are men who have considerable difficulty in overcoming their passivity and have married women whose assertiveness complements their own retiring personality. However, in our experience, there *are* couples who perhaps at first uncomfortably and somewhat stiltedly, but later naturally, can modify role relationships.

Some boys reveal their feminine identifications through physical gestures. By the time they are seen in consultation much of this display is unconscious or automatic. In order to bring it under volitional control, the child needs to be sensitized to his actions of walking, sitting, or using his hands "like a girl." Parents should be instructed to point out such behavior to the boy. In his contacts with the boy, the therapist does the same. The boy may also need actual instruction in modifying these gestures. The importance of feminine mannerisms lies in its effect on peers and the resultant social feedback. A feminine-appearing boy will be labeled "sissy" and set apart from other boys.

Unsettled issues remain. If treatment enables these boys to feel more comfortable in being male and integrate more effectively into a male peer group, what effect will this have on subsequent sexuality? While the answer will be forthcoming in time, currently we can speculate. Had these boys been on the road to transsexualism, treatment could reduce their degree of alienation from a masculine social role. The result could be less harsh incompatibility between body and identity. Thus the request (and need) for sex-change surgery might be averted.

Had these boys been on the road to exclusive homosexuality, treatment could increase their opportunities (and capacity) for bisexuality, exclusive heterosexuality, or less feminine-appearing homosexuality in a culture which censures feminine males. While the relationship between preadolescent gender-role behavior and adolescent genital sexuality is incompletely understood, peer group socialization could be one linking factor. A very feminine male adolescent may be subjected to different social forces and options than a masculine teenager. Others may react to him as though he were homosexual, thus contributing to that self-concept. Additionally, he may be less attractive as a potential partner in a heterosexual relationship and perhaps more attractive as a potential partner in a homosexual one. This is not to say that these social forces solely determine sexual orientation, but rather that intervention directed at reducing peer group alienation may expand subsequent sexual options.

Speculations aside, the question remains: What effect will puberty, with its hormonal surge resulting in heightened genital sexuality, have on these boys' behavior? Study at that transitional time may help clarify the interrelationship between (1) preschool emergence of sexual identity; (2) grade school gender-role behavior; and (3) adolescent and adult genital sexuality.

17

MASCULINE GIRLS

Tomboyishness in girls is considerably more common than sissified behavior in boys. More justifiably, it can be considered a normal passing phase. However, the childhood recollections of the female-to-male transsexuals presented in Chapter 7 demonstrate that not *all* tomboys outgrow it. Thus the research issue becomes identifying those tomboys for whom boyish behavior may not be just a passing phase but for whom the behavior represents future conflict.

A distinction may be made between basic sexual identity and gender-role preference. Thus, while many girls of seven to twelve may prefer participating in the more adventurous and autonomous activities of same-aged boys, they see themselves as female. They have adopted a masculine gender-role preference but maintain a basic female sexual identity. With adolescence, social circumstances change such that advantages accrue from being a girl, particularly if one is physically attractive. Thus, gender-role behavior becomes modified accordingly and tomboyishness typically disappears.

The task therefore becomes one of identifying tomboys who show not only a masculine gender-role preference but also a basic male sexual identity. Because tomboyishness usually arouses no concern in parents and society very few tomboys are brought for evaluation. Consequently, our understanding of the development of an enduring masculine identity in young girls is at a primitive level.

PARENTAL AND SELF-DESCRIPTIONS

In the following examples two girls are described—one by her parents and one in her own words—who appear to be more masculinely identified than the garden-variety tomboy.

Example 17-1

This mother and father are the parents of a nine-year-old girl who might be called a super-tomboy. She knows about sex-change operations and has said that she wants one. Her activities are those steadfastly avoided by the feminine boys described by their parents in Chapter 11.

Father: I think our biggest fear is this masculinity or tendencies toward masculinity, that could possibly, at a later date, develop into homosexuality. This is the biggest fear we both have.

Mother: Yes, I think that's the biggest. The wanting to be a boy, the not wanting to have anything to do with girls' toys, or playing like a girl, or being a girl; just wanting to be a boy.

Doctor: To what extent has she been doing this?

Father: Well, she seems to want to do the more active type of things. Toni does not like to sit quietly and play. She never has liked to play with dolls. And her dress, she'd rather wear pants than dresses. And her absolute insistence that when she grows up, she will become a boy.

Dr.: How long have you had these concerns?

Father: I would say we first became aware of it probably two and a half years ago, genuinely concerned within the last eighteen months.

Dr.: In looking back, what was the very earliest your daughter showed any indication of this behavior?

Father: Well, she has always been an active child. It was since she was born that she has been more or less this way. From a tiny baby she was never cuddly, where you could hold her. You would hold her a while, then she would become squirmish and active.

Contrast this feature with that typically described for the prefeminine male infant: considerable cuddliness.

Father: When I would come home and pick up her sister she would cling, where Toni never did this.

Dr.: What was her reaction to being held during the second year?

Mother: She didn't like it. She would actually push you away. If you held her on your lap, she would push her arms and get down and go get a toy to play with.

Father: I think later we probably pushed activity in encouraging her to roughhouse and do more active things than just cuddle. And we always felt she would outgrow it or settle down.

Dr. (to mother): What was it that *you* have noticed?

Mother: It became more pronounced when she went to school. She didn't want to wear dresses to school, and when she would come home and tell me what she did at school, she would always say she had been playing baseball or basketball or catch with the boys rather than hopscotch or whatever with the girls.

Dr.: Tell me about dressing, what type of clothing Toni prefers.

Father: Levi's.

Dr.: How far back does that go?

Mother: When she really started to want to wear boys' Levi's and boys' cutoff pants, I would say she was about five. She noticed the difference that girls just had little bands but boys' pants were snapped and had zippers, and she preferred those.

Dr.: And how have you felt about her preferring to wear boys' things?

Father: First, it never occurred to us. She seemed to stay a little cleaner, and it was easier to put her in those than fight with her, but in the past year or so it has been a source of concern to us, and we have tried to argue with her to wear other things. We have always more or less insisted that when she was going out, or something like that, that she dress as a girl, over and above her screams and hollers.

Dr. (to mother): And your approach to the dressing?

Mother: Well, when she goes out, she has to wear dresses. She fights and screams. She can't understand why she has to wear dresses. If I'm in capris and she is in a dress, she just pitches a fit. They have a rule at school that on a cloudy or rainy day you can wear pants, but I can't let her do that because she will carry it on every day of the school year. The other kids forget about it the next day and wear a dress, but she won't. She will want to wear pants the next day and the next day even if there is *one* cloud in the sky.

Dr.: How about toy preferences? Game preferences?

Father: Baseball, basketball, football. Anything that is active.

Dr.: How far back does this go?

Father: All the way. Even as a child, a small child, we would play active games with her because she seemed to enjoy them, and they were games more suited to her uncle and her father, so we played that way.

Dr.: How did you feel about this game preference at the beginning?

Mother: I don't think we even thought about it.

Father: No, it was just that she seemed to enjoy it, and we enjoyed it.

It was probably a lot more enjoyable for me when I got home to go out and throw a ball with her than it was to sit down and try to play dolls with her. And I think it was the same with her uncles when they would come over. It was easier for them. It was more familiar for them and for us to do this type of thing with her. It seemed to come natural. The fact that she seemed to enjoy it so much, everyone got a pleasure out of it. Lately we have tried to a certain degree to encourage her to play other types of games, but not with very much success. She spends a lot of time with her aunt, who is very active and is a physical education major, and my brother, who is athletically inclined.

Evidence exists here for reinforcement of the young girl's athletic interests. Rarely do the fathers of feminine boys describe such an avid interest in playing ball with their young sons. However, the extent to which children elicit or discourage such participation from parents, and not just the reverse, is difficult to cull from such reports.

Dr.: How about people outside the family? How did they react?
Father: Oh, "Toni's a tomboy." This type of thing.
Mother: Her aunt bought her a football for her birthday when she was six, and we had a party and some people were there and everybody was giving her dolls and things, and somebody asked her aunt why she bought a football and she said because that's what Toni wanted.
Dr.: What other things have you been concerned about?
Father: Well, about four months ago when Christine Jorgensen got back in the news, she talked about where she could go and have an operation to become a boy when she grew up. That, I think, was the first time that there was more than an activity thing with her. We did become a little deeper concerned that she now had in her mind that there was a way to become a boy. We had been telling her, "No matter what, you are going to grow up to be a girl. You're a girl and you *can't* change that." And now you get an argument because *"The guy on TV did!"*
Dr.: What does she say about that?
Mother: Just that "I can have an operation. I can have an operation. I can be a boy."
Dr.: What has been your approach to that statement?
Mother: That no, she can't just have an operation to become a boy.
Father: That when she got older we would try to explain it to her. I didn't try to get into it at that time at all with her, but she came off with it so—her attitude was so knowledgeable and determined at the time it was one of these conversations: "Well, Toni, you're going to be a girl when you grow up." "Oh, no. I can have an operation." She was very emphatic.

Modern surgical technology and public appearances by people who change sex pose a new problem in the management of the child dissatisfied with his or her gender role. It is far more difficult to convince a child who wants to change sex to learn to adapt to his or her role after a postoperative transsexual has been seen on the television screen.

Dr.: Does Toni play "house" along with all the other games?
Father: Yes, she does.
Mother: If her sister and them are playing in the house, if they are play-ing dress up she gets her dad's clothes out. Like yesterday they were playing dress up and she took one of her dad's shirts down and played with it. They were in there one day playing dress up, and I got out my wedding dress, and Toni wanted a suit of my husband's.
Father: Or when she identifies with a TV program she is the boy. She wants to be the boy. I think when we watch "The Brady Bunch" she is always the middle boy.
Dr.: How does she show that to you?
Father: She tells us. She says, "I'm him." Last night we watched "Willie the Yank," a three-part series about the Civil War, about a fifteen-year-old boy, and she's that boy. In fact, last night I asked her if the girl was pretty, the older girl coming in to relay the message that the Yanks were coming, and I said, "She's pretty, isn't she? She's helpful as a girl." And she said, "Yes, but I'm the boy." They playact, and she playacts the part of the father or the brother as actively as most kids portray the part of the mother.

In her fantasy life and role-playing she expresses character preferences just the opposite of those adopted by the feminine boy. Such prefer-ences seem to be a good reflection of a child's gender identity. A figure representing an additional aspect of a masculine girl's fantasy life is illustrated in Figure 17–1.

Dr.: What sort of stories does she prefer?
Mother: She brought home books she couldn't read on baseball, on basketball, airplanes.
Father: She brought a book which I *thoroughly enjoyed.* It was a picture history of aviation with the background—the identification of all types of airplanes. It was complicated enough for me to try to read it. She used to just sit there and look at the pictures. *World War I Aircraft* I think was the title of the book.

Example 17-2

This eleven-year-old girl describes intense feelings of wanting to be a boy, "ever since she was a kid." Having read an encyclopedia, she knows all about sex glands, transplants, bone growth, and treatment to guide the growth of facial hair.

Doctor: Why did you go see the other doctor?
Girl: Because I want to be a boy.

FIGURE 17–1.

A nine-year-old girl drew this picture of the central figure in her fantasy when she was asked to make up a story. The figure is a girl who wishes so hard to grow a "third leg" that one morning she awakens to find her wish come true.

Dr.: How old are you?

Girl: Eleven.

Dr.: How long have you wanted to be a boy?

Girl: It has been on and off for a long time.

Dr.: Are there times that you like to be a girl?

Girl: No.

Dr.: When was the very first time you remember saying to yourself, "I am a boy," or "I want to be a boy," or "I wish I'd grow up to become a boy"?

Girl: Well, when I was a *kid* I really didn't think about it much, you know. You just do the things you want to do. You don't think much. I was about ten or eleven. I always watched Roy Rogers and I always watched the Western movies. I liked to play with guns.

Dr.: What kind of kids did you like to play with?

Girl: I used to play with these two boys, Joey and David.

Dr.: Did you have any girls you used to play with when you were small?

Girl: No.

Dr.: How about when you were in school?

Girl: Well, I played with one a little bit. I can't remember her name. Lived down the street. Then there was one when I was about seven or eight or nine. Her name was Rose something or another.

Dr.: What kind of things did you like to play when you were in school?
Girl: I liked to play in the sandbox, and I remember going on the monkey bars.
Dr.: Were you different from the other girls at that time?
Girl: Yeah.
Dr.: How?
Girl: Well, I liked to climb trees and other things that they never did. I didn't really notice it then.
Dr.: Did you ever think about being a boy then?
Girl: I don't think so.
Dr.: What did you think you were?
Girl: Well, I really didn't think anything.
Dr.: But you knew you were a girl?
Girl: I guess I did, because I was raised that way.
Dr.: You were dressed like one and you had a girl's name.
Girl: Well, not really.
Dr.: What do you mean, not really?
Girl: My name is Terri, since I was real young they always called me that. Then when I went to school they said your name has to be Therese.
Dr.: Did they change it at school?
Girl: No.
Dr.: Who said it has to be Therese?
Girl: My mom, because that was my legal name. I've always been called Terri. My mom said she couldn't enroll me in school that way. No, maybe she did enroll me as Terri. I don't know.
Dr.: What do the teachers call you?
Girl: Terri.
Dr.: That sounds like a boy's name.
Girl: Yeah, I guess.
Dr.: Do you know any boys called Terry?
Girl: Yeah.

Both this girl, and the one described in Example 17–1 had been called by a gender-ambiguous name. Possibly, this influenced their self-concept as well as the manner in which others related to them. However, most of the adult female-to-male transsexuals who told their stories in Chapter 7 were *not* so named.

Dr.: As you were growing up, did your parents react to your interests? Doing boyish things more than girls' things?
Girl: They didn't say much. They just said, "Oh, she'll grow out of it."
Dr.: What did you think when you heard that? Did you think you would grow out of it?
Girl: I don't know. I knew I liked to do boy things, and I didn't think I would ever grow out of liking to do them, 'cause when you like to do things, it doesn't necessarily mean that you're going to grow out of it.
Dr.: When did you decide that you really wanted to be a boy?

Girl: Fifth or sixth grade.

Dr.: What happened then?

Girl: Well, I don't know. I liked doing things boys do, and my mom never liked me doing those things, but I still did them. And I always liked to build things. I used to build a lot of things. I don't know. I'm so puny, it sure didn't come out of the blue, but I don't know how it came. I thought about it off and on, and then I started thinking about it more and more until it stuck.

Dr:. It stuck?

Girl: Then I did something about it.

Dr.: What?

Girl: I changed my clothes. I wouldn't wear anything my mom would tell me to. I wear pants most of the time, and my mom said [mimicking mother], "You have to put a dress on," and I said I wouldn't put a dress on, so then I had to start wearing skirts and I didn't want to wear those either, but I was forced to.

Dr.: Then you started to really object to it?

Girl: Yeah. I said, "Mom, keep quiet. I can't stand being a girl so just be quiet and leave me alone, will you?"

Clothing preference and self-concept of a masculine girl are portrayed in Figure 17–2.

Dr.: Do you really want to be a boy?

Girl: Yeah.

Dr.: Why? What seems appealing to you about being a boy?

Girl: Well, being masculine. I guess I always wanted muscles and stuff. I've always played with balls and stuff like that, then the ball disappeared, and I didn't have any more balls, and I wanted to get one but my mom wouldn't let me, but finally I got one.

FIGURE 17–2.

A masculine eleven-year-old girl drew this sketch of her family. The arrow points to the figure representing herself.

One may reflect here on the symbolism behind this choice of terminology for describing some lacking ingredients of masculinity.

Dr.: What are other appealing things about being a man?

Girl: I don't know. I feel I am a boy because I like to do things like a boy. I act like a boy. I think like one.

Dr.: In what way?

Girl: Because I compare me to how my father thinks. I always did think like a boy. I always thought of getting a job, you know. I always thought of being an archaeologist, and I always just had that sort of attitude.

Dr.: Do you think you are a boy?

Girl: Well, I mean, in your mind, like, you know mentally. I think I'm a boy in a girl's body.

This is the identical summary statement describing their condition given by adult transsexuals.

Dr.: Do you think there has ever been anyone else like you before? Or do you think you're the first one?

Girl. I'm not the first one, but I don't think anyone felt as strong as me, and as distinct, you know.

Dr.: You think your mind is a boy's mind? And your body? How about your body?

Girl: Well, as far as I know it's a girl's.

Dr.: What about sexual feelings? Do you have crushes on people? Daydreams about sex, romantic feelings about people?

Girl: No, I never really liked that junk. The only one I really liked was Julie Andrews. She was an actress.

Dr.: What did you like about her?

Girl: I don't know. She was pretty; that's for sure, and I wrote a a letter to her when I was seven years old.

Dr.: What did you say?

Girl: Well, I asked her if she was married. I said I liked her. I also remember there was this lady named Sally. She's in my school group, and I always wanted to tell her she was real pretty, but I never got a chance to.

Dr.: Have you had crushes on girls? Romantic feelings that you wanted to hug them or kiss them?

Girl: I never had that with anybody. I never liked that stuff. Even since I was a kid I never liked that.

Dr.: How about your girlfriends your age? Do they have crushes on boys?

Girl: Yes.

Dr.: Have you ever had a crush on a boy or felt you wanted to neck with a boy?

Girl: No.

Dr.: Have you felt you wanted to neck with a girl?

Girl: No. At least, not *yet*.

Dr.: Think you might?
Girl: I don't know.

Here she anticipates possible homosexual attractions.

Dr.: If you do get sexual feelings or romantic feelings as you get older, do you think you would be attracted to girls or boys?
Girl: Well, it sure *won't* be a boy; that's for sure.
Dr.: Why do you say that?
Girl: I don't know. I think of them as an *equal*, not a superior or anything *different*.

Recall here the narrative in Chapter 4 in which an adult male-to-female transsexual reported an inability to be sexually attracted to females, for the analogous reason.

Dr.: In any of your dreams at night has there been any kind of love-making with anybody?
Girl: No, mine's always adventure. I always dream of flying. The only kind of daydreams I usually have is being a hero. I don't know, I've always liked to dream of that. I always dream I'm Superman, and I always used to watch "Superman" every day. Never missed it.

Study of childhood heroes and heroines again appears to be of considerable value in identifying the young child with a markedly atypical gender identity.

Dr.: How old were you when you began dreaming about Superman?
Girl: Oh, I always did. Seven or eight. I always did.
Dr.: Did you ever dream about yourself as a Superwoman?
Girl: No.
Dr.: Batgirl or anything like that?
Girl: I never dreamed of myself as a woman.
Dr.:. So, you say you want to be a boy. Well, what kind of medical help do you think is possible to become a boy?
Girl: What do you mean?
Dr.: Well, is it possible for someone like yourself to become a man?
Girl: I think so.
Dr.: How?
Girl: You get your breasts cut off. They take all these female insides out of you, and then a lot of things. If you are young enough they could possibly alter the growth of a person.
Dr.:. How?
Girl: Well, like transplant man's—what do you call those things up here? —the pituitary glands—transplant them and then kind of change your body. Like, the bones here in the hips are different, so sort of, like, move them where the man's are. And then when you grow, so they'll just keep growing, and you'll have a body like a man. We all have hair on our face, but we just need something to guide it.

Dr.: Is there anything else that would be necessary to be a man?

Girl: Well, I'd need a penis.

Dr.: Does that sound like it's medically possible to do?

Girl: Well, I don't know. All you'd have to do is close off the vagina, take a tube and put it up there—I don't know where—and then connect it to it.

Dr.: Where did you get this idea about what could be cut off, and stuff cut out from inside, and the vagina closed up? Where did you hear about it?

Girl: I read things, you know. I was curious, so I just looked up some things in the encyclopedia.

Dr.: But the thing that sounds the most difficult the way you describe it is building a penis that works like a real one.

Girl: I thought you would take it from a person who was dead.

Dr.: Well, the business about taking a penis of a dead person at this point in medical history is not possible.

Girl: I didn't think that was too possible. It was just an idea.

Dr.: The other things about the glands are also not possible.

Girl: They aren't? How come?

Dr.: Because you can't take them from one person and put them into another person.

Girl: How come?

Dr.: Because the body rejects it.

Because this girl felt that some of her life goals—a graduate degree, a career in archaeology—were attainable only if she were male, she was referred for treatment to a female psychiatrist, married, with children, herself an amateur archaeologist.

HOW THEY GET THAT WAY

As indicated earlier, there are fewer data available on the etiology of a male identity in females. Stoller, who has collected reflections from very masculine females seen in the UCLA Gender Identity Research Program, has synthesized them into a coherent story (Stoller, 1972). This cautiously advanced theory sees the common mechanism thus:

Each of the female transsexuals reports that as far back as she can remember she has felt very protective toward her mother, and had conscious thoughts of taking care of her as a husband would (but not with accompanying conscious sexual fantasies about her), and her mother has reciprocated, openly encouraging the transsexual-to-be to serve in this protective way. These mothers have been tired, long suffering, and sad or angry women, left too much alone by their husbands. In these families, just noted, the little girl moved into the vacuum created by her mother's sadness and unfilled by husband. Perhaps this child is the one chosen of all children because in infancy she strikes her parents as unfeminine in appearance or activity.

Identification theory would predict that a parent-child constellation resulting in a male identity in a female would be opposite to that associated with the emergence of a female identity in a male. Thus, one would predict a dominant father, a retiring or inadequate mother, more closeness between father and daughter, and selective reinforcement of masculine behavior. Here are reports by parents of the two preceding masculine girls describing their parent-child and marital relationships.

Example 17-3

This father had described his daughter, Example 17–1, as an active, uncuddly child. Later, in the girl's third year, her mother became unavailable as a result of hospitalizations for an emotional disorder.

Father: I didn't have the time with my second daughter to play with that I had with Toni, and I guess that is the only real difference on my part, and with my wife there was a lot of difference, of course, because she was ill with the second. [In Toni's third year.] She could not really put in the time. She was incapable at the time.

Doctor: To what extent were you able to spend time with Toni during the first year?

Father: Quite a bit. At that time I didn't have a lot of the obligations we have now, and would come home during the day, and I wouldn't go to work until late two days a week or so. I was available more in Toni's first year, and then as years went on I became more and more involved and had less time at home.

Dr.: What sort of things might you and Toni do together during the first year?

Father: Outside of normal rustle-tussle playing on the floor, not much of anything. The first year with a baby is fairly hard to do anything. I think we were mainly concerned with teaching her to walk. I spent a lot of time with that, walking her around the house, sitting on the floor rolling a ball back and forth.

Dr.: Compared to your second daughter, how would you estimate the time you had with Toni the first year?

Father: I had more time available for Toni for probably about the first three years of both their lives, because then I became consumed with my wife rather than the children. I was concerned about the children, but they were my secondary concern, and I would say between the two of them I was more mentally concerned with the second than I was with Toni, because I felt that Toni was older at three and a half and well established.

Dr.: What sort of things would you and Toni do during the second year?

Father: I think basically rough-and-tumble, wrestle. I think at that time she got her wagon and her trike, and there was never any real going-anywhere type thing.

Dr.: Compared to the second year of her sister's life, how would you rate the amount of time you had available?

Father. I had a lot more time available. [Later] it was taking more "mother" care of them that actual "father" care. Their mother was still in the hospital.

Dr.: During the years up to school—three, four, and five—to what extent were you able to spend time with her?

Father: Not very much. When she was three, her grandmother died, and all this broke loose with my wife, but we had special places we would go. I would take them in the afternoon to the park. She had her tree in the park that she would climb. We had our secret restaurant. They had the lousiest hot dog in town, but she liked it. These were our special places, and she would get a little bent out of shape when we would take her sister to her special places.

Example 17-4

This father blames his wife for his daughter's reluctance to identify as a female. The daughter's comments of wanting to be a boy were reported as Example 17-2.

Father: But there are so many things. You rack your brains why, and looking back—did this cause it?—did that cause it? Occasionally we blame each other, and occasionally we blame ourselves.

Doctor: If you have to blame each other or yourselves, what would you think it might have been?

Mother: I don't know if we blame each other in regards to things we did with her or—the only thing is, I yell quite a bit and this is one of the things I think my husband—I mean, I kind of have a temper, and I expect things from the girls, and a lot of times I kind of get on my horse and I really let loose.

Dr.: Over what kinds of things?

Father: Name it.

Mother: Lots of things.

Father: Lots of things.

Mother: I've always felt very close to her and I think my husband—

Father: I think she's expressed a certain preference for me.

Mother: Has she?

Father: I think primarily it's because of the hollering more than anything else. Although my wife does quite a bit of hollering and maybe I do, I'm more of the type that keeps things within me and rather than let everything pour out at once. My wife is the other way around, pours more out than keeps in. The only theory I have is the constant hollering.

Dr.: Why would that make her want—

Father: I don't know.

Mother: I think my husband came up with the idea why she doesn't want to be a woman. She doesn't want to be like *me.* In other words, she thinks I'm that hateful and I'm that horrible she doesn't want to be like me. Which made me feel *very good.*

Because there are but two examples here, this paucity of data will be supplemented by the childhood recollections of some female-to-male transsexuals reported in Chapter 7.

Example 17-5

Female-to-Male Transsexual: My mother wasn't too loving as far as that goes, but she said there was no trying to cuddle me. That type of thing that the rest of the kids do.

Doctor: What do you mean "Your mother isn't too loving"?

F-M TS: My mother is a very cold woman. In fact, this psychiatrist explained that she was narcissistic and that she didn't have any mother love at all. A psychiatrist tried to help me to understand her so that I could get along with her, but he recommended at that time that I go live with my father.

Dr.: What about your dad?

F-M TS: I liked him. I had a real great rapport for him, actually without anything being spoken. There was no overt affection in our family, either on his side or Mother's side. In fact, if Mother would try to kiss him in front of us kids, he'd say, "Not in front of the kids," but he was a very warm guy and a very personable guy, but he drank on the weekends. She got him out of every kind of trouble he ever got into. She'd always rescue him. I liked him. But Mother was rough on us. She had a nervous problem. She had several nervous breakdowns. Later, when I was grown up, she told me they had a sexual problem.

Dr.: What sort of sexual problem?

F-M TS: She just couldn't reach a climax. It was Mother's upbringing or something. She said it was dirty and this and that. She liked it, but she just couldn't get over the hump, and she said that my father wasn't coopera-tive. They tried everything they could, but it just didn't work. She used to beat the devil out of us because it relieved her tension from that. Of course, I was the brunt. I'd been the brunt of a lot of things in the family because I look exactly like my father, and my mannerisms and everything are just like my father. I even pretty much think like him.

Example 17-6

Doctor: What makes up your family besides yourself?

Female-to-Male Transsexual: Well, I lived with my grandmother and my aunt, and my mother is an alcoholic. I don't live with her. When I was three months old, I got sick and my grandmother took me.

Dr.: What was wrong with you?

F-M TS: I'm not really sure. I was in really bad health, I guess, and my mother was neglecting me.

Dr.: Do you remember her being an alcoholic?

F-M TS: Ever since I can remember, she's been.

Dr.: What would she be like?

F-M TS: Always constantly drinking, fighting, except for when I was a little bit older, we used to not mind it if she drank, because if she drank she was a lot friendlier and a lot of fun to be around. When she couldn't have it, she got pretty mean. There were always lots of parties. Lots of guys around the house.

Dr.: Did you know your dad when you were very little?

F-M TS: Not really. From what I understand he was real nice before he met her, except he was one of these kind that would do anything for her, and she would walk all over him.

Dr.: What sort of a man was your grandfather?

F-M TS: He was very kind. For a while he was a logger, and I used to go out with him. He liked the outdoors very much. Usually on a ranch or when he had the woods, I used to go out with him an awful lot. I know they could hardly keep me in to clean up my room long enough. In high school I would go home and do my homework, and then be gone with him outside. If they gave me something to do outside I didn't care, but anything to do inside I couldn't stand it.

Example 17-7

Female-to-Male Transsexual: Well, my parents were divorced when I was about four and my brother two. My dad wanted my brother only when they got divorced, but my mother didn't want to separate the two of us, so my father had to have both of us or none of us, so he took both of us.

Doctor: He wanted your brother?

F-M TS: Only my brother. He didn't want me. When my brother was born, I pushed him down the stairs. Once I cut his head with a razor blade because I was jealous of him.

Dr.: What kind of woman was your mother?

F-M TS: She's a begrudged woman. I can tell you that much. You do something wrong by her, and she'll remember it the rest of her life. You could never sit down and have a heart-to-heart talk with her.

Dr.: How does this compare with your father?

F-M TS: Well, with my dad I could sit down and talk to him, and he'd give me an opinion. But then he'll also say that it isn't his place to tell me this or that; it's Mother's place to do it, and I told him, "Right now you are mother *and* father to us." I didn't like my brother because he was younger and he got more attention than I did, but in a way my dad showed even attention to both my brother and I. My mother distributed love among us, but it was my stepmother I was really jealous of, because she showed more attention to my brother than to myself, yet my dad evened out his love for us.

What is lacking in the breadth of clinical material described here is compensated for by the speed with which the etiology of a male identity in a female looms clear. Give a female child a male-derivative name, provide a stable warm father, make mother an unpleasant or emotionally unavailable woman, and reinforce rough-and-tumble play. As stressed in Chapter 15 describing the routes to a female identity in a male, theorizing is simple with a few cases. Unfortunately, our thirst for understanding must first be partially quenched by considerably more subjects. Ultimately, as the numbers grow, the degree of complexity may approach that behind male femininity, previously "clarified" in Chapter 15.

18

PROBLEMS FOR
FUTURE RESEARCH

The foregoing material has converged from several vantage points toward the origins of masculinity and femininity. We began by seeing that people today labeled "sissies" and "tomboys" are not unique to this culture or this period in history. We moved to an examination of a sample of the last generation's "sissies" and "tomboys" who did not "outgrow it." From their current life situations, as described by themselves and their most intimate companions, we heard how pervasive is their cross-gender identity. We tried to detect from their recollections of childhood a means of identifying children currently experiencing what they experienced a decade or more ago. Our focus then fixed on these children and their parents. As descriptions of very feminine young boys and very masculine girls unfolded, the intriguing quality of the nature of their behavior never quite eclipsed the more fundamental issue: how did they get that way?

Where are we in answering that question? Where must we go? From the clinical data outlined in Chapter 15, it would seem that a variety of early-life circumstances may be *associated with* feminine role emergence in a male. The relative potency of *any* of these variables, whether they need to appear *in common* to exert their influence, and whether some are *potentiating* in combination, or merely *additive*, must be clarified by additional research. What is the etiologic power of exclusively female playmates from years one to three *plus* an overprotective mother *versus* father-absence and being cross-dressed by sister?

Assuming that many of the variables enumerated in Chapter 15, alone or in varying combinations, influence the emergence of feminine behavior in boys, we may still ask which affect cross-sexed *identity*, and which affect cross-gender *behavior*. Better measures are needed of identity, as distinct from activity preference. Perhaps, for example, it will be found that the role usually taken in fantasy games, and the sex of people characteristically drawn in pictures are better reflections of identity than playmate and toy preference. We need to discriminate those boys whose basic identity is male but who prefer girlish activities (perhaps because they perceive boyish behavior as threatening), from boys whose primary identity is female and whose behavior logically flows from that source. The former children would be those theoretically more responsive to environmental change as it should be easier to find appealing activities within the competence of children than to change their basic identity.

The task of discriminating basic identity from role preference may be facilitated by the fact that the boys in this study are not all feminine in the same way. Some directly state they are or want to be girls; others do not. Some talk about wanting their penis gone; others do not. Some cross-dress regularly; others do not. Some play only with girls; others can also relate to boys. Future observations on these subgroups of boys coupled with their responses to attempts at modifying their behavior may help separate enduring identities from temporary activity preferences.

A comparable situation exists with tomboys. For most masculine-behaving girls, basically identified as female, adolescence provides heightened social reward for being female *and feminine*. Thus behavior changes. Better ways are needed therefore to distinguish those tomboys who will "grow out of it" from those who are on their way to becoming transsexuals or masculine female homosexuals. By so doing, we may also understand the origins of an enduring masculine identity in a female.

The boys in this study are all clearly "feminine." But, how do we tell the prehomosexual or pretransvestic boy who is masculine? Though we are learning to identify boys with an atypical gender role preference, we do not know how to tell the masculine, rough-and-tumble, eight-year-old who at thirteen will find masturbatory fantasies exclusively occupied by males or facilitated by women's clothes. Perhaps analysis of childhood daydreams would be helpful. One boy, for example, not reported in the foregoing chapters, became aware of his homosexual orientation at thirteen. Formerly, at six, he had imagined himself overpowered by male wrestlers viewed on television. His erotic fantasies at thirteen focused on being dominated by larger males. Another patient, an adult female homosexual, also not described earlier, had been feminine as a young girl. Her childhood romantic fantasies were of being a knight on a white charger rescuing a beautiful maiden. Can such daydreams predict something about later romantic and sexual fantasy? Additionally, are there physiologic responses during prepubertal years that would be useful predictive measures? Would penile erection in a young boy in response to pictures of nude females and males hint at later patterns of sexual arousal?

What is the relationship between prepubertal gender-role behavior and postpubertal genital behavior? Why should a very feminine-behaving eight year old have a higher than average probability of being homosexually oriented during adulthood? Is it merely because he has been socialized in a feminine way and most feminine persons (typically females) are sexually attracted to males? But what of the nonfeminine boys who will also be homosexual? Furthermore, what happens to the compelling wish to be a girl in some boys who later mature into masculine homosexuals? One of the boys John Money and I studied in 1958 had at age five prayed nightly to be changed into a girl and had repeatedly improvised feminine attire. Now he is a homosexual male *without* any conscious desire to live as a woman or dress as one. When he has sexual relations with another male, he does not fantasy himself as being female. What happened to the earlier feminine identity?

Why is it that most of the feminine boys who are brought to clinics do not become transsexual, since their behavior is analogous to that retrospectively reported by adult transsexuals? Is it merely a probability basis (only thousands of children become transsexual but millions become homosexual)? Or is it the impact of the attention paid to the child's early behavior? Consider the focus of concern of the parents who bring feminine boys for clinic evaluation. They have become concerned over the *outward* manifestations of an atypical sexual identity—their sons' gender-role preference. Their attitudes have changed from those of acceptance or encouragement. Possibly, in consequence of parental disapproval, the child's gender-role behavior—dressing preferences, role-taking, and toy selection, may change. However, the parents (and researcher/therapists) have much less awareness of early behaviors which are specific harbingers of subsequent homosexuality. Thus, if the ingredients are being set into place for gender-role preference and genital sexuality, environmental manipulation may become directed toward one component only.

If such is the case, one might expect that very feminine boys whose behavior arouses concern at some time in childhood will more likely mature into masculine, homosexually oriented adults. By contrast, those boys whose parents do not attempt to discourage the feminine role behavior might be more likely to retain a cross-gender role preference *as well as* a homosexual orientation—transsexualism. Rarely, if ever, were the adult transsexuals in this study brought by their parents to a clinic while they were still children. The above is speculative, but, from such speculation testable hypotheses may evolve.

A major failing of much research into intrafamily relationships leading to certain types of behavior in children has been the inability to demonstrate why only *one* sibling falls "victim" to the behavioral oddity under study. If, for example, passive or absent fathers and overbearing mothers are responsible for producing behavior X in a male child, why don't *all* the male siblings become "afflicted" with X? None of the feminine boys in this study had feminine brothers. Why not? In some cases, such as the family reported in Chapter 14, parents describe how two brothers were treated in remarkably different ways, with the mother devoting time and attention to the prefeminine brother and the father to the premasculine brother. But this is not so in every case. Parents sometimes report that the prefeminine boy was different from the *very beginning*. Was he? Or, rather was it the parents' *attitude* toward that child, from the very beginning, that distorted perceptions and influenced the parent-child interaction? In this way a perceived difference may become a self-fulfilling prophecy.

Office interviews, contrived interactional situations to analyze marital roles, and psychologic testing (the usual strategies of the researcher) are far removed from typical daily family events. Objective appraisals of parental behaviors in their natural habitat are needed. Researchers need also travel into the home to live with families, not for hours, but for days. The myriad subtle ways that parents, siblings, and peers influence children's behavior, and the ways in which parents interact, need to be observed *in vivo*.

Consider a routine daily event as one example: Father's return home
at the end of the work day. First, how is anticipation of his return
shaped during the day? Is it "Wait until Daddy gets home, you'll get
yours!" or "Here I am working my fingers to the bone in a hot kitchen
while your father sits in an air-conditioned office"; or "Won't it be nice
when Daddy comes home so you can both go out and play a while
before dinner?" Second, what happens when Daddy does return? How
is his re-entry into the home greeted? Does mother interrupt her activity
to meet him at the door and impart some physical gesture of welcome?
Do the children interrupt their play or television viewing? What is the
correlation between the mother's response and those of the children?
Third, what effect on the family milieu is brought about by father's
presence?

Predictive studies are needed. If certain family variables appear to
cluster as the search for etiology continues, would similar families,
deemed likely to produce a feminine boy with their next son, do just
that? Could the extent of masculinity and femininity in both boys and
girls be predicted for the children of just-married couples using data
being collected in current studies? Furthermore, families that theoretically should be highly likely to yield a feminine boy but that do *not*
should come under close study to find out "what went right." For
example, a population of masculine boys with female siblings should be
found who have been separated from their fathers before the second
year, have had but minimal residual contact with him, and whose
mothers have not remarried. Whence their masculinity?

Cultural differences in child-rearing and patterns of gender identity
also offer great research promise. The study described here needs to
be repeated in cultures with different basic family patterns, and with
different expressions of childhood masculinity and femininity. Anthro-
pologic data (Chapter 1) have documented the *existence* of gender-
deviant behavior in many societies, but not its *etiology*. Contrasting
factors producing cross-gender identity and behavior (of whatever types)
in markedly different cultures would be an outstanding addition to
understanding psychosexual differentiation in the *human being*, not
merely the southern Californian.

Indeed, cultural attitudes pervade much of the process of the work
described here. They influence how patients see themselves and affect
decisions about treatment intervention. Much of the distress these people experience is the consequence of the culture in which they live.
What if the way in which this society views "masculinity" in men and

women and "femininity" in women and men continues to change? What if the social consequences of evolving in an atypical life-style were radically modified? Would the motivation for sex-change surgery be as great for males if the society were fully tolerant of their deviant sexuality? Speculation has it that one reason there are fewer females who choose (or need to resort to) surgical and hormonal sex change is the less harsh societal opprobrium with which their behavior is met.

Western society of the early 1970s is characterized as moving in a unisex direction, with blurring of sex roles. If social pressures on males for aggressive competitiveness were to diminish, with less dichotomy of boy-girl behavior, would this reduce the stress on some boys who prefer less competitive feminine activities? If so, then one might expect to find less gravitation by these boys toward female companions and those behavioral attributes that remain culturally feminine. Perhaps too, adult males with greater latitude for cross-sexed expression will not feel as compelling a need for surgically induced change. A question to be answered, though, would be the degree to which the desire for genital change in an adult male is derived secondarily from social sanctions against homosexuality or femininity, or springs primarily from a female identity. If from the former, requests for surgery might be related to the extent to which the culture becomes more tolerant. If from the latter, harsh anatomic incompatibility with one's self-concept would still remain.

The chapters on treatment intervention into the lives of adults and children with sexual identity conflicts, for the reasons stated earlier, focused on helping these people adjust to their society. What can be done to help society adjust to these people? Can the behavioral scientist also be effective as a social activist? Can the researcher/therapist modify societal attitudes so that atypical sexual life-styles which do not infringe on the liberties of others do not cause conflict for the atypical individual? Can this society move closer to the cultural acceptance of variants in gender-role expression demonstrated by other cultures described in Chapter 1?

Can we expect cultural biases to erode before the press of scientific data or be erased with the stroke of the legal pen? Can we extirpate the cultural disparity between males and females which contributes so heavily to the sexual identity conflict experienced by these patients? The interface between one's role as behavioral scientist, therapist, and facilitator of social change is a labyrinthine plexus. It presents a challenge which cannot be ignored.

Thus far, environmental experiences contributing to sexual identity have held center stage. However, all babies are not created equal. Observations in nurseries reveal that children are not the same at birth, not only in physical appearance, but also in behavior. Some research already points to inborn influences on later sexuality. Currently the most provocative signpost is the linkage between prenatal male hormone levels and postnatal masculine activity. These data were summarized in Chapter 3 with the accounts of female monkeys and humans exposed to excessive male hormone before birth who were more "tomboyish" than normal females, and of males exposed to excessive female hormone who appeared less aggressive and athletic than typical males.

While hormones may influence the developing brain in modifying the ultimate expression of sexual identity, it may be that their role is that of the supporting cast rather than a principal player. Possibly a nonspecific input such as cuddliness or aggressivity is hormone-influenced so that parent-child and peer-child relations are affected. As children shape parental behavior, and not just the reverse, mothers deriving more satisfaction from holding responsive children will tend to hold them more, and perhaps cultivate within them less autonomy. Indeed, the study noted in Chapter 2 that found thirteen-month-old female infants staying closer to their mother than boys, had also found that the female infants were held more at five months of age. Whether the increased degree of holding was due to the mother's greater desire to hold a girl or to the girl's greater responsivity to being held is not clear. It is also unclear whether greater differences for cuddliness exist *between* boys and girls or *among* children of either sex. It may be significant that the majority of families in our research described their prefeminine boy as having been more cuddly than *any* of his siblings, male or female. Whether this is an objective assessment and constitutes a first ingredient brought into the system by the infant to produce a unique mother-child relationship *or* is a product of the mother's bias, which is *itself* the first ingredient, is an additional question. During later childhood, possibly also as a product of an inborn difference, boys' aggressivity levels may vary so that father-son interaction and peer-group socialization are influenced. A low level of aggressivity may result in a boy's accommodating more easily to the activities and companionship of women and girls. "Boys play too rough!" is a familiar cry of the feminine boy.

Until recently, assessment of prenatal hormone levels in the human bordered on science fiction. However, current obstetrical procedures that allow removal of samples of amniotic fluid during pregnancy, coupled with exquisitely sensitive hormonal assays, introduce the possibility of correlating prenatal levels in the fetus with postnatal behavior in the child. Additionally, the mother's plasma levels during pregnancy may be measured. Are her hormone levels while carrying one son different than while carrying another? It might be rewarding to study children with high and low intrauterine androgen exposure on such parameters as neonatal cuddliness and activity, early childhood aggressivity, and later gender-role preferences. It will also be rewarding to examine the feminine and masculine children in the current study, as they enter puberty and adolescence, for levels of gonadal hormones.

Skeptics of a prenatal hormonal influence on postnatal behavior may well ask, "What does the hypothalamus know about firemen's hats and trucks?" Unquestionably, culturally imposed learning must play a role in shaping behavior. Yet there are hints that even some toy and activity preferences may not be entirely learned. Consider doll play and infant care, more commonly shown by girls and feminine boys (Chapter 13). Are these entirely cultural accidents? Could there be here any heritage from subhuman species?

Observations of monkeys have yielded new reflections on the genesis of some aspects of human behavior. With respect to interest in infants, great differences appear at a strikingly early age between male and female monkeys. Infant females, who are but nine months old and themselves not yet weaned, show a considerable interest in newborns. By contrast, males of *any* age rarely show maternal behavior toward a newborn infant (Lancaster, 1971). These sex differences appear to be innate and not modeled after adult behavior. Juvenile monkeys raised without the opportunity to witness their mothers or *any* adult female show these same differences (Chamove et al., 1967). The quantitative difference in maternal holding of human male and female infants also has a parallel in the nonhuman. Young female monkeys too are held more by their mothers, with greater physical autonomy asserted by males (Jenset et al., 1968; Mitchell, 1968; Rosenblum, 1974). Thus, there is considerable value in studying nonhuman primates to gain a broader perspective from which to view roots of human mother-infant behavior.

Other pithy questions remain. What will be the sexual identity of children raised by two persons of the same genetic sex, when one is a postoperative transsexual? What middle-life crises a decade or two later await those young adults who undergo sex-change surgery? Is there a "menopausal" dilemma for the postoperative transsexual? . . . But enough.

Let us neither despair from the weight of unanswered questions nor revel in the extent of our current knowledge. Rather, let us quietly and systematically press on with our research.

EPILOGUE

It would be unfair to leave the reader with a sense of frustration engendered by having just contemplated a train of as yet unanswered questions. That frustration (and its accompanying excitement) is the lot of the researcher.

The foregoing questions ought not be marshalled to bolster a philosophy of nihilism. We *have* been accumulating knowledge into the origins of those behaviors which constitute sexual identity. Theories and strategies for studying these origins abound. At first glance, they seem disparate and perhaps incompatible: the observations made during the neonatal period by the human ethologist, the symbolic formulations of the psychoanalyst, the learning theory principles of the psychologist, and the laboratory animal models of the psychobiologist. Yet, these varied tongues are quite amenable to translation into a common language. Where not translatable, they are complementary and not incompatible.

As each research strategy converges toward the centrum of human sexual identity, let us demand of each of its proponents that their vocabulary speaks to us all. Furthermore, let us label our theories for what they are: hypotheses to be *tested*. They must be formulated in ways that *are* testable, and must be freely abandoned should they fade under the glare of scientific scrutiny. Let us be immodest while formulating questions but bashful while stating answers. The process of inquiry should erode the confidence of the dogmatist while igniting the curiosity of the eclectic.

Theories demand the evolution of research strategies. We have presented ours for an understanding of the origins of sexual identity. We speak with dramatically atypical adults and inquire about their parents and childhood. We are not spent by the distance between the adulthood reflection and the childhood experience. Rather, we look for children whose behavior approximates those reflections. We study these children, and their parents, directly.

Theories also demand the development of research tools. Toward this end, we have made progress. We ask parallel questions of parents with feminine or masculine boys and assess how they see themselves and their children. We talk with the children in conflict over their sexual identity and hear their perceptions of the nature of that conflict. We develop and administer psychological tests that reveal differences between feminine boys and masculine boys and compare feminine boys with typical girls.

However, while our academic lust for knowledge proceeds, we researchers cannot ignore the distress of those we study. People whose sexual identity is markedly atypical experience considerable conflict. Sensitive to these persons' conflicts, we cannot avoid the challenge of that plight. With adults, we accede, in selected cases, to their desperate pleadings to bring the outer body into closer conformity with the inner identity. With children, we are pained by the distress already experienced and disturbed further by the prospects for its augmentation in ensuing years.

In consequence of hormonal and surgical treatment with adults, we have, at times, incurred the wrath of other health professionals who see this intervention as treating merely the symptom while ignoring the underlying cause. Yet medical science has so far not yielded a more effective means to reduce their suffering.

In consequence of psychological intervention with children, we have, at times, incurred the wrath of those who assert that children should be free to adopt whatever behaviors they wish, whether the culture defines them as gender-appropriate or inappropriate, providing they do no one else harm. This is truly an ideal to be strived for. Yet, these children hurt. We hope we can reduce their current pain and permit them a wider range of social options in the future. We hope they will be less driven toward behavior which the culture continues to stigmatize.

Concurrently the researcher turned clinician wears yet another hat. It is that of educator and mediator of social change. He works for revision of public laws and private attitudes so that persons of any age whose sexual identity is atypical may live in dignity.

In closing, let us return one final time, to our sample of feminine boys. What will be their sexual behavior during adulthood? Follow-up assessments on these children will permit correlation of many specific preadolescent behavioral and family features with long-term outcome. It should permit better understanding of what promotes and evolves into transsexualism, transvestism, homosexuality, and the most common subgroup of all, heterosexuality.

REFERENCES

Among these references will be found both those works cited in the text and those works recommended for further reading on the subjects of each chapter.

1
HISTORICAL AND CROSS-CULTURAL SURVEY

Bastian, A. 1860. Der mensch in der geschichte. Cited in Crawley, E. *The mystic rose*, 1927.

Benjamin, H., and Masters, R. 1964. A new kind of prostitute. *Sexology* 30:446–48.

Bloch, I. 1933. *Anthropological studies on the strange sexual practices of all races and all ages.* New York: Anthropological Press.

Bogoras, W. 1907. *The Chukchee religion.* Memoirs of the American Museum of Natural History, vol. XI. Leiden: E. J. Brill.

Brown, D. 1961. Transvestism and sex-role inversion. In *Encyclopedia of Sexual Behavior*. A. Ellis and A. Abarbanel, eds. New York: Hawthorne.

Bulliet, C. 1928. *Venus Castina: Famous female impersonators, celestial and human.* New York: Covici, Friede.

Carstairs, G. 1956. Hinjra and Jiryan: Two derivatives of Hindu attitudes to sexuality. *Brit. J. of Med. Psychol.* 29:128–138.

Crawley, E. 1927. *The mystic rose.* New York: Boni and Liveright.

Creekmore, H., tr. 1963. *The satires of Juvenal.* New York: Mentor/New American Library. Passage from "Against Hypocritical Queens" reprinted by permission of the publisher.

Czaplicka, M. 1914. *Aboriginal Siberia.* Oxford: Clarendon Press.

De Magalhaens, Gandavo, P. Histoire de la province de Sancta Cruz, que nous nommons ordinairement le Brazil, cited in Crawley, 1927.

De Savitsch, E. 1958. *Homosexuality, transvestism and change of sex.* London: William Heinemann Medical Books.

Devereux, G. 1937. Institutionalized homosexuality of the Mohave Indians. *Human Biol.* 9:508–27.

Dubois, C. 1969. Transsexualism and cultural anthropology. *Gynecologie Pratique.* 20:431–40.

Durrell, L. 1962. *Pope Joan.* London: World Distributors (Manchester).

Ford, C. 1931. University of California Publications in American Archaeology and Ethnology, vol. 28.

Frazer, J. G. 1955. *The golden bough*, pt. IV, vol. 2. London: Macmillan.

Gifford, E. 1933. University of California Publications in American Archaeology and Ethnology, vol. 31.

Gilbert, O. 1926. *Men in woman's guise.* London: John Lane.

Graves, R. 1955. *The Greek myths.* Baltimore: Penguin Books.

Grinnell, G. 1923. *The Cheyenne Indians.* New Haven: Yale University Press.

Hammond, W. 1887. *Sexual impotence in the male and female*. Detroit: George S. Davis.

Herodotus, cited by Krafft-Ebing, *Psychopathia sexualis*, 1931.

Hippocrates. *Air, water and environment*, cited by Hammond, 1887.

Howitt, A. 1844. Some Australian ceremonies of initiation. *JAI* 13:448. Cited in Crawley, 1927.

Joshi, P. 1886–89. On the evil eye in the Konkan. *J. of Anthropol. and Sociol.* 1:123, cited in Crawley, 1927.

Krafft-Ebing, R. 1931. *Psychopathia sexualis*. Brooklyn: Physicians and Surgeons Book Co.

Langsdorf, G. Voyages and travels in various parts of the world during the years 1803–07, cited in Crawley, 1927.

Leach, M., ed. 1949. *Standard dictionary of folklore, mythology and legend*. New York: Funk and Wagnalls.

Masters, R. 1962. *Eros and evil*. New York: The Julian Press.

———. Effeminacy and the homosexual, unpublished.

Nixon, E. 1964. The Chevalier d'Eon: A case of double identity. *History Today* 14:126–34.

Powers, S. *Tribes of California*, 1877, cited in Crawley, 1927.

Shortt, J. 1873. The Kajas of Southern India. *JAI* 2:406, cited in Crawley, 1927.

Siddigui, T. and Rehman, M. 1963. Eunuchs of India and Pakistan. *Sexology* 29:824–26.

Spier, L. 1933. *Yuman tribes of the Gila River*. Chicago: University of Chicago Press.

Westermarck, E. 1917. *The origin and development of the moral ideas*, vol. 2. London: Macmillan.

Yawger, N. 1940. Transvestism and other cross-sex manifestations. *J. Nerv. Men. Dis.* 92:41–48.

2

PSYCHOLOGIC THEORIES

Bell, R., and Costello, N. 1964. Three tests for sex differences in tactile sensitivity in the newborn. *Biol. Neonat.* 7:335–47.

Biller, H. 1968. A multi-aspect investigation of masculine development in kindergarten age boys. *Genet. Psychol. Monogr.* 78:89–138.

———. 1969. Father absence, maternal encouragement and sex role development in kindergarten age boys. *Child Develop.* 40:539–46.

Bridges, W., and Birns, B. 1963. Neonates' behavioral and autonomic responses to stress during soothing. In *Recent Advances in Biological Psychiatry*, ed. J. Wortis 5:1–6.

Colley, T. 1959. The nature and origins of psychological sexual identity. *Psychol. Rev.* 66:165–77.

Fenichel, O. 1945. *The psychoanalytic theory of neurosis*. New York: Norton.

Freud, S. 1935. *A general introduction to psychoanalysis*. New York: Boni and Liveright.

Goldberg, S., and Lewis, M. 1969. Play behavior in the year-old infant: Early sex differences. *Child Develop.* 40:21–31.

Hampson, J., and Hampson, J. 1961. The ontogenesis of sexual behavior in man. In *Sex and internal secretions*, vol. 2, ed. W. Young. Baltimore: Williams and Wilkins.

Hetherington, E. 1965. A developmental study of the effects of the sex of the dominant parent on sex role preference, identification and imitation in children. *J. Person. and Soc. Psychol.* 2:188–94.

———. 1966. Effects of paternal absence on sex-typed behaviors in Negro and white preadolescent males. *J. Person. and Soc. Psychol.* 4:87–91.

Horney, K. 1933. The denial of the vagina. In *Psychoanalysis and female sexuality*, ed. H. Ruitenbeck. 1966. New Haven: College and University Press.

Kagan, J. 1958. The concept of identification. *Psychol. Rev.* 65:296–305.

Kagan, J., and Lewis, M. 1965. Studies of attention in the human infant. *Merrill-Palmer Quarterly* 11:95–127.

Kleeman, J. 1971a. The establishment of core gender identity in normal girls, I. *Arch. Sex. Behav.* 1:103–16.

———. 1971b. The establishment of core identity in normal girls, II. *Arch. Sex. Behav.* 1:117–29.

Kohlberg, L. 1966. A cognitive-developmental analysis of children's sex-role concepts and attitudes. In *The development of sex differences*, ed. E. Maccoby. Stanford: University Press.

Kohlberg, L., and Zigler, E. 1967. The impact of cognitive maturity on the development of sex-role attitudes in the years 4 to 8. *Genet. Psychol. Monogr.* 75:89–165.

Lewis, M.; Kagan, J.; and Kalafat, J. 1966. Patterns of fixation in the young infant. *Child Develop.* 37:331–41.

Lynn, D. 1959. A note on sex differences in the development of masculine and feminine identification. *Psychol. Rev.* 66:126–35.

Mead, M. 1949. *Male and female*. New York: New American Library.

———. 1961. Cultural determinants of sexual behavior. In *Sex and internal secretions*, vol. 2, ed. W. Young. Baltimore: Williams and Wilkins.

Mischel, W. 1966. A social-learning view of sex differences in behavior. In *The development of sex differences*, ed. E. Maccoby. Stanford: Stanford University Press.

Money, J.; Hampson, J.; and Hampson, J. 1955. An examination of some basic sexual concepts: The evidence of human hermaphroditism. *Bull. Johns Hopkins Hosp.* 97:301–19.

———. 1957. Imprinting and the establishment of gender role. *Arch. Neurol. Psychiat.* 77:333–36.

Moss, H. 1967. Sex, age, and state as determinants of mother-infant interaction. *Merrill-Palmer Quarterly* 13:19–36.

Nisbett, R., and Gurwitz, S. 1970. Weight, sex, and the eating behavior of human newborns. *J. Comp. and Physiol. Psychol.* 73:245–53.

Panborn, R. 1959. Influence of hunger on sweetness preferences and taste thresholds. *Amer. J. Clin. Nutrition* 7:280–87.

Rebelsky, F., and Hanks, C. 1971. Fathers' verbal interaction with infants in the first three months of life. *Child Develop.* 42:63–68.

Rosenblum, L. Forthcoming 1974. Sex differences, environmental complexity and mother-infant relations. *Arch. Sex. Behav.*

Sears, R. 1965. Development of gender role. In *Sex and behavior*, ed. F. Beach. New York: John Wiley.

Sears, R.; Rau, L.; and Alpert, R. 1965. *Identification and child rearing*. Stanford: Stanford University Press.

Stern, G.; Caldwell, B.; Hersher, L.; Lipton, E.; and Richmond, J. 1969. A factor analytic study of the mother-infant dyad. *Child Develop.* 40:163–81.

Stoller, R. 1968. *Sex and gender: On the development of masculinity and femininity*. New York: Science House.

———. 1969. Parental influences in male transsexualism. In *Transsexualism and sex reassignment*, ed. R. Green and J. Money. Baltimore: Johns Hopkins Press.

Thoman, E.; Leiderman, P.; and Olson, J. 1972. Neonate-mother interaction during breast-feeding. *Develop. Psychol.* 6:110–18.

Thompson, C. 1942. "Penis envy" in woman. In *Psychoanalysis and female sexuality*, ed. H. Ruitenbeck. 1966. New Haven: College and University Press.

Todd, G., and Palmer, B. 1968. Social reinforcement of infant babbling. *Child Develop.* 39:591–96.

Watson, J. 1966. Operant conditioning of visual fixation in 14 week old infants:

A reward modality by sex difference. Paper read at American Psychological Association Annual Meeting. Published in *Develop. Psychol.* 1:508–16, 1969.

Whiting, J.; Kluckhohn, R.; and Anthony, A. 1958. The function of male initiation ceremonies at puberty. In *Readings in Social Psychology,* ed. E. Maccoby et al. New York: Holt, Rinehart, and Winston.

Yarrow, L., and Goodwin, M. 1965. Some conceptual issues in the study of mother-infant interaction. *Amer. J. Orthopsychiat.* 35:473–81.

3

BIOLOGIC STUDIES

Baker, H., and Stoller, R. 1968. Sexual psychopathology in the hypogonadal male. *Arch. Gen. Psychiat.* 18:361–434.

Ball, J. 1968. A case of hair fetishism, transvestism, and organic cerebral disorder. *Acta. Psychiat. Scandinav.* 44:249–54.

Bardin, C., and Peterson, R. 1967. Studies of androgen production by the rat. *Endocrinol.* 80:38.

Blumer, D. 1969. Transsexualism, sexual dysfunction and temporal lobe disorder. In R. Green and J. Money, eds. *Transsexualism and sex reassignment.* Baltimore: The Johns Hopkins Press.

Christian, J. 1955. Effect of population size on the adrenal glands and reproductive organs of male mice in populations of fixed size. *Amer. J. Physiol.* 182:292.

Ehrhardt, A.; Epstein, R.; and Money, J. 1968. Fetal androgens and female gender identity in the early-treated adrenogenital syndrome. *Johns Hopkins Med. J.* 122:160–67.

Ehrhardt, A.; Evers, K.; and Money, J. 1968. Influence of androgen and some aspects of sexually dimorphic behavior in women with the late-treated adrenogenital syndrome. *Johns Hopkins Med. J.* 123:115–22.

Ehrhardt, A., and Money, J. 1967. Progestin-induced hermaphroditism: IQ and psychosexual identity in a study of ten girls. *J. Sex Research* 3:83–100.

Evans, R. 1972. Physical and biochemical characteristics of homosexual men. *J. Consult. and Clin. Psychol.* 39:140–47.

Freemon, F., and Nevis, A. 1969. Temporal lobe sexual seizures. *Neurol.* 19:87–90.

Freud, S. 1920. The psychogenesis of a case of homosexuality in a woman. In J. Strachey, ed. *The standard edition of the complete psychological works of Sigmund Freud.* 1955. London: Hogarth Press, p. 171.

Gillespie, A. 1971. Paper read at the Second International Congress on Gender Identity, Elsinore, Denmark.

Goldfoot, D.; Feder, H.; and Goy, R. 1969. Development of bisexuality in the male rat treated neonatally with androstenedione. *J. Comp. Physiol. Psychol.* 67:41–45.

Grady, K.; Phoenix, C.; and Young, W. 1965. Role of the developing testis in differentiation of the neural tissues mediating mating behavior. *J. Compar. Physiol. Psychol.* 59:176–82.

Greenson, R. 1967. Dis-identifying from mother: Its special importance for the boy. Paper presented at the International Psycho-Analytical Congress.

Harris, G. 1964. Sex hormones, brain development, and brain function. *Endocrinol.* 75:627–48.

Jones, J. 1971. Paper read at the Second International Congress on Gender Identity, Elsinore, Denmark. *Arch. Sex. Behav.* 2:251–56.

Jost, A. 1947. Recherches sur la differenciation sexuelle de l'embryo de lapin. *Arch. Anat. Microscop. et Morphol. Exper.* 36:151–200; 242–70; 271–319.

Kolarsky, A.; Freund, K.; Machek, J.; and Polak, G. 1967. Male sexual deviation. *Arch. Gen. Psychiat.* 17:735–43.

Kolodny, R.; Masters, W.; Hendryx, J.; and Toro, G. 1971. Plasma testosterone and semen analysis in male homosexuals. *New Eng. J. Med.* 285:1170–74.

Kluver, H., and Bucy, P. 1939. Preliminary analysis of functions of the temporal lobes in monkeys. *Arch. Neurol. and Psychiat.* 42:979–1000.

Kreuz, L.; Rose, R.; and Jennings, J. 1972. Suppression of plasma testosterone levels and psychological stress. *Arch. Gen. Psychiat.* 26:479–82.

Loraine, J.; Ismail, A.; Adamopoulos, A.; and Dove, G. 1970. Endocrine function in male and female homosexuals. *Brit. Med. J.* 4:406–08.

Luttge, W., and Whalen, R. 1970. Dihydrotestosterone, androstenedione, testosterone: Comparative effectiveness in masculinizing and defeminizing reproductive systems in male and female rats. *Hormones and Behavior* 1:265–81.

Migeon, C.; Rivarola, M.; and Forest, M. 1969. Studies of androgens in male transsexual subjects. In R. Green and J. Money, eds., *Transsexualism and sex reassignment*. Baltimore: The Johns Hopkins Press.

Mitchell, W.; Falconer, M.; and Hill, D. 1964. Epilepsy with fetishism relieved by temporal lobectomy. *Lancet* 2:626–30.

Margolese, S. 1970. Homosexuality: A new endocrine correlate. *Horm. and Behav.* 1:151–55.

Money, J. 1968. *Sex errors of the body*. Baltimore: The Johns Hopkins Press.

Money, J.; Ehrhardt, A.; and Masica, D. 1968. Fetal feminization induced by androgen insensitivity in the testicular feminizing syndrome. *Johns Hopkins Med. Bull.* 123:105–111.

Money, J., and Pollitt, E. 1964. Cytogenetic and psychosexual ambiguity: Klinefelter's Syndrome and transvestism compared. *Arch. Gen. Psychiat.* 11:589–95.

Rivarola, M.; Saez, J.; Meyer, W.; Kenney, F;. and Migeon, C. 1967. Studies of androgens in the syndrome of male pseudohermaphroditism with testicular feminization. *J. Clin. Endocrin. Metab.* 27:371–78.

Roeder, F., and Muller, D. 1969. The stereotaxic treatment of pedophilic homosexuality. *German Med. Monthly* 14:265–71.

Rose, R. M.; Bourne, P.; and Poe, R. 1969. Androgen responses to stress. *Psychosom. Med.* 31:418–36.

Simmer, H.; Pion, R.; and Dignam, W. 1965. *Testicular feminization*. Springfield, Ill.: Charles C Thomas.

Terzian, H., and Dalle Ore, G. 1955. Syndrome of Kluver and Bucy reproduced in man by bilateral removal of the temporal lobe. *Neurol.* 5:373–80.

Tourney, G., and Hatfield, L. 1972. Androgen metabolism in schizophrenics, homosexuals and normal controls. Paper presented at Annual Meeting, Society of Biological Psychiatry.

Walinder, J. 1965. Transvestism, definition and evidence in favor of occasional derivation from cerebral dysfunction. *Internat. J. Neuropsychiat.* 1:567–73.

Whalen, R., and Luttge, W. 1971. Testosterone, androstenedione, and dihydrotestosterone: Effects on mating behavior of male rats. *Horm. and Behav.* 2:117–25.

Whalen, R.; Peck, C.; and LoPiccolo, J. 1966. Virilization of female rats by prenatally administered progestin. *Endocrinol.* 78:965–70.

Yalom, I.; Green, R.; and Fisk, N. 1973. Prenatal exposure to female hormones. Effect on psychosexual development in boys. *Arch. Gen. Psychiat.* 28:554–61.

Young, W.; Goy, R.; and Phoenix, C. 1964. Hormones and sexual behavior. *Science* 143:212–18.

4

MEN WHO WANT TO BECOME WOMEN

Benjamin, H. 1966. *The transsexual phenomenon*. New York: Julian Press.

Green, R., and Money, J., eds. 1969. *Transsexualism and sex reassignment*. Baltimore: Johns Hopkins Press.

Stoller, R. 1968. *Sex and gender: On the development of masculinity and femininity.* New York: Science House.

6

TREATMENT OF MEN WHO WANT
TO BECOME WOMEN

Benjamin, H. 1966. *The transsexual phenomenon.* New York: Julian Press.

Green, R. 1970. Persons seeking sex-change: Psychiatric management of special problems. *Amer. J. Psychiat.* 126:1596–1603.

Money, J. 1971. Prefatory remarks on outcome of sex reassignment in 24 cases of transsexualism. *Arch. Sex. Behav.* 1:163–66.

Pauly, I. 1968. Current status of the change of sex operation. *J. Nerv. Ment. Dis.* 47:460–71.

Randell, J. 1969. Preoperative and postoperative status of male and female transsexuals. In *Transsexualism and sex reassignment,* ed. R. Green and J. Money. Baltimore: Johns Hopkins Press.

Stoller, R. 1968. *Sex and gender: On the development of masculinity and femininity.* New York: Science House.

7

WOMEN WHO WANT TO BECOME MEN

Benjamin, H. 1966. *The transsexual phenomenon.* New York: Julian Press.

Green, R., and Money, J., eds. 1969. *Transsexualism and sex reassignment.* Baltimore: Johns Hopkins Press.

Stoller, R. 1968. *Sex and gender: On the development of masculinity and femininity.* New York: Science House.

8

GIRLFRIENDS AND WIVES OF
FEMALE-TO-MALE TRANSSEXUALS

Hoffman, M. 1968. *The gay world: Male homosexuality and the social creation of evil.* New York: Basic Books.

Masters, W. H., and Johnson, V. E. 1966. *Human sexual response.* Boston: Little, Brown.

9

TREATMENT OF WOMEN WHO
WANT TO BECOME MEN

Laub, D. 1971. Paper read at Second International Congress on Gender Identity, Elsinore, Denmark.

13

FEMININE BOYS: PSYCHOLOGIC TESTING

Alkire, A. 1969. Social power and accuracy of communication in families of disturbed and non-disturbed pre-adolescents. *J. Person. and Soc. Psychol.* 13:335–49.

Back, K.; Festinger, L.; Hymovitch, B.; Kelley, H.; Schachter, S.; and Thibault, J. 1950. The methodology of studying rumor transmission. *Human Relat.* 3:307–12.

Bandura, A. 1965. Influence of models' reinforcement contingencies on the acquisition of imitative responses. *J. Person. and Soc. Psychol.* 1:589–95.

Brown, D. 1956. Sex role preference in young children. *Psychol. Monogr.* 70, no. 14 (whole no. 421).

Green, R. 1971a. Family-Doll Preference Test. Copyright 1971, Richard Green, M.D.

———. 1971b. Parent and Activity Preference Test. Copyright 1971, Richard Green, M.D.

Hurwitz, J.; Zander, A.; and Hymovitz, B. 1960. Some effects of power on the relations among group members. In *Group dynamics*, 2d ed., ed. D. Cartwright and A. Zander. New York: Harper and Row.

Jolles, I. 1952. A study of some hypotheses for the qualitative interpretation of the H-T-P for children of elementary school age: I. Sexual identification. *J. Clin. Psychol.* 8:113–18.

Kelley, H. 1951. Communication in experimentally created hierarchies. *Human Relat.* 4:307–12.

14
"IDENTICAL" TWIN BOYS: ONE MASCULINE,
ONE FEMININE

Bene, E., and Anthony, J. 1957 Family Relations Test. Copyright 1957, Eva Bene and James Anthony.

Brown, D. 1956. Sex role preference in young children. *Psychol. Monogr.* 70 No. 14 (whole no. 421).

Davison, K.; Brierly, M.; and Smith, C. 1971. A male monozygotic twinship discordant for homosexuality. *Brit. J. Psychiat.* 118:675–82.

Green, R. 1971. Parent and Activity Preference Test. Copyright 1971, Richard Green, M.D.

Jolles, I. 1952. A study of validity of some hypotheses for the qualitative interpretation of the H-T-P for children of elementary school age: I. Sexual identification. *J. Clin. Psychol.* 8:113–18.

Kallmann, F. J. 1952. Comparative twin study of the genetic aspects of male homosexuality. *J. Nerv. Ment. Dis.* 115:283–98.

———. 1960. Discussion of paper by J. Rainer et al. *Psychosom. Med.* 22:259.

Klintworth, G. 1962. A pair of male monozygotic twins discordant for homosexuality. *J. Nerv. Ment. Dis.* 135:113–25.

Stoller, R. 1968. *Sex and gender: On the development of masculinity and femininity.* New York: Science House.

15
FEMININE BOYS: HOW THEY GET THAT WAY

Bandura, A. 1965. Influence of model's reinforcement contingencies on the acquisition of imitative responses. *J. Person. and Soc. Psychol.* 1:589–95.

Current Population Reports, Population Characteristics, Marital Status and Family Status: March, 1970. Washington, D.C., U.S. Department of Commerce Publications.

Fenichel, O. 1945. *The psychoanalytic theory of neurosis.* New York: Norton.

Stoller, R. 1968. *Sex and gender: On the development of masculinity and femininity.* New York: Science House.

16
FEMININE BOYS: TREATMENT

Allyon, T. 1963. Intensive treatment of psychotic behavior by stimulus satiation and food reinforcement. *Behav. Res. and Ther.* 1:53–62.

Bieber, I. et al. 1962. *Homosexuality.* New York: Basic Books.

Bijou, S., and Baer, D. 1966. Operant methods in child behavior and development. In *Operant behavior: Areas of research and application,* ed. W. Honig. New York: Appleton-Century-Crofts.

Green, R.; Newman, L.; and Stoller, R. 1972. Treatment of boyhood "transsexualism": An interim report of four years' duration. *Arch. Gen. Psychiat.* 26:213–17.

Greenson, R. 1966. A transvestite boy and a hypothesis. *Int. J. Psycho-Anal.* 47:396–403.

Lebovitz, P. 1972. Feminine behavior in boys. Aspects of its outcome. *Amer. J. Psychiat.* 128:1283–89.

Money, J. 1972. Strategy, ethics, behavior modification, and homosexuality. *Arch. Sex. Behav.* 2:79–82.

Patterson, G., and Gullion, M. 1968. *Living with children.* Champaign: Research Press.

Sherman, J., and Baer, D. 1969. Appraisal of operant therapy techniques with children and adults. In *Behavior therapy: Appraisal and status,* ed. C. Franks. New York: McGraw-Hill.

Zuger, B. 1966. Effeminate behavior present in boys from early childhood. *J. Pediat.* 69:1098–1107.

17
MASCULINE GIRLS

Brown, D. 1957. The development of sex-role inversion and homosexuality. *J. Pediat.* 50:613–19.

Lynn, D. 1969. *Parental and sex role identification.* Berkeley: McCutchen.

Stoller, R. 1972. Etiological factors in female transsexualism: A first approximation. *Arch. Sex. Behav.* 2:47–64.

18
PROBLEMS FOR FUTURE RESEARCH

Chamove, A.; Harlow, H.; and Mitchell, G. 1967. Sex difference in the infant-directed behavior of preadolescent rhesus monkeys. *Child Develop.* 38:329–35.

Ehrhardt, A.; Epstein, R.; and Money, J. 1968. Fetal androgens and female gender identity in the early-treated adrenogenital syndrome. *Johns Hopkins Medical J.* 122:160–67.

Hore, B. 1973. Two transsexual males in one family. *Arch. Sex. Behav.* In press.

Jensen, G.; Bobbitt, R.; and Gordon, B. 1968. Sex differences in development of independence of infant monkeys. *Behav.* 30:1–14.

Lancaster, J. 1971. Play-mothering: The relations between juvenile females and young infants among free-ranging vervet monkeys. *Folia Primat.* 15:161–82.

Mitchell, G. 1968. Attachment differences in male and female infant monkeys. *Child Develop.* 39:611–20.

Rosenblum, L. 1974. Sex differences, environmental complexity and mother-infant relations. *Arch. Sex. Behav.* In press.

Stoller, R., and Baker, H. 1973. Two transsexual males in one family. *Arch. Sex. Behav.* 2:323–28.

Young, W.; Goy, R.; and Phoenix, C. 1964. Hormones and sexual behavior. *Science* 143:212–18.

INDEX

A

Adoption, female-to-male transsexuals and, 120, 129, 138–139

Adrenogenital syndrome: hormonal production and, 35–36; intersexed children, studies of, 25

Aleut Indians, 11

Alkire, A., 197, 202

Alpert, R., 24

Amazons, 4–5, 12

American Indians, transsexualism among, 9–11, 174

Ancient history, transsexualism in, 3–6

Androgen: effects of administration of, to female-to-male transsexual, 131; female hormonal development and, 35–36

Animal research, hormonal studies and, 29–30, 303

Anthony, A., 26–27

Anthony, J., 209

Anthropological observations of transsexualism, 26–27, 28

Aphrodite, 4

Arthur, Chester, 8

B

Back, K., 203

Baer, D., 275

Baker, H., 37, 40, 70

Ball, J., 32

Bardin, C., 39

Bastian, A., 12

Beauty of feminine boys, 213, 225

Becarelli, 7

Bell, R., 16

Bene, E., 209

Bene-Anthony Test of Family Relations, differences in twins' scores on, 209

Benjamin, H., 6, 87

Bieber, I., 243

Bijou, S., 275

Biller, H., 24

Biologic studies, 29–41

Birns, B., 16

Bloch, I., 11

Blumer, D., 32

Bogoras, W., 11

Brain destruction, focal, as treatment of atypical sexuality, 33

Brazil, transsexualism in, 12

Bridges, W., 16

Brierly, M., 205

Brown, D., 8, 192, 209

Bucy, P., 31

Bulliet, C., 4, 6, 7, 8, 9

C

California Indians, 10

Castration fears: feminine boys and, 170, 183, 187, 188, 213, 229–230; male-to-female transsexuals and, 46–47; psychoanalytic theories of, 19, 21

China, ancient, transsexualism in, 12

Choisy, Abbé de, 7

Christian, J., 39

Chukchee Indians, 11

Clitoris: androgen administration effects on, 131, 136; female-to-male transsexual's use of, 128

Cocopa Indians, 9–10

Colley, T., 23

Cornbury, Lord, 8

Costello, N., 16

Counseling: diagnostic and preoperative, male-to-female transsexuals, 82–92; family, for male-to-female transsexuals, 96–99; female-to-male transsexuals and, 131–139; feminine boys and,